Journal of Critical Infrastructure Policy

Volume 4, Number 1 • Fall 2023

Also from Westphalia Press
westphaliapress.org

- The Idea of the Digital University
- Dialogue in the Roman-Greco World
- The History of Photography
- International or Local Ownership?: Security Sector Development in Post-Independent Kosovo
- Lankes, His Woodcut Bookplates
- Opportunity and Horatio Alger
- The Role of Theory in Policy Analysis
- The Little Confectioner
- Non-Profit Organizations and Disaster
- The Idea of Neoliberalism: The Emperor Has Threadbare Contemporary Clothes
- Social Satire and the Modern Novel
- Ukraine vs. Russia: Revolution, Democracy and War: Selected Articles and Blogs, 2010-2016
- James Martineau and Rebuilding Theology
- A Strategy for Implementing the Reconciliation Process
- Issues in Maritime Cyber Security
- A Different Dimension: Reflections on the History of Transpersonal Thought
- Iran: Who Is Really In Charge?
- Contracting, Logistics, Reverse Logistics: The Project, Program and Portfolio Approach
- Unworkable Conservatism: Small Government, Freemarkets, and Impracticality
- Springfield: The Novel
- Lariats and Lassos
- Ongoing Issues in Georgian Policy and Public Administration
- Growing Inequality: Bridging Complex Systems, Population Health and Health Disparities
- Designing, Adapting, Strategizing in Online Education
- Pacific Hurtgen: The American Army in Northern Luzon, 1945
- Natural Gas as an Instrument of Russian State Power
- New Frontiers in Criminology
- Feeding the Global South
- Beijing Express: How to Understand New China
- The Rise of the Book Plate: An Exemplative of the Art

Journal of Critical Infrastructure Policy

Volume 4, Number 1 • Fall 2023

Richard M. Krieg, PhD, editor-in-chief

Westphalia Press
An imprint of Policy Studies Organization

Journal of Critical Infrastructure Policy
Volume 4, Number 1 • Fall 2023

All Rights Reserved © 2023 by Policy Studies Organization

Westphalia Press
An imprint of Policy Studies Organization
1367 Connecticut Avenue NW
Washington, D.C. 20036
info@ipsonet.org

ISBN: 978-1-63723-637-6

Cover and interior design by Jeffrey Barnes
jbarnesbook.design

Daniel Gutierrez-Sandoval, Executive Director
PSO and Westphalia Press

Updated material and comments on this edition
can be found at the Westphalia Press website:
www.westphaliapress.org

Journal of Critical Infrastructure Policy
Volume 4, Number 1 • Fall 2023
© 2023 Policy Studies Organization

Richard M. Krieg, PhD, Editor-in-Chief
TABLE OF CONTENTS

Editor-in-Chief's Letter 1
Richard M. Krieg

Revolutionizing the Global Electricity System through Multi-Day
Battery Storage 7
Editor's Interview with Form Energy CEO Mateo Jaramillo

Editorial: Artificial Intelligence – A Perspective 17
Pramode Verma

Cybersecurity Preparedness of Critical Infrastructure: A National
Review 21
Maryam Roshanaei

PJM: Charting the Path to the Grid of the Future 45
Kenneth Seiler

In the Polycrisis Era, Infrastructure Defenders Need to Broaden,
Not Tighten, Their Focus 51
Andrew Bochman

New SEC Cybersecurity Disclosure Protocols: Enhanced
Transparency, Short Deadlines 61
Brian Walker

National Infrastructure Bank: A Permanent Solution and Timely
Budget Workaround 67
Stanley Forczyk

Archival Section: Overview 83
Richard M. Krieg

Progress toward Resilient Infrastructures: Are we falling behind
the pace of events and changing threats? 87
David A. Woods and David Alderson

(Cont'd.)

Energy Supply Changes and Change 101
Diane Graziano, Elisa Alonso, Fletcher Fields and Diana Bauer

Electromagnetic Pulse Resilience of United States Critical
Infrastructure: Progress and Prognosis 125
George E. Baker

The 2021 Texas Electric Grid Failure: Causes, Consequences and
Cures 137
Thomas Popik and Richard Humphreys

Nuclear Policy in the States: A National Review 165
Daniel Shea

Incentivizing Good Governance Beyond Regulatory Minimums:
The Civil Nuclear Sector 181
Debra Decker and Kathryn Rauhut

Evolution and Trends of Industrial Control System Cyber Incidents
since 2017 207
Robert Grubbs, Jeremiah Stoddard, Sarah Freeman, and Ron Fisher

Journal of Critical Infrastructure Policy

Founding Editor

Richard Krieg, PhD

Editor-in-Chief

Richard Krieg, PhD

Associate Editors

Noah Dormady, PhD

Camille Palmer, PhD

Thomas Sharkey, PhD

Editorial Board

Bilal Ayub, PhD

Morgan Bazilian, PhD

Chuck Bean, MA

Sharon Cardash, JD

Stephen Cauffman, BS

Arrietta Chakos, MA

Amb. Henry Cooper, PhD

Noah Dormady, PhD

David Flanigan, PhD

Ronald Gibbs, MA

Richard Krieg, PhD

Mary Lasky, MA

Richard Little, MS

Pamela Murray-Tuite, PhD

Sean O'Keefe, MPA

Camille Palmer, PhD

Edward Pohl, PhD

Kevin Quigley, PhD

Craig Rieger, PhD

Liesel Ritchie, PhD

Thomas Sharkey, PhD

Editor-in-Chief's Letter

Richard M. Krieg, PhD

This double issue of JCIP includes both new articles and an archival section which provides a curated revisit to some of the pioneering articles that helped to shape *JCIP*'s trajectory to date. The criteria used to select the archived contributions are presented along with commentary on each of the articles in my Archival Section Overview.

The current issue begins with our **Editor's Interview with Mateo Jaramillo**, CEO of Form Energy ("Revolutionizing the Global Electricity System through Multi-Day Battery Storage"). A vanguard in the energy storage industry, Form Energy is carving a niche with its groundbreaking iron-air battery technology, which boasts an impressive electricity storage capacity of up to 100 hours. This positions it as a viable and cost-efficient adjunct to conventional power plants. The company's vision leverages Jaramillo's rich experience at Tesla, where he pioneered their stationary energy storage program. His journey from Gaia Power Technologies to Tesla and now to Form Energy underscores a consistent trajectory toward innovative energy solutions. With the iron-air battery, Form Energy introduces a "multi-day storage" (MDS) concept, aiming to fortify grid reliability against the backdrop of increasingly frequent extreme weather events, a challenge underscored by the Texas power crisis during Winter Storm Uri.

Form Energy's strategic underpinnings are bolstered by strong public policy support, illustrated by the company's collaboration with federal and state governments, such as the Inflation Reduction Act and state-level incentives. This support has catalyzed the company's trajectory, enabling the construction of its first state-of-the-art battery factory in West Virginia and a significant pilot project in New York. The federal and state endorsement not only accelerates the commercialization of Form Energy's transformative technology but also signifies a commitment to grid decarbonization and a transition to clean energy. With leadership that I describe as a "dream team," Form Energy's culture is steeped in mutual respect and a collective mission to address climate change—a mission that is now translating into tangible economic benefits and job creation, particularly in the communities hosting their operations.

Between our last edition and now, Artificial Intelligence (AI) has emerged as a transformative force, heralding what could be the next major technological revolution. In his editorial: "Artificial Intelligence—A Perspective," **Pramode Verma** offers a reflective perspective on AI's evolution and potential, comparing it to historical technological leaps such as the printing press and the steam engine. Verma articulates the dual nature of AI's expansion: the incredible capability to extend human intellect, and the imperative to harness such growth responsibly to mitigate potential harm. He explores the generative aspects of AI that have begun to challenge the boundaries between human creativity and machine learning, raising questions about the future of this human-machine continuum.

The discussion moves to the ethical and practical challenges presented by AI, particularly in the realms of misinformation and the necessity for regulation. Verma suggests that AI's growth, powered by sophisticated algorithms and extensive data, is inevitable, yet must be regulated with awareness of the rights and protections for those it could harm. The author proposes solutions for regulating the spread of misinformation, advocating for the positive identification of information sources online, akin to the Know Your Customer (KYC) policies in financial institutions. He also addresses the need for oversight in broadcast media and public databases to ensure the authenticity and accuracy of information disseminated, especially in sensitive areas like healthcare.

In the broader context of AI, Verma's editorial echoes a global conversation about the integration of AI into the fabric of society. While AI's capabilities inch ever closer to human intelligence, surpassing it in some areas, the editorial raises profound questions about the essence of human consciousness and emotion, which AI has yet to touch. It acknowledges the transformative potential of AI on employment and digital literacy, and the consequential widening of the socio-economic divide. The editorial serves as a call to navigate the AI revolution with a conscious effort to balance technological prowess with ethical foresight, ensuring that AI serves as a benefactor rather than a disruptor to the collective human experience.

In "Cybersecurity Preparedness of Critical Infrastructure: A National Review," **Maryam Roshanaei** notes that critical infrastructures, such as transportation networks, power grids, water systems, telecommunications, and financial systems, are the bedrock of modern society, integral to the daily operations of governments, businesses, and communities. The U.S., while heavily reliant on these systems, faces challenges in safeguarding them against increasingly sophisticated domestic and international threats. The article discusses the challenges modern societies face in protecting critical infrastructures, emphasizing the need for robust cybersecurity readiness to ensure that systems can withstand and recover from disruptive events.

The article continues to underscore the importance of collaborative, comprehensive strategies that integrate Information, Communication, and Technology (ICT) platforms with innovative technologies for enhanced protection. With critical infrastructures becoming more interconnected and digitized, they are more susceptible to cyber threats, making cybersecurity readiness an essential aspect of national security. Furthermore, it highlights the varying security needs of IT and Operational Technology (OT) within critical infrastructures, particularly emphasizing the unique requirements of OT systems for safety and reliability. The need for resilient strategies that protect against all types of threats and the urgency of developing such measures are central themes of the discussion.

The article's analytic findings illuminate the stark reality that CI installations have been recurrently compromised. The Energy and Transportation sectors are particularly vulnerable, having faced a substantial number of incidents over the years. The data suggest a trend of escalating sophistication in cyberattacks, with a notable spike in disruptions due to ransomware and malware—underscoring an urgent call for reinforced cybersecurity readiness. By charting the landscape of past breaches, the article serves as a clarion call for a fortified stance against potential future threats. It is buttressed by Grubbs et al. in "Evolution and Trends of Industrial Control System Cyber Incidents Since 2017," which is presented in the Archival Section.

In "PJM: Charting the Path to the Grid of the Future," **Kenneth Seiler** notes that the electric grid stands as one of the most crucial yet complex systems in modern society, a silent enabler of our daily lives and economic activities. He summarizes the electric grid's evolving landscape from the perspective of planning for a grid operator that services an extensive region, including 13 states and the District of Columbia. He explores the challenges and transformations the grid is undergoing, delving into the intersection of customer preferences, clean energy goals, policy choices, and technological advancements, painting the picture of an industry at a pivotal point of change.

Seiler's article is timely, as it addresses the escalating need to balance reliability and innovation in the face of retiring conventional energy generators and the increasing frequency of extreme weather events. The piece highlights PJM Interconnection's important role in managing these challenges while maintaining an uninterrupted power supply, a task that is becoming increasingly complex and urgent. The discussion revolves around not just the need for effective operation but also the need for strategic planning and market adaptations to ensure the resilience and reliability of the grid in unprecedented scenarios. Seiler's perspective is particularly valuable given PJM's position as the largest regional transmission organization in the United States, emphasizing the scale and impact of the issues discussed.

The article further explores the practical aspects and implications of transitioning to a grid that increasingly relies on renewable energy sources, such as wind and solar. This transition, while important for a sustainable future, presents unique challenges in maintaining the reliability of the power supply. The author examines these challenges in depth, including the need for new planning processes, the impact of regulatory and market structures, and the critical role of policy in facilitating this transition.

Andrew Bochman's "In the Polycrisis Era, Infrastructure Defenders Need to Broaden, Not Tighten, Their Focus," delves into the complexity of our current period, characterized by overlapping and interlinked crises that collectively threaten global infrastructure. The author highlights the need for a strategic rethink in infrastructure protection, emphasizing the interdependencies between operational technology cybersecurity and climate-induced physical risks. Acknowledging the evolving and compound nature of threats, from climate change to rapid technological advancement, the paper underscores the urgency of holistic resilience planning and intersectoral collaboration.

In detailing the components of the Polycrisis Era, the author reflects on historical precedents, current vulnerabilities, and the inadequacies of existing frameworks to address multifaceted challenges. A particular focus is placed on the systemic failures to manage complex social, ecological, and technological systems, and the consequent economic and societal repercussions. The article argues for a shift from siloed defense strategies to integrated approaches that recognize the cascade of impacts from climate events and cyber threats.

The article introduces the concept of Critical Function Assurance (CFA), advocating for proactive risk management and preparedness for "black sky events"—extreme, prolonged outages affecting multiple states—and "black swan" events—unpredictable, catastrophic occurrences. It proposes a cross-disciplinary strategy that leverages diverse expertise and calls for enhanced communication among infrastructure defenders. By examining both cyber and physical climate risks, the paper suggests that shared knowledge and coordinated defenses can bolster resilience in the face of unprecedented global challenges.

The vast majority of U.S. critical infrastructure is owned by private sector companies. In "New SEC Cybersecurity Disclosure Protocols: Enhanced Transparency, Short Deadlines," **Brian Walker** discusses the final rule issued by the SEC on Cybersecurity Risk Management, Strategy, Governance, and Incident Response. Finalized on July 26, 2023, the rule requires SEC-regulated companies to disclose significant cybersecurity incidents and their cyber risk management processes. It aims to provide investors with more transparency into the cyber risks and mitigation strategies of SEC-regulated companies. The rulemaking process, which lasted eighteen months and began in March 2022, involved heated debate and divergent viewpoints. Walker highlights the challenges companies will face in adapting to these new regulations, particularly those with less structured cyber risk management approaches.

In outlining the new rules for annual cyber risk disclosures, the article focuses on two areas: Cyber Risk Management and Cyber Risk Governance. Under rule provisions, affected companies must describe strategies and processes for managing cyber risk, and the roles and responsibilities of those involved in monitoring and managing such risk. In addition to annual disclosures, companies must also report significant cyber-related incidents within four business days of determining their materiality. Companies will need to focus on foundational capabilities like incident classification, response, crisis response plans, and regular testing to comply effectively with the SEC's new cybersecurity rules. While the finalized rules do not provide detailed guidance on these disclosures, they emphasize transparency, leaving the specifics to each company's leadership.

[Editor's note: in terms of some of its climate change disclosures, the SEC's current posture is part of a broader global trend towards integrating environmental, social, and governance (ESG) factors in financial reporting. However, it highlights the ongoing debate in the United States about the role of regulators in addressing climate change and the extent to which companies should be held accountable for disclosing climate-related risks. The contentious nature of this rulemaking reflects broader societal divisions over climate policy and the role of business in mitigating environmental impacts.]

Stanley Forczyk, in "National Infrastructure Bank: A Permanent Solution and Timely Budget Workaround," highlights the critical state of America's public infrastructure, which is strained by both underinvestment and the impacts of climate change. The recent Infrastructure Investment and Jobs Act (IIJA) of 2021, while a substantial measure, only covers a fraction of the nation's vast, unfunded infrastructure needs. The proposed solution is the establishment of a $5 trillion National Infrastructure Bank (NIB), outlined in HR4052, which would address this funding gap without additional taxes or debt, by using private sector Treasury swaps for equity in the bank.

The article underscores the role of robust infrastructure in economic vitality and social equity. It illustrates the negative consequences of inadequate investment in public infrastructure—hampering efficiency, innovation, and disproportionately affecting disadvantaged communities. It also details how a well-funded and modernized infrastructure is crucial for businesses, particularly for supply chain efficiency and overall national competitiveness.

The proposed NIB is intended to complement existing federal programs and to catalyze economic growth by providing low-cost loans for critical infrastructure projects. This would facilitate strategic, sustainable investments across diverse sectors such as transportation, water management, and housing. The author posits that the Bank's self-sustaining model, which mirrors successful historical precedents, is intended to appeal across the political spectrum, emphasizing infrastructure investment as a bipartisan priority that could drive America's future prosperity and international competitiveness.

Revolutionizing the Global Electricity System through Multi-Day Battery Storage

Editor-in-Chief's Interview with Form Energy CEO Mateo Jaramillo

Form Energy is a trailblazing American company in the energy storage sector, specializing in the development and commercialization of an innovative iron-air battery. The battery stands out for its ability to store electricity for up to 100 hours, offering a cost-effective solution comparable to traditional power plants. CEO Mateo Jaramillo is co-founder and CEO of Form Energy. He was formerly Vice President of Products and Programs for Tesla's stationary energy storage program, an effort he started. In that role, he was responsible for Tesla Energy's product line and business model definition, as well as global policy and business development. Mateo joined Tesla in 2009 as the Director of Powertrain Business Development, serving as commercial lead on over $100M in new development and $500M in production contracts signed for electric powertrain sales. Prior to Tesla, Mateo was Chief Operating Officer and part of the founding team at Gaia Power Technologies, a pioneering distributed energy storage firm. He serves on the Board of the American Clean Power Association. He earned his A.B. in Economics from Harvard University and a Masters in Theology from Yale Divinity School.

Krieg Long Duration Energy Storage (LDES) systems seem poised to revolutionize energy system decarbonization, offering bulk power benefits and resilience to behind-the-meter applications. Given the increasing prevalence of extreme weather events, these technologies may become pivotal in enhancing local and regional grid resilience and reducing grid expansion costs. Can you delve deeper into their significance and potential?

Jaramillo "Long duration" is an imprecise term which, as used today in the industry, currently covers everything from 6 to 1,000+ hours of rated discharge. The term "long duration" typically refers to storage systems that can discharge for longer periods than the most deployed lithium-ion systems today, which are usually designed to discharge for 2-4 hours at full capacity and in practice, "long duration" is used today to refer to storage systems ranging from lithium-ion batteries that can provide 6-8 hours of storage capability, to 10-hour flow batteries, to 12-hour mechanical or thermal storage systems. Form's electrochemical battery can discharge energy continuously for 100+ hours and solves a different problem from other "long duration" storage technologies; we prefer to use the term "multi-day" storage (MDS) to refer to our approach.

MDS is an essential part of a reliable, cost effective, decarbonizing grid. Multi-day weather events such as extreme cold, extreme heat, and prolonged cloudy doldrums present the primary reliability challenge to present day and future grids. This fact was tragically demonstrated by the four-day outage that Winter Storm Uri inflicted on Texas. MDS can harness low-cost clean energy during periods of abundance and use that energy to provide a low carbon backstop to the grid during these prolonged periods of grid stress. But MDS isn't just a "rainy day fund." While catastrophic events like Winter storm Uri happen relatively infrequently, grid operators are tasked with managing the more minor heat waves and winter storms that occur many times each year—MDS presents an economic solution to these challenges. Further, MDS complements today's storage technologies to support renewable energy firming, providing flexible power as the sun sets and as the breeze dissipates. In that light, the U.S. Department of Energy noted that the grid will need between 225 and 460 gigawatts of LDES to enable decarbonization, with 180 – 200 GW coming from MDS.[1]

Krieg With growing reliance on solar and wind for energy generation, the challenge of seasonal fluctuations in electricity supply becomes prominent. A low-carbon power system needs to provide clean energy even during non-peak solar and wind periods. How can long-term energy storage reshape grid dynamics in such scenarios?

Jaramillo Seasonal fluctuations in clean energy present an economic opportunity for MDS. During spring and fall months, demand for electricity tends to be relatively low due to mild weather. However, clean energy supply tends to be strong as days are often long, clear, and breezy. As a result, energy tends to be clean and inexpensive —an ideal opportu-

---

1 U.S. Department of Energy, 2023. Pathways to Commercial Liftoff: Long Duration Energy Storage. https://liftoff.energy.gov/wp-content/uploads/2023/10/Pathways-to-Commercial-Liftoff-LDES-May-5_UPDATED-v10.pdf

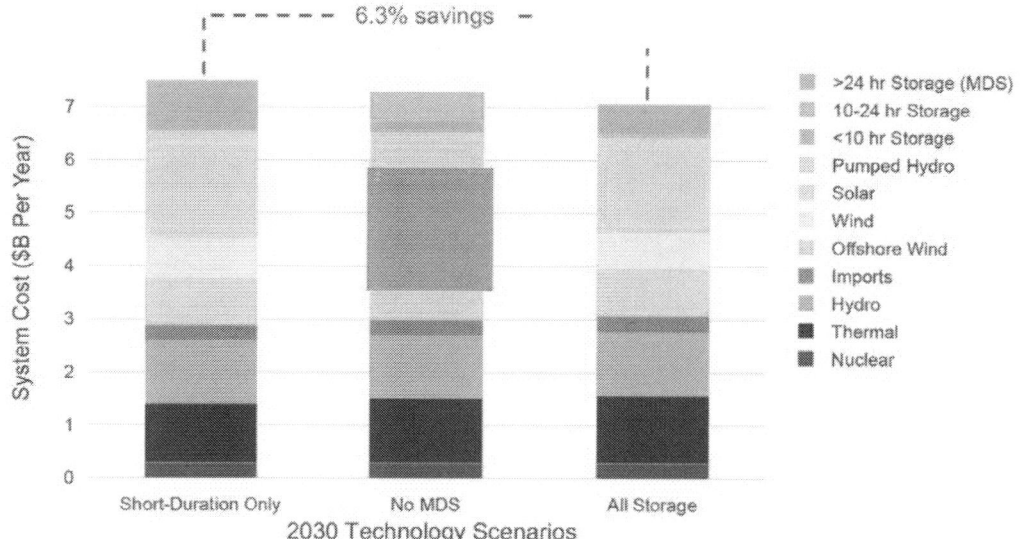

nity for MDS. In our modeling we see MDS taking advantage of this abundant, low-cost clean energy during spring and fall months to shift energy seasonally—as shown in the chart below, taken from a recent study Form Energy published focused on supporting New England's clean energy goals.[2] The figure shows how MDS charges throughout spring and fall months, followed by discharges throughout summer and winter grid stress periods. The result of this economic behavior is that MDS dramatically increases the utilization of renewable energy, cutting renewable energy waste—curtailment—by up to 83% in our modeled scenarios.

Krieg It would be hard not to view your senior management group as a "dream team." Each member is a respected veteran in his or her specialty. It strikes me as providential that you're working together rather than competing in the LDES development and implementation space. Could you describe Form Energy's core leadership team as well as your mission and shared values?

Jaramillo Thank you, Richard. Form Energy was created when two early-stage companies working on breakthrough energy storage battery technologies joined together. Our teams combined because everyone valued having the best shot at making a meaningful impact on climate change more than their particular company achieving singular success. As

---

[2] Form Energy, 2023. Clean, Reliable, Affordable: The Value of Multi-Day Storage in New England. https://formenergy.com/wp-content/uploads/2023/09/Form-ISO-New-England-whitepaper-09.27.23.pdf

co-founders, we knew it made good business sense to join forces, but it was our mutual respect and ability to connect as human beings that sealed the deal. The Form Energy origin story is an unusual one, free of the egotism that can often accompany venture-funded tech startups. Our company was founded on human connection, mutual respect, and deep motivation and inspiration to create a better world.

Krieg The federal and state governments are vigorously promoting LDES system development. DOE, under Secretary Granholm, has scoped out multiple pathways for commercial liftoff of these technologies. With funding in the Inflation Reduction Act and through other means, the agency wants to improve critical certainty for private investment. Construction of your first battery factory in West Virginia relies in part on asset-based performance financing from the State. And in New York, you received a sizable grant from the state's Research and Development Authority (NYSERDA) to deploy a 10 MW/1,000 MWh pilot battery project by 2026. How has the supportive public policy environment impacted the company's trajectory?

Jaramillo We are racing against the clock to commercialize an entirely new battery chemistry for grid-scale multi-day storage. It took about 30 years from when the first lithium-ion battery was used in a camcorder to becoming the mainstream battery that powers all the electric cars in the world. We have about ⅓ of the development time to get our product to market, and this will only be possible with a supportive public policy environment at the federal, state, and local levels.

The Inflation Reduction Act supports the U.S. manufacturing sector broadly, and the entire domestic battery manufacturing industry specifically, in addition to other industries such as solar and wind, with manufacturing credits for the production of PV cells, wafers, inverters, and wind components, especially in the case of offshore wind. Although we have not yet received any IRA funding, it is already having a positive impact. For instance, when the IRA passed last summer, we had already received an executed term sheet for a Series E funding and were well underway in our site selection process for our first high-volume manufacturing facility. With the passing of the IRA, it became clear the entire electric industry was about to shift into high gear. Our investors soon grasped the impact; our in-process funding round doubled in size, and we all pushed forward to close quickly and finalize our site selection process. West Virginia state officials, as well as the local county and city officials, stepped up to bring the revitalization of the old Weirton Steel site to fruition by offering a substantial state incentive package, a pro-business landscape, streamlined processes, and a serious commitment to workforce development.

Across the country, more and more states are setting targets for LDES. For instance, in a first among states, California approved $126 million in incentives to demonstrate new long-duration storage technologies. Massachusetts came out with its 2022 Massachusetts Climate Bill, which recognized the potential of long-duration and other storage technologies to enable the state's ambitious climate goals. And, as you mentioned New York State has a long-duration energy storage grant program, a $17 million fund intended to expedite commercialization of promising technologies offering 10 to 100+ hours of energy storage.

We believe that the demonstrated leadership at the local, state, and federal level will result in meaningful climate impact and will allow us to meet our country's energy goals: enhancing grid resilience and security, increasing grid reliability and safety, creating well-paying jobs and economically benefiting local communities, and ensuring the inventions that secure our energy future are built right here in the United States. However, to do this in a relevant timeframe, there must be a new focus on coordination and alignment between the federal level and the local level to provide greater certainty and expediency around clean energy and infrastructure deployments. For instance, there will need to be dedicated efforts to streamline permitting processes, enhance grid modeling and planning tools, create new market structures, and provide the necessary support to scale up domestic manufacturing.

Krieg It's noteworthy that in New York and West Virginia, you're on the ground in the nation's 4th and 40th largest states. I'm particularly interested in West Virginia because Form Factory One is a historic facility—both in terms of the iron-air batteries to be produced there and its impact on West Virginia's economy. Am I correct that the Weirton WV site was selected from a slate of some 500 locations? What led you to select this site, and what do you think the facility's economic impact might be?

Jaramillo Yes, you are correct. We led a year-long, robust nationwide selection process for the site of our first full-scale battery manufacturing plant. Our team started by identifying over 500 candidate locations across 16 states, narrowing the search to three locations. After evaluating several promising manufacturing site locations, we landed on a great site in Weirton, West Virginia. We appreciated the proximity to our existing pilot manufacturing facility in Eighty-Four, PA and were also impressed with West Virginia's pro-business landscape, streamlined processes, and commitment to workforce development.

As we look to our future, when we are receiving hundreds of thousands of tons of iron every year by rail or barge and turning it into electrodes in batteries, there were only a few places in the United States that made sense to build these batteries because the infrastructure and know-how is already there. Weirton is a historic steel community—sits on a river—has direct access to rail and hardened highways —and has the know-how to make great things out of iron.

Regarding economic impact, our first commercial production line in Weirton will result in the creation of over 750 good-paying jobs when it is in full operation by 2028. We have already hired more than 20 West Virginians and will ramp up hiring for Form Factory 1 later this year and into next year. The majority of factory employees will be machine operators, assemblers, material handlers, maintenance and repair technicians, lab technicians, and shipping and receiving associates. We will also be looking to hire leadership positions at all levels—manufacturing associate leads up through supervisors, managers, and directors. In addition, we'll also be hiring employees to support the finance, human resources, engineering, environmental health and safety, supply chain, and logistics teams.

There will also be indirect economic benefits to the community, and in fact we are already seeing this, as we construct the factory. Many of the subcontractors working on the construction of the factory are within the region and hire local tradespeople. We now have teams of employees who are in Weirton regularly for work, staying at the local hotels, eating at the local restaurants, and supporting the community through their patronage; this will only increase as we begin to hire more employees to work at Form Factory 1.

Krieg Turning attention to New York, a recent analysis by a Stanford University team highlighted the critical role of various energy storage solutions, including LDES and multi-day storage (MDS), to effectively decarbonize the State's electric grid. These solutions were shown to be the least cost approach to meeting New York's needs for dispatchable, emissions-free resources. What else did the study show?

Jaramillo I am not familiar with this specific analysis but Form Energy also studied the decarbonization of New York's power grid in line with the Empire State's goals.[3] Our research shows that investing in a diversity

---

3   Form Energy, 2023. Modeling Multi-Day Energy Storage in New York Storage Portfolios that Can Enable a Reliable, Zero Carbon Grid. https://formenergy.com/wp-content/uploads/2023/09/Form-Modeling-Multi-Day-Energy-Storage-in-NY-whitepaper-8.8.23.pdf

of storage resources—including short duration (<10 hour), medium duration (10 - 24 hour) and multi-day (>24 hour) storage—presents the least cost, most reliable path for New York to meet its goals. Our study shows that a technology pathway that supports all storage types can save the state hundreds of millions of dollars per year by 2030 and roughly $9 billion dollars per year by 2030, relative to a path that focuses exclusively on today's lithium-ion technologies. These savings are primarily driven by the ability of multi-day storage technologies to provide dispatchable, emissions free power; without multi-day storage, the State would need to "over build" other types of storage resources in order to ensure reliability during extreme weather conditions and prolonged renewable energy lulls. In fact, in 2030, one megawatt of multi-day storage reduces the need for roughly 2.33 megawatts of other resources, including wind, solar, and storage. The resulting impact is a lower cost, lower land use, more efficient system.

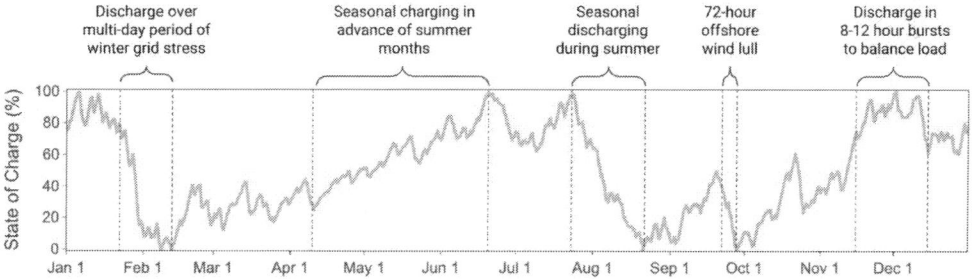

Krieg Nationally, DOE estimates suggest a potential cumulative benefit of up to $530 billion in the next 25 years, provided LDES technologies gain sufficient market traction by 2030. This includes over 2 million job years in engineering and construction. Do these projections align with your own expectations and vision for LDES?

Jaramillo The stability of the electric grid is increasingly important as we electrify more and more of society. However, recent severe weather events—ranging from heat waves to cold snaps to thousand-year rains—have highlighted the weakness of our electric grid, which is increasingly reliant on low-cost—and weather driven—renewable energy. Energy storage would be an obvious solution to this, however while we have cost-effective batteries for up to a few hours, in order to run the grid reliably and affordably, we need new, transformative energy storage technologies capable of cost-effectively storing electricity for longer durations, and specifically multiple days.

We believe there is tremendous potential for LDES to gain market traction in the U.S. and beyond. The global market for these systems is expected to grow tremendously in the coming years. A study by the nonprofit LDES (Long Duration Energy Storage) Council pegs the long-duration energy storage market at between 80 and 140 terawatt-hours by 2040.

Krieg Form Energy has operated in one of the most scientifically challenging corners of the rapidly evolving energy sector. Over the past five years, I've been impressed that unlike many startups—in energy, water supply and in other critical infrastructure sectors—you've consistently avoided the exaggerated claims that investors sometimes hear. Reflecting on your journey over the past half-decade, how would you characterize Form Energy's current position and accomplishments?

Jaramillo Form Energy has progressed quickly since our founding in 2017. We now have more than 650 employees working across the United States. Our mission and focus from the very beginning has been on impact, and until we are manufacturing at scale, we know we haven't achieved our goal. All of our progress to date is viewed by the company in that context.

We are headquartered in Somerville, MA, where our team is focused on electrochemical research and development, innovation, and continuous learning and improvement. We have facilities in Berkeley, CA, where our team is focused on product engineering and design, assembly development, as well as full scale battery validation and testing. Eighty-Four, PA is home to our manufacturing engineering team, where we operate a pilot manufacturing line to test our manufacturing processes and prepare for the scale up and broad commercialization of our iron air battery systems. And as noted above, we are constructing our first high-volume manufacturing facility in Weirton, WV, where we will begin manufacturing iron air battery systems for broad commercialization starting in 2024.

We continue to make tremendous progress on the commercial front. We partnered with Minnesota's second-largest electric utility, Great River Energy, to jointly deploy a 1.5 megawatt/150-megawatt hour pilot project to be located in Cambridge, MN. We announced a partnership with Xcel Energy to jointly deploy a 10 megawatt / 1,000 megawatt-hour multi-day storage system at the Sherburne County Generating Station in Becker, Minnesota and a 10 megawatt / 1,000 megawatt-hour multi-day storage system at the Comanche Generating Station in Pueblo, Colorado. Both projects are expected to come online as early as 2025.

We are also collaborating with Georgia Power, the largest electric subsidiary of Southern Company, to deploy a 15 megawatt/1500-megawatt hour energy storage system in the utility's service area. This project is expected to come online in 2026. We were awarded a $12 million grant from the New York State Energy Research and Development Authority to accelerate the deployment of a 10 megawatt / 1,000 megawatt-hour iron-air battery system in New York State, expected to come online by 2026. And most recently, we announced a partnership with Dominion Energy to provide a 5 megawatt / 500 megawatt-hour iron air battery storage system as part of the Darbytown Storage Pilot Project in Virginia. We have several other commercial negotiations underway and will have more news to share later in the year.

Krieg Looking a decade ahead, considering the possibilities and economic viability in the long-term energy storage industry, where would you like Form Energy to be?

Jaramillo Iron-air batteries can cost-effectively facilitate access to renewable energy sources, boost the stability and reliability of power grids, and ultimately accelerate grid decarbonization. Our internal analytics predict that over the next decade, achieving Form's cost and performance targets will unlock tens of gigawatts of demand for multi-day storage in the U.S. and accelerate the country's trajectory towards a more reliable and resilient grid. At such levels of deployment, Form's technology will catalyze billions of dollars in savings to American electricity consumers.

Editorial: A Perspective on Artificial Intelligence

Pramode Verma[*]

[*] Professor Emeritus of Electrical and Computer Engineering,
University of Oklahoma, pverma@ou.edu

In some ways, Artificial Intelligence (AI) has already started the next technological revolution. Compared to the past technological revolutions like the printing press (1436), the steam engine (1759), automobile (1672), or the information technology (1960s), the AI revolution appears to be different.

Critical analyses of the potential of AI are showing up everywhere at an increasingly rapid rate. Scientists and technologists are working hard to continuously enhance the potential of AI to match, possibly exceed, the capabilities normally attributed to humans. Social scientists, on the other hand, are struggling to develop adequate safety mechanisms that will limit the damage AI can inflict on unsuspecting individuals or organizations. The euphoria to push the bounds of AI to higher levels in the servitude of mankind appears to have suddenly given way to the fear of a dark outcome looming on the horizon.

Human intelligence aided by machines when put into practice has consistently benefited mankind. Is AI a tipping point where machine intellect might be too good for humanity? This article attempts to address ways in which AI can inflict damages and proposes how the damages can be contained, if not eliminated.

Artificial Intelligence is by no means a new endeavor. Dating back to the 1950s, AI researchers have tried to create machines that could mimic or surpass the capabilities of humans. Until most recently, AI was viewed as offering a human-machine continuum with a flexible boundary. The flexibility depended on needs of the task and the human element responsible for the task.

The generative properties of AI have challenged this notion. Generative AI can draw pictures, write a book, compose a poem, or generate text with little guidance. Generative AI is based on patterns and similarities in the underlying data and the relationship to its label or descriptor. Machine learning continuously enhances the depth and scope of such relationships by mining the massive amounts of data that Generative AI has access to along with the contextual application of relationships.

AI algorithms are driven by techniques used by neural networks. The algorithms use autocorrelation techniques choosing the most likely word, phrase, or icon based on the statistical analysis of hundreds of gigabytes of Internet text. The repertoire of information is growing at an exponential rate thus enhancing the capabilities of AI. In many instances, the outcomes delivered by Generative AI, have surprised the developers, and surpassed their expectations.

Can AI replace human beings in their entirety? This remains an open question because humans also display consciousness, feelings, emotions, and sensations. Some of these attributes arise because of the intricate relationship between mind and body. Furthermore, the sensory mechanisms of the human body are complex and distributed and include such attributes as touch, taste, and smell. While it's possible to build mechanisms to mimic these features in a robot, possibly in a limited way, the potential benefits of such an undertaking are questionable from a commercial perspective. Artificial Intelligence applications in the day-to-day businesses are the major drivers of the science and technology of AI currently.

How should one regulate AI? Given the fact that AI is driven by algorithms and processing capabilities along with access to massive amounts of data, the innate growth of AI is unstoppable. We posit that regulation of AI should be looked upon from the perspective of those who it has the potential to inflict damage on. In other words, rights of the recipients who AI can hurt should drive the AI regulation.

The ability of AI to create misinformation is potentially its most damaging outcome. Unfortunately, no one can control the ability to generate misinformation any more than one can control the thought process associated with human beings. Once generated, misinformation can be delivered through the Internet on a person-to-person basis or through a broadcast medium. Another compelling example is misinformation generated by a database, such as a medical database, which is delivered to an inquiring customer over the Internet. The availability of instantaneous transport of misinformation worldwide adds to the gravity of the situation.

Let's first consider misinformation delivered over the Internet. The most important part is to positively identify the sender at the behest of the receiving entity. This can be accomplished through a variety of means. One possibility is the use of public and private keys. However, the computational overhead consumed in such a scheme will likely make it unattractive to most consumers.

An alternative is to require every ISP to positively identify its customer. The receiving entity in such a network should have the choice to require the network to forward information from only those entities whose vetted credentials are forwarded along with the message. This contrivance should not violate the freedom of speech or expression; it merely empowers the receiving entity to limit access to it by an unknown or an unapproved entity. And it's no more limiting than locking the door of your home to strangers.

The positive identification of a client by the entity to which the client has a relationship is prevalent among many institutions. In financial institutions, it's known as the Know Your Customer (KYC) requirement. The implementation of forwarding the sender's identity to a discerning receiver should not be difficult.

Any digital device connected to the Internet can be uniquely identified by the network through its Layer 2 address. This can be supplemented by the Layer 3 address (such as a password) that can uniquely identify an individual, a process, or an institution. Indeed, this positive identification is already implemented by financial institutions. This identification can be forwarded to a discerning end point.

Let us now take up the case of broadcast media. Such media are, in most countries, regulated. The regulation can easily require that that any content the medium broadcasts has been vetted for the authenticity of the content originating entity. This can be displayed as part of the broadcast.

The third element that requires regulation is access to publicly available databases using Artificial Intelligence. One leading example is a health-related database that is publicly available. Such databases should be vetted by the concerned regulatory bodies or public institutions at large. A database, for example, answering queries related to health should be measured and rated for the level of accuracy it delivers in its response by the medical establishment of the country.

In some ways, human intelligence has grown too fast for the good of humanity. Every time technology has enhanced our capabilities to produce goods at a level unimaginable with human labor alone, there have been collateral damages.

Like any new technology that comes into practice, AI will cause collateral damage. There will be job losses especially for the most vulnerable members of the society, e.g., those who cannot easily adapt to changed modes of operation such as the elderly or those disadvantaged in other ways. Since AI is so heavily dependent on digital literacy, countries that are less literate in technology will be left further behind. And increased resource gaps between and among nations is not a good option for humanity as a whole.

Undoubtedly, AI will be growing closer and closer to the human brain, even possibly surpassing it. Arguably, it already has. As to whether it reaches the human mind which shows consciousness, instincts, and feelings, we do not know currently.

Author Capsule Bio

Pramode Verma is Professor Emeritus of Electrical and Computer Engineering at the Gallogly College of Engineering of the University of Oklahoma. Prior to that he was Professor, Williams Chair in Telecommunications Networking, and Director of the Telecommunications Engineering Program. He joined the University of Oklahoma in 1999 as the founder-director of a graduate program in Telecommunications Engineering. He is the author/co-author of over 150 journal articles and conference papers, and several books in telecommunications engineering. His academic credentials include a doctorate in electrical engineering from Concordia

University in Montreal, and an MBA from the Wharton School of the University of Pennsylvania. Dr. Verma has been a keynote speaker at several international conferences. He received the University of Oklahoma-Tulsa President's Leadership Award for Excellence in Research and Development in 2009. He is a Senior Member of the IEEE and a Senior Fellow of The Information and Telecommunication Education and Research Association. Prior to joining the University of Oklahoma, over a period of twenty-five years, he held a variety of professional, managerial and leadership positions in the telecommunications industry, most notably at AT&T Bell Laboratories and Lucent Technologies. He is the co-inventor of twelve patents.

Cybersecurity Preparedness of Critical Infrastructure—A National Review

Maryam Roshanaei[*]

[*]Assistant Professor of Cybersecurity & IST,
Pennsylvania State University Abington, mur45@psu.edu

Abstract

Critical infrastructures are the foundational pillars of modern society, encompassing essential systems and assets that support our daily lives, economy, and national security. These infrastructures, including transportation networks, power grids, water supplies, telecommunications, and financial systems, play a vital role in ensuring the smooth functioning of governments, businesses, and communities. Safeguarding these critical infrastructures from both physical and cyber threats is of utmost importance in our interconnected world. The global landscape presents various threats that can impact infrastructures, such as the Covid-19 pandemic, the activities of state and non-state hackers, and extreme weather events. Therefore, it is crucial to prioritize the development of resilient infrastructures capable of withstanding crises and maintaining stability. This entails adopting information, communication, and technology (ICT) platforms that leverage emerging and innovative technologies to enhance infrastructure protection. As ICT systems evolve and become more interconnected, collaborative, and holistic strategies are necessary to protect critical infrastructure assets from an ever-increasing number of evolving cyber threats and disruptive cyberattacks. Safeguarding high-risk critical infrastructure assets, which are vital to safety, efficiency, and reliability, presents serious challenges. Recognizing the importance of protecting critical infrastructure from all types of threats and implementing resilient strategies is paramount. This article begins by describing the challenges faced by the United States in protecting critical infrastructure and assessing its Cybersecurity readiness. It then explores strategies for resilience and the urgent need for critical infrastructure protection. Finally, the authors evaluate the resilience and readiness strategies in place for protecting critical infrastructure in the United States.

Keywords: Information, Communication, and Technology (ICT), Critical Infrastructures Protection, Cybersecurity Readiness

Introduction

Critical infrastructures are indispensable for the continuous functioning of society. They provide vital services that support economic growth, public safety, and overall well-being. Transportation networks facilitate the movement of goods and people, powering commerce and daily commutes. Power grids supply electricity, enabling industries, hospitals, and homes to operate. Telecommunications systems connect individuals across the globe, facilitating communication, commerce, and emergency services. Water supply systems ensure access to clean water, a fundamental necessity for health and sanitation. Financial systems underpin economic transactions, facilitating trade, investment, and prosperity. Any disruption or failure in these infrastructures can have severe consequences, affecting individuals, businesses, and nations at large. The United States heavily relies on the reliable and functioning critical infrastructure (CIs) for national and economic protection. However, it is crucial to recognize the increased risks associated with this dependency. Today, highly digitized, and interconnected CIs, such as healthcare and energy sectors, face numerous domestic and nation-state-sponsored threats. The cybersecurity readiness in critical infrastructure must ensure the confidentiality, integrity, and availability of assets. This includes protecting the creation, processing, storage, and transmission of assets within the system, preventing persistent, sophisticated, systematic, and well-funded attacks from both internal and external threat actors.

Critical infrastructure operators (Ross, 2018), along with their operational technologies (OT), operate complex industrial control (IC) systems, such as Supervisory Control and Data Acquisition (SCADA). These IC systems and equipment monitor and control devices, processes, and events in sectors like power, water, transportation, manufacturing, and other essential services. SCADA manages programmable systems or equipment that interacts with the physical environment in critical infrastructures. Ensuring the safety of critical infrastructure operators and their OT, as well as recognizing the need for cybersecurity readiness to protect IT infrastructure assets, must be a top priority for critical infrastructure stakeholders. IT assets in critical infrastructure are considered sensitive resources within IT systems and technologies. Addressing system vulnerabilities and effectively responding to attacks is essential for business continuity.

On the other hand, OT assets within critical infrastructure (IEC Technology Report, 2019), specifically power systems, have different security requirements and constraints. These OT power systems include cyber-operational and physical systems, each with specific security needs, such as availability, authentication, authorization, integrity, and safety levels. Disruptive incidents impacting OT assets can harm the safety and reliability of power systems, leading to catastrophic consequences. Safety-related incidents may result in intentional or accidental mis-operation of OT assets, potentially causing harm or even fatalities, while reliability-related incidents affect the performance of power system components like generators, breakers, transformers, power, and gas lines. Addressing vulnerabilities in OT, including poorly protected operational systems, control systems, and connected devices, has lagged IT infrastructure protection. Table 1 illustrates the priorities and security requirements (confidentiality, integrity, and availability) of critical infrastructure IT and OT systems.

Priority	C.I.A	Description
IT system	Confidentiality Integrity Availability	Prioritizes confidentiality to protect sensitive and private information
OT system	Availability Integrity Confidentiality	Prioritizes availability for safe and reliable operations

Table 1 – IT and OT C.I.A priorities and security requirement

Information Protection in Critical Infrastructures

The Whitehouse fact sheet (White House Fact Sheet, 2021) reported that the United States of America ranks 13th globally for overall quality of infrastructure protection even though it is considered as the wealthiest country in the world. To support the economy and security interests, it is important to ensure sufficient trustworthiness of systems, products, and services providing Critical Infrastructures Protection (CIP) to strengthen the critical infrastructure operators and their operational technologies. The urgency of protecting critical infrastructures should be recognized against cyber threats, natural disasters, and nation sponsor terrorist activities to avoid direct effect on the security and resilience of numerous sectors that could cause harm with catastrophic consequences.

Providing CIP for critical infrastructure prepare all the sectors to the highest standard for disaster preparedness, response, and recovery. For decades industries and administration (Global Forum on Cyber Expertise Report 2017) prioritized protecting critical infrastructures a range of physical challenges and threats attacks, such as terrorist acts, sabotage, or natural disasters. These events can cause significant damage and disruption to essential services, affecting public safety and economic stability. Additionally, the increasing reliance on technology and interconnected systems has led to the emergence of cyber threats. Cyberattacks targeting critical infrastructures can disrupt operations, compromise sensitive data, and potentially inflict widespread damage. The ever-evolving nature of these threats necessitates proactive measures to identify vulnerabilities and enhance protection.

Critical Information Infrastructures (CIIs) refer to the systems and networks that are vital to the functioning of a nation, organization, or society. These infrastructures primarily rely on information and communication technologies (ICT) to operate and provide essential services to the public, government, and various sectors of the economy. CIIs are crucial for the functioning of sectors such as energy, transportation, finance, healthcare, telecommunications, and government services. Increasing connectivity is a characteristic of CII that recognizes the growing interconnectedness of systems and devices. This connectivity enables efficient data exchange and integration across various components of the infrastructure, facilitating remote monitoring and management. It is essential to recognize the need for Critical Information Infrastructures Protection (CIIP) in place for effective CIIs. CIIP refers to the policies, strategies, and measures implemented to safeguard and secure critical information infrastructures against cyber threats and attacks. Figure 1 shows the interconnection between CI, CII and ICT infrastructures.

It is crucial for governments, organizations, and stakeholders to collaborate and align their efforts to develop and implement integrated strategies that encompass CIP, CIIP, and Cybersecurity to ensure the security, resilience, and continuity of critical systems and infrastructure in the face of emerging threats and challenges. Elements and concepts of Critical Infrastructure Protection (CIP), Critical Information Infrastructure Protection (CIIP), and Cybersecurity strategies are interrelated and complementary in safeguarding critical systems and assets. Figure 2 shows CIP, CIIP, and Cybersecurity strategies share common goals of protecting critical systems, assets, and information from threats and disruptions.

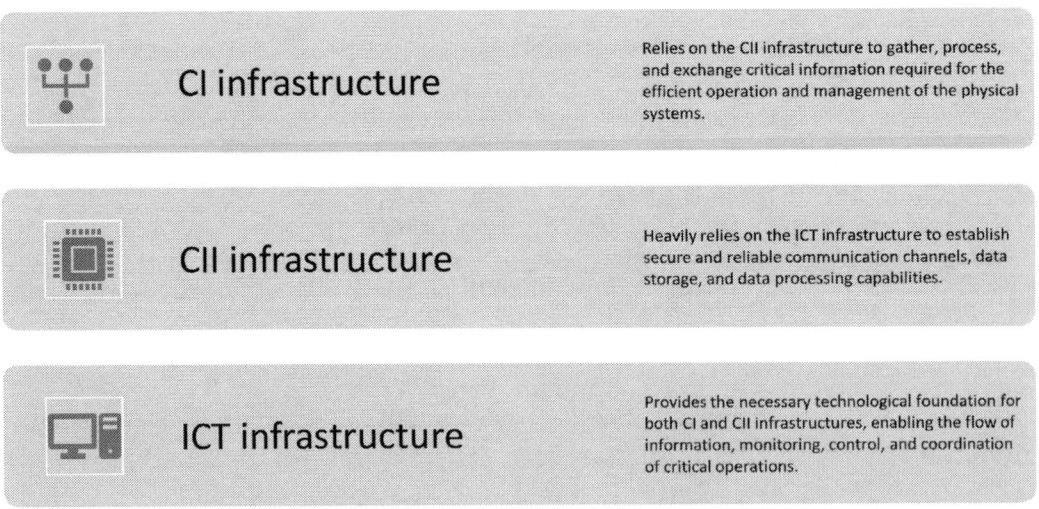

Figure 1 – Interconnection between CI, CII, and ICT infrastructures

Elements of Critical Infrastructure Protection (CIP)

Include identifying critical infrastructure sectors, conducting risk assessments, implementing protective measures, and establishing response and recovery plans.

Elements of Critical Information Infrastructure Protection (CIIP)

Elements of CIIP include risk assessments, security controls, incident response mechanisms, and information sharing frameworks to protect against cyber threats targeting critical information infrastructure.

Cybersecurity Strategies

Align with CIP and CIIP by addressing cyber threats that can disrupt critical infrastructure operations and compromise the security and resilience of information systems.

Figure 2 – Perspective on CIP, CIIP, and Cybersecurity strategies how their elements and concepts align

Threats and Risks impacts

Critical infrastructure is susceptible to a range of threats and risks that can have significant consequences for societies and economies. The 2023 global risks report (World Economic Forum Report, 2023) recognized the cybers threats among the top 10 risks. Figure 3 illustrates the threats and risks associated with critical infrastructure.

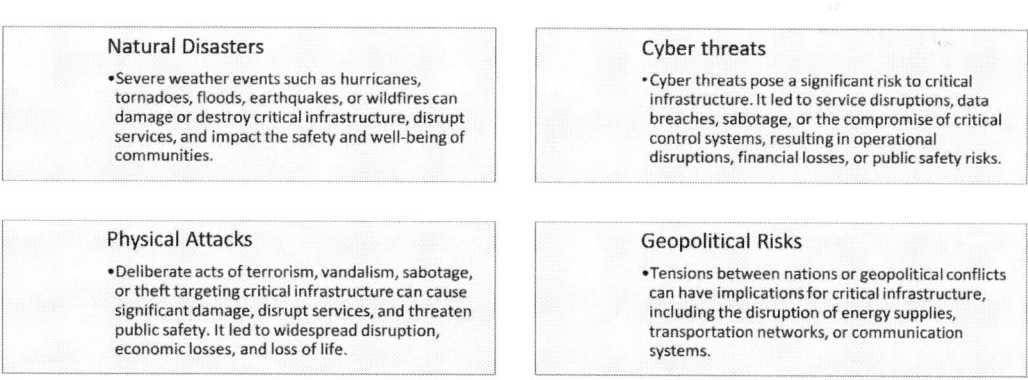

Natural Disasters
- Severe weather events such as hurricanes, tornadoes, floods, earthquakes, or wildfires can damage or destroy critical infrastructure, disrupt services, and impact the safety and well-being of communities.

Cyber threats
- Cyber threats pose a significant risk to critical infrastructure. It led to service disruptions, data breaches, sabotage, or the compromise of critical control systems, resulting in operational disruptions, financial losses, or public safety risks.

Physical Attacks
- Deliberate acts of terrorism, vandalism, sabotage, or theft targeting critical infrastructure can cause significant damage, disrupt services, and threaten public safety. It led to widespread disruption, economic losses, and loss of life.

Geopolitical Risks
- Tensions between nations or geopolitical conflicts can have implications for critical infrastructure, including the disruption of energy supplies, transportation networks, or communication systems.

Figure 3 – Ranking threats and risks associated with critical infrastructure 2023

Addressing these threats and risks requires a multi-faceted approach, including risk assessment and management, investment in resilient infrastructure, implementation of robust cybersecurity measures, emergency preparedness and response planning, public-private partnerships, and ongoing monitoring and mitigation efforts. Governments, organizations, and communities must collaborate to enhance the resilience and security of critical infrastructure to ensure the continued functioning and safety of societies.

Cyber Incidents Timeline

The cyber incidents highlight the increasing sophistication and impact of cyberattacks on critical infrastructure. They underscore the importance of robust cybersecurity readiness, risk assessments, incident response capabilities, and collaboration between public and private sectors to safeguard critical systems and minimize the potential for disruptions. The (Center for Strategic & International Studies, 2023) identified the timeline of significant global cyber incidents since 2006 focusing on state actions, espionage, and cyberattacks. These incidents illustrate the global nature of cyber threats targeting government agencies, defense, and critical infrastructures, highlighting the need for robust cybersecurity measures, readiness, and constant vigilance to protect sensitive information and ensure the resilience of essential systems. Figure 4 shows the substantial global cyber incidents between 2006 to March 2023.

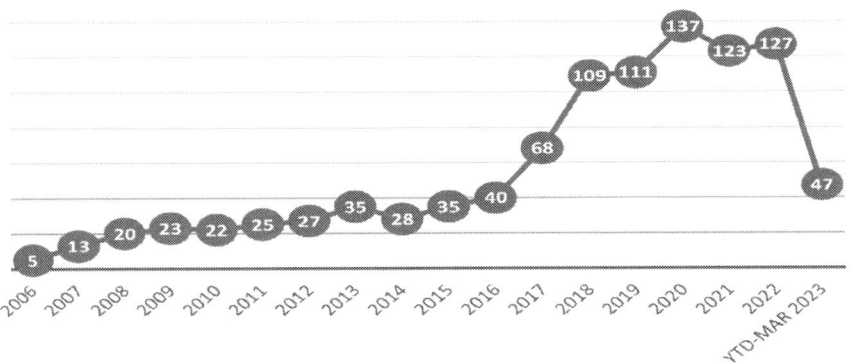

Figure 4 – Timeline of significant global cyber incidents

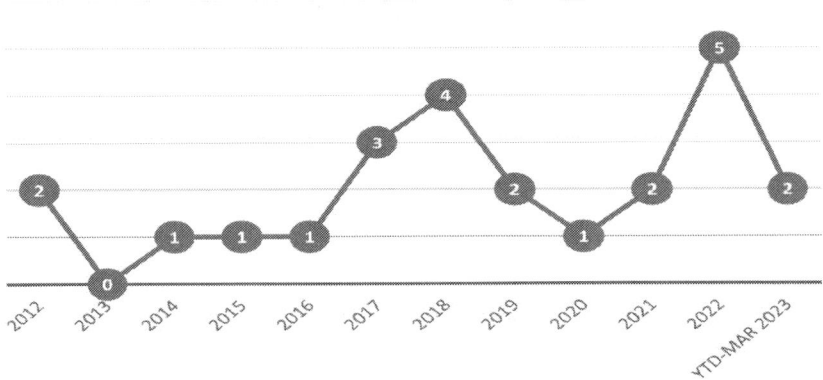

Figure 5 – Timeline of significant global cyber incidents targeting critical infrastructure

Figure 5 shows the substantial global cyber incidents on critical infrastructure between 2006 to March 2023. The incidents highlight the growing sophistication and impact of cyber-attacks on critical infrastructure globally. They underscore the need for robust cybersecurity measures, continuous monitoring, and international collaboration to defend against such threats and protect critical systems. The (Washburn and Sin, 2019) dataset collected significant incidents worldwide, utilizing publicly available information, targeting various domains of critical infrastructures from January 1, 2009, to November 15, 2019. It comprises a total of 130 incidents specifically directed at critical infrastructure sectors. Figure 6 illustrates the notable incidents within different critical infrastructure sectors documented during the period spanning from 2009 to 2019.

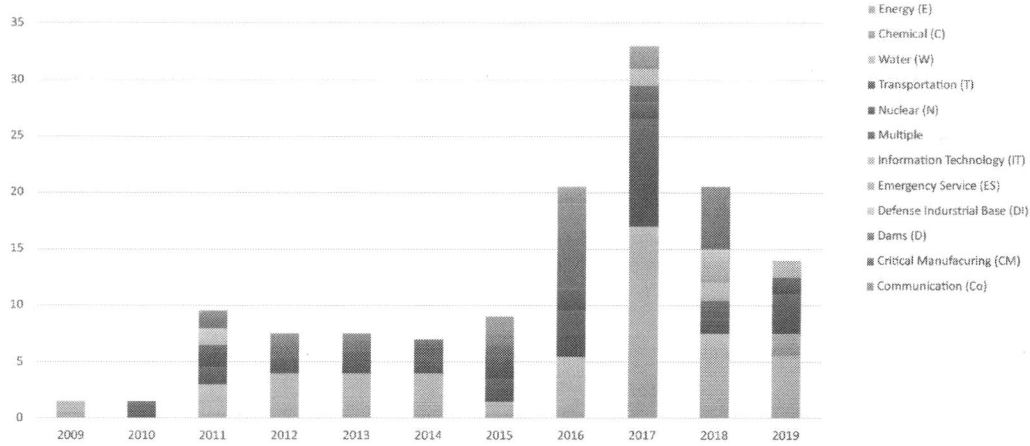

Figure 6 – notable incidents within different critical infrastructure sectors from 2009 to 2019

Based on the graph provided, notable observations can be made regarding the disruption of critical infrastructure sectors, particularly in the Energy and Transportation sectors. These sectors experienced a significant spike in incidents, followed by the critical manufacturing and nuclear sectors, respectively. This spike can be attributed to ransomware attacks like WannaCry and destructive malware such as NotPetya, which occurred in 2017. The dataset encompasses two key factors: disruptive cyber-physical incidents and disruptive cyber-operational incidents. In the case of cyber-physical incidents, malicious activities executed by state or nonstate threat actors have had disruptive effects on operational technology (OT) systems, devices, and processes, thereby compromising Industrial Control (IC) systems. On the other hand, cyber-operational incidents involve threat actors conducting malicious activities that disrupt IT systems connected to ICS or Internet of Things (IoT) systems and devices. These incidents can be aimed at managing inspections, intelligence preparation of the battlefield (IPB), or stealing intellectual property (IP) for economic purposes. Figure 7 displays the cases of disruptive incidents categorized as cyber-physical incidents, cyber-operational incidents, or cases with unknown factors. The data covers the period from January 1, 2009, to November 15, 2019.

Figure 7 – Disruptive incidents

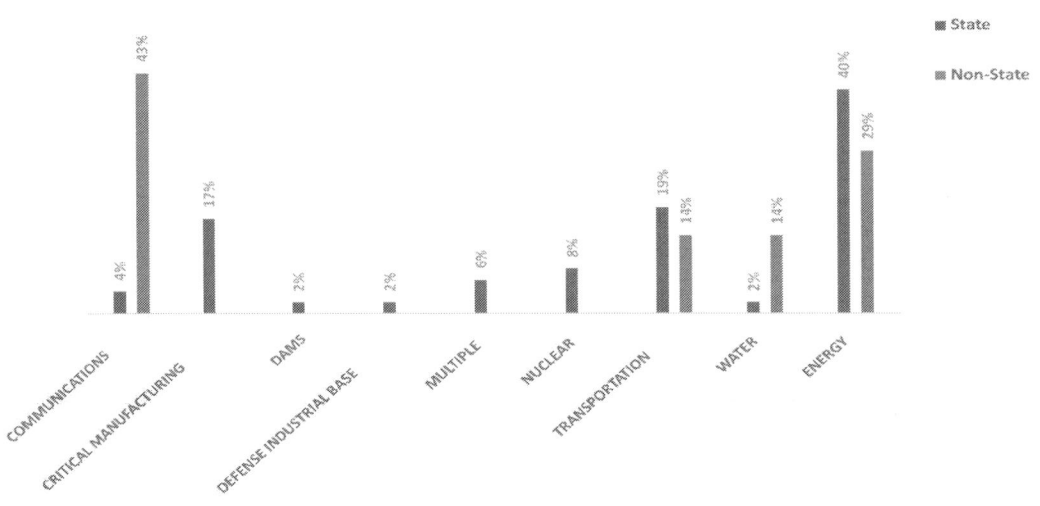

Figure 8 – Critical infrastructure sectors targeted by various threat agents

Based on the data collected, as depicted in Figure 8, it is evident that critical infrastructure sectors have been targeted by various threat agents. The dataset reveals that the number of incidents attributed to state agents is higher compared to non-state agents. This trend can be attributed to the fact that non-state incidents in the cyber domain often remain anonymous, making it challenging to attribute them to specific entities or actors.

Critical Infrastructure Protection (CIP) in the United States

Reliable critical infrastructures serve as a lifeline for the United States, supporting essential aspects of daily life such as access to clean water, power supply, transportation, and communications. The definition of critical infrastructures was redefined under the Patriot Act of 2001 (Patriot Act of 2001) to encompass a wide range of assets, systems, operational technologies, and other vital elements within both the physical and cyber environments. Recognizing the importance of protecting these critical infrastructures, the United States made it a top national priority, leading to the initiation of Executive Order 13636 (Executive Order 13636, 2013) in 2013. This order aimed to enhance the cybersecurity of critical infrastructures by promoting the development and implementation of effective measures. Its policy directive is to bolster the security and resilience of the nation's critical infrastructures while fostering an efficient, innovative, and economically prosperous cyber environment. Additionally, the order emphasizes the importance of maintaining safety, security, business confidentiality, privacy, and civil liberties.

Cybersecurity Enhancement Act 2014 (CEA)

In the United States, critical physical and cyber infrastructures are primarily owned and operated by entities in the private sector, as well as federal, state, or regional governments. In alignment with the directives of Executive Order 13636, the Cybersecurity Enhancement Act 2014 (CEA) (S.1353 -113th Congress, 2014) was enacted. This legislation authorized the National Institute of Standards and Technology (NIST) to lead efforts in developing a framework aimed at reducing risks to critical infrastructures. The CEA focuses on several key areas on in order to enhance the overall cybersecurity posture, collaboration between the public and private sectors is crucial. By encouraging cooperation and information sharing, both sectors can benefit from shared knowledge and resources, leading to improved cyber defense capabilities.

Additionally, promoting cybersecurity research and development plays a significant role in strengthening the security of critical infrastructures. This involves advancing technologies, tools, and techniques to stay ahead of evolving threats and vulnerabilities. Another key aspect is education and workforce development. Supporting programs and initiatives aimed at developing a skilled cybersecurity workforce is essential for addressing the growing demand for cybersecurity professionals. By increasing awareness of cybersecurity best practices, individuals and organizations can better protect themselves against cyber threats. Raising public awareness about cybersecurity threats and promoting preparedness measures is also vital. This includes educating the public about common cyber threats, such as phishing and malware, and providing guidance on how to protect personal information and sensitive data. Additionally, fostering an understanding of the potential impact of cyberattacks can encourage individuals and organizations to take proactive measures to mitigate risks.

Lastly, the advancement of cybersecurity technical standards is crucial for improving the security and resilience of critical infrastructures. By facilitating the development and adoption of technical standards, such as encryption protocols and secure network architectures, we can establish a strong foundation for cybersecurity across various sectors. These standards help ensure interoperability, promote best practices, and foster a more secure digital environment overall. Through the implementation of these initiatives, the CEA aims to enhance the protection of critical infrastructures by fostering collaboration, research, education, preparedness, and the establishment of technical standards in the field of cybersecurity.

The aim is to establish a framework that enables owners and operators of critical infrastructures to effectively address cyber risks in a prioritized, flexible, repeatable, performance-based, and cost-effective manner. This involves implementing information security measures and controls that can be voluntarily adopted. In 2013, Executive Order 13691 (Executive Order 13691, 2013) was issued to promote cybersecurity information sharing and engage the private sector in exchanging information about cybersecurity risks and disruptive incidents.

The United States Critical Infrastructure Sectors

The United States recognizes sixteen critical infrastructure sectors (CISA Year in Review 2022, 2022) that are essential for the functioning of society and the economy. These sectors, as identified by the Cybersecurity and Infrastructure Security Agency (CISA) (H.R.3359-115th Congress, 2018). The critical infrastructure of a nation comprises various sectors, each playing a vital role in the functioning of society.

The Chemical Sector involves facilities engaged in the production, storage, and distribution of chemicals, which are essential for numerous industries. The Commercial Facilities Sector includes shopping malls, sports arenas, and other commercial buildings that provide spaces for business activities and public gatherings. The Communications Sector encompasses the infrastructure and services responsible for transmitting and distributing communication signals, such as telecommunications networks and broadcasting systems. The Critical Manufacturing Sector comprises industries involved in manufacturing essential goods and materials, including automotive, aerospace, and defense. The Dams Sector encompasses dams and related infrastructure, such as reservoirs and levees, which play a crucial role in water management and energy production. The Defense Industrial Base Sector supports defense and military operations by providing the necessary industrial complex. The Emergency Services Sector encompasses organizations involved in providing emergency response and management services, including law enforcement, fire services, and emergency medical services. The Energy Sector covers the production, transmission, and distribution of energy resources, such as electricity, oil, natural gas, and renewable energy sources. The Financial Services Sector involves institutions engaged in banking, investment, insurance, and other financial activities. The Food and Agriculture Sector plays a critical role in the production, processing, and distribution of food and agricultural products, ensuring food security and supply. The Government Facilities Sector includes facilities and infrastructure that support government operations, such as administrative buildings and public transportation systems. The Healthcare and Public Health Sector comprises healthcare facilities, hospitals, medical supply manufacturers, and public health organizations. The Information Technology Sector involves industries responsible for designing, developing, and maintaining information technology systems and networks, facilitating communication, and data management. The Nuclear Reactors, Materials, and Waste Sector includes nuclear power plants, facilities for handling nuclear materials, and sites for the disposal of radioactive waste. The Transportation Systems Sector encompasses various modes of transportation, including aviation, maritime, rail, and road transportation systems. Lastly, the Water and Wastewater Systems Sector covers facilities involved in water supply, treatment, distribution, and wastewater management, ensuring clean and accessible water resources for communities. These sectors collectively form the critical infrastructure that underpins the functioning and security of a nation, requiring careful attention and protection.

These sectors are interconnected and rely on each other to ensure the reliable operation of critical infrastructure. They represent various industries and infrastructure components that are vital for the functioning of the nation. Each sector has its own unique characteristics, risks, and vulnerabilities. CISA, along with sector-specific agencies and stakeholders, works to enhance the security, resilience, and preparedness of these critical infrastructure sectors. By addressing risks and implementing appropriate protective measures, the aim is to ensure the continued operation and protection of these essential sectors in the face of various threats and hazards. Table 1 presents the sixteen critical infrastructure sectors and their corresponding Sector-Specific Agencies, as outlined in Presidential Policy Directive-21 and the 2013 National Infrastructure Protection Plan (National Infrastructure Protection Plan 2013).

Sector-Specify Agency	Critical infrastructure sectors
Department of Homeland Security (DHS)	Chemical Sector
	Communications Sector
	Dam Sector
	Emergency Services Sector
	Government Facilities Sector
	Information Technology Sector
	Transportation system Sector
	Commercial facilities Sector
	Critical Manufacturing Sector
	Nuclear Reactors, Materials & Waste Sector
Department of Treasury	Financial Services Sector
General Services Administration (GSA)	Government Facilities Sector
Department of Transportation (DOT)	Transportation system Sector
Department of Defense (DOD)	Defense Industrial Base Sector
Department of Energy (DOE)	Energy Sector
Department of Agriculture (USDA)	Food & Agriculture Sector
Department of Health & Human Services (HHS)	Food & Agriculture Sector
Environmental Protection Agency (EFA)	Water & Wastewater systems sector

Table 2 – CISA Critical Infrastructure Sectors

The 16 critical infrastructure sectors in the United States are interconnected and mutually dependent on each other to ensure reliable operations. Consequently, any disruption or loss experienced in one of these critical sectors will directly impact the security and resilience of not only the affected sector but also the operational technologies of other sectors. It is crucial to recognize and comprehend the interdependencies among these sectors in order to assess potential risks and vulnerabilities. Figure 9 provides a visual representation of the interdependencies among the U.S. critical infrastructure sectors.[1]

The private sector is responsible for owning and operating the majority of critical infrastructure sectors in the United States. Establishing strong partnerships between the private and public sectors is crucial to enhance security and resilience through integrated collaboration and interaction. These partnerships play a central role in implementing information sharing and awareness programs, ensuring efficient dissemination of critical threat information, risk mitigation strategies,

---

[1] Critical infrastructure sectors - https://www.cisa.gov/topics/critical-infrastructure-security-and-resilience/critical-infrastructure-sectors

and other sensitive information from state, local, tribal, territorial governments, and international partners.

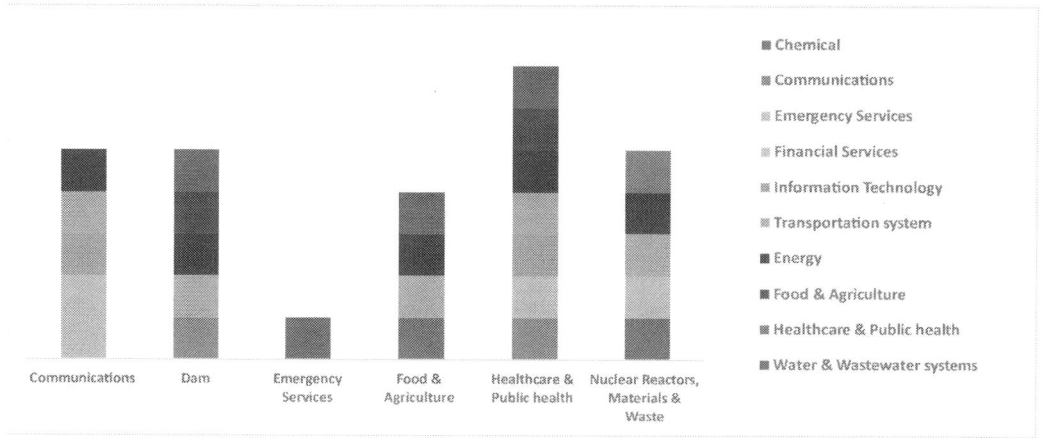

Figure 9 – Critical infrastructure sectors and their Interdependencies

Collaboration Between Public and Private Sector Partners

The Department of Homeland Security (DHS) and the Cybersecurity and Infrastructure Security Agency (CISA) actively collaborate with public and private sector partners to effectively manage and safeguard the critical infrastructure of the United States. This collaboration is vital for enhancing the security and resilience of the nation's critical infrastructure. Together, these agencies work closely with stakeholders from both sectors to ensure a comprehensive and coordinated approach to protecting critical infrastructure. To support this unified and coordinated approach, various councils and initiatives play significant roles. They focus on promoting collaboration, information sharing, and efficient resource allocation, all of which contribute to enhancing the overall protection and continuity of critical infrastructures.

> *National Infrastructure Protection Plan (NIPP)* – (National Infrastructure Protection Plan, 2013) serves as a strategic document, guiding federal, state, local, tribal, and territorial governments, as well as private sector entities, in collaborating and coordinating efforts to protect critical infrastructures. The NIPP emphasizes the importance of partnerships and collaboration as key components of a successful security and resilience strategy. It encourages the formation of public-private partnerships and partnerships between government agencies at all levels to leverage resources, expertise, and information sharing. Additionally, there are several councils that play vital roles in supporting critical infrastructure protection and resilience.

Critical Infrastructures Partnership Advisory Council (CIPAC) – (Charter of Critical Infrastructure Protection Advisory Council, 2010) serves as an advisory body, facilitating collaboration and information exchange between public and private sector stakeholders. It helps identify and address cross-sector issues, vulnerabilities, and interdependencies, while supporting the development and implementation of strategies, policies, and programs to enhance the protection, preparedness, response, and recovery capabilities of critical infrastructures.

Critical Infrastructures Cross-Sector Council (CICSC) – (Critical Infrastructure Cross Sector Council Charter, 2018) focuses on addressing cross-sector issues and interdependencies among different critical infrastructure sectors. It promotes collaboration and coordination among sector-specific agencies, industry representatives, and other stakeholders to identify and mitigate cross-sector risks and vulnerabilities. Through the exchange of best practices and actionable information, the CICSC contributes to effective risk management, incident response, and recovery capabilities across multiple sectors.

Federal Senior Leadership Council (FSLC) – (Federal Senior Leadership Council Charter, 2021) comprises senior officials from federal departments and agencies who provide leadership, coordination, and guidance to enhance the protection and resilience of critical infrastructures at the federal level. The FSLC facilitates collaboration and coordination among federal agencies involved in critical infrastructure protection, aligning efforts, and ensuring effective resource utilization.

State, Local, Tribal, and Territorial Government Coordinating Council (SLTTGCC) – (State, Local, Tribal, and Territorial Government Coordinating Council, 2016) serves as a platform for coordination and collaboration among state, local, tribal, and territorial (SLTT) governments. The council enables information sharing, enhances preparedness and response capabilities, and ensures a coordinated and integrated approach to critical infrastructure protection within SLTT jurisdictions.

Regional Consortium Coordinating Council (RC3) – (Regional Consortium Coordinating Council Charter, 2018) facilitates coordination and collaboration among regional consortiums, bringing together stakeholders within specific geographic areas. The RC3 supports information sharing, the development of regional strategies, and the integration of regional efforts into the larger framework of critical infrastructure protection and resilience.

Through the collaborative efforts of these councils and initiatives, a unified and coordinated approach is fostered, strengthening the security and resilience of critical infrastructures. They promote effective communication, resource utilization, and the sharing of best practices, ultimately safeguarding essential services and ensuring the well-being and prosperity of the country.

Information Sharing and Partnerships

Collaborative partnerships, both voluntary and regulatory, along with information sharing facilitation and awareness initiatives, play a pivotal role in safeguarding the security and resilience of critical infrastructures [21]. These programs are essential for establishing a robust knowledge system that enables the exchange and upkeep of critical threat information, risk mitigation strategies, and other sensitive assets. By fostering information sharing, collaboration, and coordination, these programs, and platforms bolster cybersecurity capabilities, fortify the resilience of critical infrastructures and communities, and ensure their enhanced protection.

> *Traffic Light Protocol (TLP)* – (Traffic Light Protocol 2.0 User Guide, 2022) provides a standardized framework for classifying and distributing information based on its sensitivity and intended audience. Information is categorized into different levels within the TLP, each serving a specific purpose. TLP Red designates highly sensitive information that should be restricted to individuals with a specific need-to-know within a specific organization or agency. Its distribution is strictly limited to that trusted circle. TLP Amber represents sensitive information that can be shared with a broader audience on a need-to-know basis, especially if it involves specific operational details or potential risks that require limited distribution. TLP Green signifies unclassified information that can be shared more freely within a community or with trusted partners, such as general awareness, best practices, or general threat information. TLP White indicates unclassified information that can be openly shared with the public, including general information, public advisories, or educational resources. By adhering to the TLP, organizations ensure the appropriate handling and control of sensitive information, promoting effective communication, information sharing, and collaboration while maintaining necessary levels of confidentiality and security. The TLP helps prevent unnecessary disclosure and potential risks, enabling organizations and individuals to share sensitive information appropriately.
>
> *Cyber Information Sharing and Collaboration Program (CISCP)* – (Critical Infrastructure and Key Resources Cyber Information Sharing and Collaboration Program, 2023) is a program aimed at facilitating the sharing of cyber threat information and promoting collaboration among participating organizations. It provides a structured framework for sharing valuable cyber threat intelligence, including indicators of compromise, attack patterns,

and vulnerability information. By sharing this information in a timely and secure manner, organizations can enhance their situational awareness, improve their cyber defenses, and respond effectively to emerging threats. The program encourages collaboration between public and private sector entities, fostering the exchange of best practices, lessons learned, and technical expertise. It also fosters partnerships between government agencies, industry stakeholders, and other organizations, creating a collaborative ecosystem for addressing cyber threats and improving cybersecurity posture. Participating organizations benefit from access to timely and actionable cyber threat information, enabling them to make informed decisions and take proactive measures to protect their networks and systems. The program also supports the development of standardized processes, tools, and protocols to streamline information sharing and collaboration.

Information Sharing and Analysis Centers (ISACs) – (Vijayan, 2022) are industry-specific organizations that facilitate the sharing of cyber threat information and best practices within a particular sector. They serve as trusted hubs for information exchange, collaboration, and coordination among stakeholders to enhance cyber threat awareness and response capabilities. ISACs bring together organizations operating within the same sector, such as companies, government agencies, academic institutions, and non-profit organizations. The primary goal of ISACs is to promote timely and effective sharing of actionable threat intelligence, incident reports, and mitigation strategies. They play a vital role in enhancing sector-wide cybersecurity resilience by fostering collaboration, developing sector-specific incident response plans, and advocating for policy improvements. ISACs also serve as liaisons between their sector and government agencies, enabling information exchange and coordination of cybersecurity efforts.

Information Sharing and Analysis Organizations (ISAOs) – (Vijayan, 2022) are entities that facilitate the sharing of cybersecurity information and collaborate with stakeholders to enhance cybersecurity capabilities. They serve as trusted platforms for information exchange, analysis, and coordination among organizations within a specific sector, community, or region. ISAOs encourage the voluntary sharing of cybersecurity-related data, including threat intelligence, incident reports, and best practices. Their primary objective is to foster collaboration and enable members to collectively address cybersecurity challenges. Participating organizations gain access to tailored threat intelligence and analysis, enhancing situational awareness and incident response capabilities. ISAOs also coordinate incident response efforts, share timely alerts and warnings, and provide services such as training and education. They collaborate with government agencies and industry partners to advocate for policy improvements and promote industry-specific standards and best practices. ISAOs contribute to overall resilience by creating a collective defense environment that strengthens cybersecurity across communities or sectors.

Automated Indicator Sharing (AIS) – (Automated Indicator Sharing, 2016) is a system and process that enables organizations to exchange cybersecurity threat indicators in an automated and machine-readable format. It enhances timely detection and response to cyber threats by sharing actionable intelligence such as indicators of compromise (IOCs) with trusted partners. AIS automates the collection, processing, and dissemination of this information, improving the speed and efficiency of sharing. The goal is to proactively detect and respond to cyber incidents by incorporating real-time updates into security systems. AIS operates on trust and compliance with data sharing standards, ensuring privacy and protection of sensitive information. It integrates with existing security infrastructure for correlation and analysis, strengthening collective cyber defense capabilities.

Protected Critical Infrastructure Information (PCII) – (Protected Critical Infrastructure Information, 2023) refers to sensitive information related to critical infrastructure that is shared with the government and receives certain legal protections. PCII is a designation established by the United States Department of Homeland Security (DHS) under the Critical Infrastructure Information Act of 2002. Its purpose is to encourage private sector entities to voluntarily share sensitive information about their critical infrastructure assets, systems, and operations with the government. PCII includes vulnerabilities, threats, and protective measures. The shared information helps the government understand risks and develop strategies to enhance security and resilience. PCII is protected by law, exempt from public disclosure under the Freedom of Information Act (FOIA). This protection ensures the confidentiality and privacy of shared information and alleviates concerns about legal or competitive consequences. The sharing of PCII follows established channels and processes, prioritizing information protection. Organizations that submit PCII receive certification, recognizing and safeguarding their information. The PCII program fosters a trusted partnership between the government and the private sector, promoting information sharing for critical infrastructure security and resilience. It facilitates the exchange of valuable information, enabling the government to understand the critical infrastructure landscape, mitigate risks, and collaborate effectively with private sector stakeholders to respond to threats.

Homeland Security Information Network (HSIN) – (Homeland Security Information Network Annual Report, 2022) is a secure web-based platform operated by the United States Department of Homeland Security (DHS).

It facilitates information sharing and collaboration among homeland security stakeholders, including federal, state, local, tribal, territorial governments, and private sector organizations. HSIN allows authorized users to exchange sensitive but unclassified information, collaborate on operational activities, and access resources for protecting the homeland. It provides a secure environment for sharing situational awareness, threat intelligence, incident reports, and best practices. The platform offers features like discussion boards, file sharing, real-time chat, and notification systems. HSIN supports various homeland security missions and initiatives, serving as a central hub for accessing timely information, coordinating activities, and collaborating on joint projects. Robust security measures ensure the confidentiality, integrity, and availability of shared information, with access restricted to authorized individuals.

National Cyber Awareness System (NCAS) – (National Cyber Awareness System, 2023) is a program operated by the United States Department of Homeland Security (DHS). Its main goal is to provide timely and actionable information about cybersecurity threats, vulnerabilities, and best practices. The NCCIC serves as a centralized repository for cybersecurity resources and disseminates alerts, advisories, and notifications to individuals, organizations, and the public. The information is carefully vetted and validated before sharing. The NCCIC offers customizable notifications through various channels and provides educational resources and guidance to improve cybersecurity. Its aim is to empower individuals and organizations to protect their digital assets and contribute to the resilience of the nation's digital infrastructure.

National Information Exchange Model (NIEM) – (National Information Exchange Model, 2021) is a framework and set of standards developed by the United States government to facilitate the exchange of information between different organizations and agencies. It provides a common language and structure for data sharing, ensuring interoperability, and consistency. NIEM addresses information sharing challenges across various domains and sectors by promoting standardized data exchange. It includes data standards, exchange specifications, and supporting infrastructure. NIEM streamlines information sharing processes, reduces data translation efforts, and enhances accuracy. It enables disparate systems to exchange data in a consistent manner, fostering efficient collaboration. NIEM is a collaborative effort involving the government, agencies, tribal governments, international partners, and industry stakeholders. It breaks down data silos, improves communication, and supports various government operations.

Threat Information Guidelines

To streamline the exchange of threat information between private and public critical infrastructure sectors, a comprehensive set of guidelines has been implemented. These guidelines serve as a framework that facilitates the sharing of information and expedites its flow among these sectors. The objective is to establish robust information sharing platforms that enhance collaboration and enable swift dissemination of threat intelligence between private and public entities within the critical infrastructure sectors.

Cybersecurity and Infrastructure Security Agency's (CISA) Infrastructure Security Division – (Infrastructure Security Division, 2023) focuses on protecting and enhancing the security of critical infrastructure in the United States. Its main mission is to collaborate with public and private sector partners to identify, assess, and mitigate risks to critical infrastructure, thereby safeguarding national security and public safety. The division works across multiple sectors, providing services such as risk assessments, incident response coordination, information sharing, and technical assistance. Its responsibilities include conducting thorough risk assessments, coordinating response efforts during incidents, facilitating information sharing among partners, offering technical expertise to infrastructure owners and operators, and establishing partnerships with public and private sector entities. By leveraging its expertise and partnerships, the division works towards enhancing the security and resilience of critical infrastructure, ensuring the availability of essential services, and protecting the well-being of the nation's citizens.

Information sharing tools – promote the sharing of information within and between the various sectors of critical infrastructures, including Homeland Security Information Network - Critical Infrastructures (HSIN-CI) (Homeland Security Information Network - Critical Infrastructures, 2023), Infrastructures Protection Gateway (IP Gateway) (Infrastructures Protection Gateway, 2023), National Infrastructures Coordinating Center (NICC) (National Infrastructures Coordinating Center, 2008), National Risk Management Center (NRMC) (National Risk Management Center, 2023), Protected Critical Infrastructures Information (PCII) Program, Protective Security Advisors (PSAs) (Protective Security Advisors, 2023) and TRIPwire (Technical Resource for Incident Prevention) (TRIPwire, 2023).

Critical Infrastructures Threat Information Sharing Framework and Environment –(Critical Infrastructure Threat Information Sharing Framework, 2016) a structured approach and set of guidelines that facilitate the sharing of threat information related to critical infrastructure. It establishes policies and procedures, builds trust, standardizes data formats, and utilizes dedicated platforms and tools to enable effective information sharing. The framework includes mechanisms for timely reporting and coordinated response, automation of sharing through technologies like AIS, sector-specific information sharing groups, and continuous improvement and evaluation. By implementing this framework, organizations can enhance their ability to detect, prevent, and respond to threats, ensuring the security and resilience of critical infrastructure. The Sharing Environment is a collaborative effort that enhances the sharing of critical infrastructure information among government agencies, private sector organizations, and stakeholders. It provides a platform for exchanging threat intelligence, best practices, and situational awareness specific to critical infrastructure sectors. It facilitates sector-specific information sharing, develops trusted communities, supports incident reporting and collaboration, offers analytical capabilities, and fosters government-private sector partnerships. It ensures a secure environment for sharing information, maintains confidentiality, and adapts to evolving threats and sector requirements. Participating in this environment enables organizations to access valuable insights, enhance their security posture, and collectively address critical infrastructure challenges for national security and public safety.

Conclusion

Critical infrastructure is a vital requirement for the survival of any society. This article highlights the importance of recognizing security and resilience as critical requirements for effective protection strategies in the United State. It explores various cybersecurity assessment frameworks and strategies with a shared goal of enhancing cybersecurity capacity and effectiveness. These assessments primarily focus on evaluating the level of cybersecurity capabilities by promoting best practices, safeguarding information, guiding cybersecurity activities, and managing risks within organizations. They also contribute to maintaining the desired security posture, assessing the current state of cyber preparedness, and fostering operational resilience. To further enhance the frameworks for protecting critical infrastructure, it is recommended to develop a measurement system that evaluates the capabilities of assessment methods. This system should measure the effectiveness of activities and action plans using meaningful indicators on a shared platform. Moreover, transitioning from voluntary and self-assessment methods to a more consistent and comprehensive approach would be beneficial.

Author Capsule Bio

Maryam Roshanaei, Ph.D. is as an assistant professor specializing in cybersecurity and Information Sciences and Technology at the Pennsylvania State University Abington. She earned her Ph.D. in Computer Networks and Security from University of Kingston London, UK. Before coming to Pennsylvania, she held the position of Associate Professor of Cybersecurity at the University of Greenwich in London, United Kingdom (UK). With over two decades of experience, she is a dedicated and enthusiastic educator, having taught and developed courses at both undergraduate and graduate levels in the fields of Cybersecurity, Information Security, and related subjects in both the USA and UK. She is an active researcher whose areas of expertise encompass various domains including AI for Good, Cyber Trust, Cyber hygiene, Critical Infrastructure Protection, Future Networks (FN), Cybersecurity, Digital Forensics and Crime, Internet privacy, and surveillance. Her involvement extends to esteemed organizations such as the British Standard Institute (BSI), International Standard Organization (ISO), and International Telecommunication Union (ITU) Data Communication standards committees. Within these groups, she serves in significant capacities such as Committee Chair and Principal Expert. Her contributions span standardization and journal publications across a diverse range of applied research projects, including AI for Good, Future Network (FN), Mobility, and Service Composition.

References

Automated Indicator Sharing (AIS). 2016. HDS. Retrieved from https://www.dhs.gov/sites/default/files/publications/privacy_pia_nppd_ais_update_03162016.pdf.

Center for Strategic & International Studies (CSIS). 2023. Significant Cyber Incidents Since 2006.Retrieved from https://www.csis.org/programs/strategic-technologies-program/significant-cyber-incidents

Charter of Critical Infrastructure Protection Advisory Council. 2010. HDS. Retrieved from https://www.dhs.gov/xlibrary/assets/cipac/cipac_charter.pdf.

CISA Year in Review 2022. CISA. 2022. CISA Year in Review 2022. Retrieved from https://www.cisa.gov/2022-year-review

Critical Infrastructure and Key Resources Cyber Information Sharing and Collaboration Program. 2023. HDS. Retrieved from https://www.cisa.gov/sites/default/files/c3vp/CISCP_20140523.pdf.

Critical Infrastructure Cross Sector Council Charter. 2018. CISA. Retrieved from https://www.cisa.gov/sites/default/files/publications/chartercscapp-508.pdf.

Critical Infrastructure Sector Partnerships. 2023. CISA. Retrieved from https://www.cisa.gov/topics/partnerships-and-collaboration/critical-infrastructure-sector-partnerships-0.

Critical Infrastructure Threat Information Sharing Framework: A Reference Guide for the Critical Infrastructure Community, 2016. DHS. Retrieved from https://www.cisa.gov/sites/default/files/publications/ci-threat-information-sharing-framework-508.pdf.

Executive Order 13636. 2013. Improving Critical Infrastructure Cybersecurity. Retrieved from https://www.federalregister.gov/documents/2013/02/19/2013-03915/improving-critical-infrastructure-cybersecurity.

Executive Order 13691.2013—Promoting Private Sector Cybersecurity Information Sharing. https://obamawhitehouse.archives.gov/the-press-office/2015/02/13/executive-order-promoting-private-sector-cybersecurity-information-shari.

Federal Senior Leadership Council Charter. 2021. CISA. Retrieved from https://www.cisa.gov/sites/default/files/publications/fslc-charter-2021-508.pdf.

Global Forum on Cyber Expertise Report. 2017. GFCE Global Good Practices Critical Information Infrastructure

Protection (CIIP). Retrieved from https://thegfce.org/wp-content/uploads/2020/06/CriticalInformationInfrastructureProtectionCIIP.pdf.

H.R.3359 — 115th Congress. 2018. Cybersecurity and Infrastructure Security Agency Act of 2018. Retrieved from https://www.congress.gov/bill/115th-congress/house-bill/3359/text

Homeland Security Information Network – Critical Infrastructures (HSIN-CI). 2023. DHS. Retrieved from https://www.dhs.gov/hsin-critical-infrastructure.

Homeland Security Information Network Annual Report, 2022. DHS. Retrieved from https://www.dhs.gov/sites/default/files/2023-05/23_0512_hsin-2022-annual-report-508-version.pdf.

IEC Technology Report. 2019. Cyber Security and Resilience Guidelines for the Smart Energy Operational Environment. Retrieved from www.iec.ch/basecamp/

cyber-security-and-resilience-guidelines-smart-energy-operational-environment.

Infrastructure Security Division. 2023. CISA. Retrieved from https://www.cisa.gov/about/divisions-offices/infrastructure-security-division.

Infrastructures Protection Gateway (IP Gateway), 2023. DHS. Retrieved from https://www.cisa.gov/sites/default/files/publications/ip-gateway-fact-sheet-11-15-508.pdf.

National Cyber Awareness System, 2023. CISA. Retrieved from https://www.cisa.gov/resources-tools/services/national-cyber-awareness-system.

National Information Exchange Model. 2021. NIEM Report. Retrieved from https://www.niem.gov/sites/default/files/2022-02/NIEM_2021AnnualReport%20FINAL.pdf.

National Infrastructure Protection Plan (NIPP) 2013: Partnering for Critical Infrastructure Security and Resilience. Cybersecurity and Infrastructure Security Agency (CISA). Retrieved from https://www.cisa.gov/resources-tools/resources/nipp-2013-partnering-critical-infrastructure-security-and-resilience.

National Infrastructures Coordinating Center (NICC), 2008. DHS. Retrieved from https://www.fema.gov/pdf/emergency/nrf/nrf-core.pdf.

National Risk Management Center, 2023. CISA. Retrieved from https://www.cisa.gov/sites/default/files/publications/fact_sheet_nrmc_508_1.pdf.

Patriot Act of 2001. Retrieved from https://www.justice.gov/archive/ll/highlights.htm.

Presidential Policy Directive-21. 2013. Critical Infrastructure Security and Resilience. Retrieved from https://obamawhitehouse.archives.gov/the-press-office/2013/02/12/presidential-policy-directive-critical-infrastructure-security-and-resil.

Protected Critical Infrastructure Information. 2023. CISA. Retrieved from https://www.cisa.gov/sites/default/files/2023-02/pcii-program-fact-sheet-012022_0.pdf.

Protective Security Advisors (PSAs). 2023. CISA. Retrieved from https://www.cisa.gov/sites/default/files/publications/CISA%2520Fact%2520Sheet%2520-%2520PSA%2520Program%2520-%2520508c_IAA%2520Final.19MAR2020.pdf.

Regional Consortium Coordinating Council Charter. 2018. CISA. Retrieved from https://www.cisa.gov/sites/default/files/publications/regional-consortium-coordinating-council-charter-2018-508.pdf.

Ross, Ron. 2018. Risk Management Framework for Information Systems and Organizations: A System Life Cycle Approach for Security and Privacy (Special Publication (NIST SP) No. 800-37r2). National Institute of Standards and Technology. Retrieved from https://doi.org/10.6028/NIST.SP.800-37r2.

S.1353 — 113th Congress. 2014. Cybersecurity Enhancement Act 2014 (CEA). Retrieved from https://www.congress.gov/bill/113th-congress/senate-bill/1353/text.

State, Local, Tribal, and Territorial Government Coordinating Council. 2016. HDS. Retrieved from https://www.cisa.gov/sites/default/files/publications/slttgcc-fact-sheet-2017-508.pdf.

Traffic Light Protocol 2.0 User Guide. 2022. CISA. Retrieved from https://www.cisa.gov/sites/default/files/2023-02/tlp-2-0-user-guide_508c.pdf.

TRIPwire (Technical Resource for Incident Prevention), 2023. DHS. Retrieved from https://www.cisa.gov/resources-tools/resources/technical-resource-incident-prevention-tripwire-portal#:~:text=Developed%20and%20maintained%20by%20the,Explosive%20Device%20(IED)%20incidents.

Vijayan, Jaikumar. 2022. "What is an ISAC or ISAO? How this cyber threat information sharing organizations improve security." CSO. Retrieved from https://www.csoonline.com/article/3406505/what-is-an-isac-or-isao-how-these-cyber-threat-information-sharing-organizations-improve-security.html.

Washburn, Ryan, and Sarah Sin. 2019. Research Brief: Significant Multi-Domain Incidents against Critical Infrastructure (SMICI) Dataset. College Park, MD: START. Retrieved from https://www.start.umd.edu/publication/research-brief-significant-multi-domain-incidents-against-critical-infrastructure-smici.

White House Fact sheet. 2021. The American Jobs Plan. Retrieved from https://www.whitehouse.gov/briefing-room/statements-releases/2021/03/31/fact-sheet-the-american-jobs-plan/.

World Economic Forum Report. 2023. The Global Risks Report 2023. Retrieved from https://www.weforum.org/reports/global-risks-report-2023/.

PJM: Charting the Path to the Grid of the Future

Kenneth Seiler[1]

[1] Senior Vice President – Planning, PJM Interconnection

The electric grid is undergoing a revolutionary transformation—customer preference, corporate clean energy aspirations, and state and federal policy choices are dramatically changing how energy is generated, and the retirement of conventional generators threatens to outpace the construction of new resources.

Technology is offering customers new ways to interact with the system, blurring traditional distinctions between how electricity is generated and transmitted long distances and how it is delivered to homes and businesses. At the same time, the frequency of extreme weather events—and the stresses they put on the system—continues to increase.

All of these forces present challenges for operating the largest and most complex machine on earth for a product that is produced, transported and consumed in an instant.

PJM Interconnection, the grid operator for 65 million people in 13 states and the District of Columbia, along with the many stakeholders with a voice in our operations and policies, is tasked with forging solutions without sacrificing the uninterrupted power supply that allows modern society to function.

As the country's largest regional transmission organization, PJM's No. 1 job is keeping electricity flowing, and doing it cost-effectively, every moment of the day. Affordable, reliable electricity is essential for everything we do as a society—starting with powering the country's critical infrastructure we rely on, from transportation and communication to emergency services and health care.

This responsibility demands that the wholesale electricity market we oversee provides economic incentives to attract the investment needed to build and resources that maintain system reliability, as it has for over 25 years. It also requires us to plan for broader trends and events to make sure the grid is resilient enough to operate through and recover from rare, extreme and high-impact events that PJM has never experienced before.

Reliability Risks on the Horizon

PJM's combined functions of operations, markets and planning have worked together successfully to keep the lights on since 1927, providing up to $4 billion in efficiencies for our customers in the process. But there are working trends on the horizon.

In a recent report, PJM analysis showed that 40 GW of existing generation—mostly coal, gas and oil generators representing 21% of our installed capacity—is at risk of retiring by 2030. Some industry forecasts predict that renewable energy will provide nearly half the power to the country by 2032, but currently those renewable resources are not being built at the rate we need to replace those traditional generators.

As the generation fleet moves to a lower-carbon footprint, reliant on intermittent energy resources (like sun and wind), the planners and operators of the bulk electric system have to plan for a much different kind of system with different physical characteristics—and get it right. Peoples' livelihoods and lives depend on it.

This means PJM and its stakeholders have been hard at work crafting a reliable path forward through our core functions of planning, markets and operations.

We have synthesized these efforts into our Ensuring a Reliable Energy Transition initiative, dedicated to finding answers to reliability challenges through intensive, data-driven research and analysis and collaboration across government and industry.

New Fuel Mix Challenges Reliability

The story of this energy transition is told in our New Services Queue, where generation projects come to interconnect with the PJM system. More than 97 percent of the resources requesting to join the PJM system are wind, solar or batteries, or a hybrid of both.

These smaller, weather-dependent resources generate energy in a whole different way than traditional thermal generators powered by coal, oil, gas or nuclear, introducing a new set of physical dynamics and characteristics.

Underlying the new reality of grid operations is the fact that intermittent and limited-duration resources like batteries do not replace "1 for 1," but rather require multiple megawatts to replace 1 MW of dispatchable generation due to their limited availability in certain hours of the day and seasons of the year.

As generators increasingly rely on renewable energy sources like wind and solar, PJM has identified trends that could realize a shortage of generating resources as early as 2027:

- The demand for power is growing with the electrification of transportation, industrial and building sectors, along with the development of energy-intensive data centers—driven in part by the increase in artificial intelligence and machine learning processes—at an unprecedented rate.

- At the same time, fossil fuel generators that balance the grid today are retiring at a significant rate.

- Replacement generation is made up of primarily intermittent and limited-duration resources that require multiple megawatts to replace 1 MW of dispatchable generation.

- Renewable resources that have passed through PJM's vetting process are not being built at the pace required to replace these resources, through factors beyond PJM's control, like supply chain issues, cost of capital and permitting.

The related analysis is detailed in our most recent paper in the Energy Transition in PJM series.

New Planning Process Begins

Critical to getting generation online, PJM this summer began transitioning to a new "first-ready, first-served" interconnection process that improves project cost certainty for network upgrades and significantly improves the overall process by which new and upgraded generation resources are studied and introduced onto the electrical grid.

In the transition period to our new interconnection process, we will study enough interconnection requests to replace the entire generation fleet of nearly 200 GW and far more than make up for retiring coal, oil and gas generators.

The key question is: Will the new generation actually come online?

Right now, we have more than 40,000 MW of projects that have completed PJM's study process and should be moving to construction.

Yet in 2022, we saw just 2,000 MW in projects built, and only 700 MW of those were renewables. So far in 2023, we have seen 620 MW of solar, 285 MW of wind, and 41 MW of storage come online, along with 3,100 MW of natural gas.

Many projects coming through the queue are not being built because of siting, financing or supply chain issues. These factors are out of PJM's control.

PJM is not alone in having stalled projects. This same issue is happening across the country. But we are leading the pack in clearing our queue. A recent S&P Global Market Intelligence analysis of U.S. interconnection queues found that PJM has the shortest project turnaround time of all grid operators in the country.

Reliability-First Policies

These reliability concerns are not unique to the PJM grid. As this year's North American Electric Reliability Corporation's (NERC) summer assessment showed, roughly two-thirds of the U.S. (but not the PJM region) already faced increased resource adequacy risk this past summer.

However, we believe this risk is avoidable. How? Through policies that accelerate the rate of entry of new generation (such as through permitting reform) and slow the exit of the traditional thermal generation we use to balance the grid today. This will give time for replacement generation to be installed and operating at the required scale.

In addition, PJM advocates an approach to policymaking that expressly considers reliability impacts in the development phase of the policy—not after the fact.

We continue to work with both state and federal policymakers to ensure that reliability considerations are built into all environmental and renewable generation policies.

PJM Steps Up as Independent Industry Leader

The energy transition presents a broad set of challenges and opportunities, and PJM is making headway in a number of areas, including:

- Enacted major interconnection reform, which is expected to result in the processing of over 250 GW of new generation requests in the next three years and produce a more predictable, streamlined process for new generators to connect with the system

- Filed with FERC a set of proposals to better recognize the relative contribution of all generation resources in meeting reliability needs

- Engaged stakeholders in developing a long-range transmission planning protocol that will enable us to analyze the longer-term needs of the system under multiple long-range scenarios to optimize a set of solutions based on the changing fleet and electrification

- Developed new rules to remove barriers to renewable resources participating in PJM's capacity market

- Performed groundbreaking work with the state of New Jersey to advance the buildout of its ambitious offshore wind program—a model that is being considered by other states

Our Ensuring a Reliable Energy Transition initiative proposes an initial set of actions to support reliability that PJM can take with its stakeholders, government and industry over the immediate, near-term and upcoming time frames to keep pace with these trends:

- **Immediate**: Ensuring the performance of existing generation resources

- **Near Term**: Maintaining adequate generation resources and deliverable megawatts to meet electricity demand

- **Upcoming**: Attracting and maintaining (as needed) resources that have essential reliability services

Essential reliability services are defined by NERC as the ability of a generation resource to provide services such as voltage control, frequency support, and ramping capability to balance the electrical grid and maintain the reliable delivery of electricity.

PJM has documented in its research that the more we depend on intermittent resources, the more we will need to share electricity with our neighboring systems to account for fluctuations in supply. PJM is already a leader in this area and regularly exports and imports electricity to adjoining systems; we are currently working both internally and externally to determine just how much of that interregional transfer capability we will need to build.

Helping States Achieve Their Goals

Another action we're taking as part of our reliability initiative is offering states a way to incorporate their policy goals into our Regional Transmission Expansion Plan (RTEP).

The first state to do this was New Jersey. In October 2022, the New Jersey Board of Public Utilities (NJBPU) selected a package of onshore transmission solutions that, in conjunction with prior action, will enable the injection of 7,500 MW of offshore wind capacity by 2035.

The NJBPU order was informed by technical analysis performed by PJM staff under the State Agreement Approach (SAA), through which states can access PJM's expertise and existing planning process to cost-effectively develop and optimize the transmission improvements necessary to support the reliable interconnection of certain desirable resources.

The SAA enables a state or group of states to propose a project that could potentially realize public policy requirements as long as the state (or states) agrees to pay all costs of the state-selected buildout included in the RTEP.

The first engagement of the SAA was so successful, New Jersey returned to PJM in April and requested to partner on a second stage to enable an additional 3,500 MW of offshore wind energy. New Jersey's experience can serve as a template for PJM's other coastal states.

Together, We Will Find Solutions

PJM has sufficient generation to meet the needs of our system today. However, as we look further out, we are concerned by the trends we see.

Despite PJM's healthy reserve margins, recent winter storms have provided a sobering reminder of the critical role that resource adequacy will play through the energy transition. For the first time in recent history, PJM could be at risk of facing resource adequacy challenges.

Decarbonizing the grid will be a challenge, for all of us, but it will happen. We're all going to have to work together to find solutions, including state and federal policymakers.

The solutions are there; this country has proven that time and time again, it simply requires dedicated resources and brainpower. PJM will find those solutions but will need all stakeholders at the table to do so.

Author Capsule Bio

Kenneth Seiler leads PJM's System Planning Division. He is responsible for all activities related to resource adequacy, generation interconnection, interregional planning and transmission planning, including the development of the Regional Transmission Expansion Plan. Previously, Seiler was the executive director of System Operations and was responsible for the reliable operation and coordination of the bulk power system, including PJM's real-time dispatch operations and near-term reliability studies. Seiler oversaw the dispatcher training and certification functions, as well as the markets coordination function, to ensure the efficient and most cost-effective dispatch of the generation fleet.

Seiler is on the board of directors of ReliabilityFirst, one of the eight Federal Energy Regulatory Commission-designated regional entities responsible for ensuring the reliability of the North American bulk power system. He is also on the board of PJM Environmental Information Services Inc. In addition, he is an instructor for the Mayfly Project, a national organization that uses fly fishing as a catalyst to mentor and support children in foster care and introduce them to their local water ecosystems, with a hope that connecting them to a rewarding hobby will provide an opportunity for foster children to have fun, build confidence and develop a meaningful connection.

Prior to joining PJM, Seiler was employed by Metropolitan Edison Company/GPU Energy for nearly 14 years. He held the positions of operations manager, transmission engineering manager, relay protection and control engineer, and substation/transmission construction and maintenance engineer. He earned a Bachelor of Science in electrical engineering from The Pennsylvania State University and a Master of Business Administration from Lebanon Valley College.

In the Polycrisis Era, Infrastructure Defenders Need to Broaden, not Tighten, Their Focus

Andrew Bochman[1]

[1] Senior Grid Strategist, Idaho National Laboratory Homeland Security Directorate, andybochman@gmail.com

Abstract

Marked by multiple concurrent overlapping and interconnected challenges, the Polycrisis Era portends an unprecedented mix of threats to infrastructure protection and demands more resilience planning and preparation than ever before. This article explores some distinct facets of the Polycrisis Era, tracing its emergence, its unique characteristics, and the societal implications of failing to adequately address these challenges. Importantly, the case is made that infrastructure defenders in the operational technology (OT) cyber space and those primarily concerned with physical climate risks should consider enhanced communication and collaboration with each other. Put another way, in an age of simultaneous, interwoven crises, it is advantageous for infrastructure defenders to think beyond their traditional domains. In order to examine this topic and to facilitate productive collaboration, an exploratory typology is advanced.

The Polycrisis Era

From wars and industrial revolutions to the dawn of cyber threats, infrastructure defense has evolved in tandem with the nature of challenges faced. However, the evolving Polycrisis Era is distinct, marking an epoch of compounded and multifaceted vulnerabilities. The term "Polycrisis" denotes a period characterized by multiple, overlapping crises. These are not isolated incidents but are interconnected, often exacerbating each other. As early as five years ago, the National Academies of Sciences, Engineering, and Medicine predicted some of these challenges:

> Climate change and extreme weather grab headlines and present a fundamental challenge to the ability of infrastructure to protect communities. But beneath the seemingly endless cascade of catastrophes lie consistent, systemic failures in current approaches to infrastructure. One common failure is an overconfidence, bordering on hubris, in the ability to tightly control complex social

and ecological systems through the management of technological systems. Another is the failure often associated with managing interdependent infrastructure systems. And there are failures in the ability of institutions that manage infrastructure to generate, communicate, and utilize knowledge.[1]

What differentiates this era from the past includes, but is not limited to:

- *Complex Interdependencies*: Crises are no longer isolated. For instance, climate change intensifies natural disasters, which in turn disrupts socio-economic systems and challenges digital infrastructures. As global temperatures rise and weather patterns shift, the intensity and frequency of natural disasters such as hurricanes, floods, and wildfires have notably increased. These environmental calamities don't just wreak havoc on the natural world; they also severely disrupt socio-economic systems, causing dislocation, impacting supply chains, and challenging critical infrastructures—including high priority digital networks. In the tightly knit global landscape, it is evident that challenges in one domain can have cascading effects on others, prescribing the need for more comprehensive solutions.

- *Rapid Technological Advancement*: The rate of technological innovation, while beneficial, has introduced a slew of vulnerabilities. These vulnerabilities, especially in our increasingly interconnected digital networks, pose compound threats. For example, cyber-attacks can destabilize power grids.[2] When such critical infrastructures are compromised, the cascading effects may be profound, impacting vital sectors like healthcare and transportation, potentially leading to widespread disruptions and crises.

- *Economic Repercussions*: A single crisis—whether emanating from the OT cyber side or a major climate disaster—can snowball into global economic downturns, leading to unemployment, inflation, and societal unrest. Economies are more intricately interwoven now than ever before. A disturbance in one sector or region can have a domino effect, leading to global financial downturns. Examples from the 2008 financial crisis or the economic impacts of the COVID-19 pandemic serve are harbingers of the cascading impacts we will witness in this new era

---

1 Rethinking Infrastructure in an Era of Unprecedented Weather Events, National Academies of Sciences, Engineering and Medicine, Winter, 2018.

2 This risk will become greater still as the U.S., fueled by federal funds from the Bipartisan Infrastructure and Inflation Reduction Act, will stimulate enormous amounts of new distributed energy resources (DERs). These will be deployed over the next five to ten years. Otherwise known as inverter-based resources (IBRs), inverters are sourced almost entirely from the U.S.'s main cyber adversary: China. So as we make DERs responsible for a higher percentage of generation, we will also potentially be enabling China to hold that higher percentage at risk.

- *Societal Fragmentation*: Discontentment stemming from unaddressed crises can result in polarization, mistrust in institutions, and potential civil unrest. Simultaneous crises have historically produced societal discord, leading to a rise in extremist ideologies and a breakdown of social cohesion. An underlying sentiment of inequality (real or perceived), gets exacerbated, leading to larger rifts in society, and if anything, AI promises to sow further distrust.

- *Environmental Degradation*: Beyond the preservation of critical infrastructures, ignoring the environmental components of a polycrisis might lead to irreversible ecological damage, impacting biodiversity and human survival. Climate change-induced natural disasters, coupled with infrastructural collapses, can wreak havoc on ecosystems, making regions uninhabitable, leading to the mass migration of both humans and wildlife.

- *Socio-political Tensions*: Geopolitical discord, stemming from territorial disputes, ideological differences or other factors, can escalate into crises where the attack surfaces of adversaries are exploited in a highly concentrated fashion. Supply chains can be severely impacted. Whether launched by state-sponsored entities or groups affiliated with particular governments, cyberattacks may target a nation's critical infrastructure, impact large regions or metropolitan areas, or spread misinformation to destabilize societies. It is axiomatic that state actors will attempt to hijack sensitive data to gain strategic advantages. As the digital realm increasingly joins with the physical, addressing such threats requires wholistic, cross disciplinary thinking.

Black Skies and Black Swans

I first met Dr. Paul Stockton at the 2018 Winter meeting of the National Association of Regulatory Utility Commissioners (NARUC). Paul had previously served as Assistant Secretary of Defense for Homeland Defense and Americas' Security Affairs, where he was responsible for Defense Critical Infrastructure Protection, Western Hemisphere security policy, domestic crisis management, continuity of operations planning, and a range of other responsibilities. He served from 2009–2013 with distinction, but, by far, his greatest test came in the form of a hurricane named Sandy, a so-called superstorm.

As one climatologist put it, Sandy "was a hurricane wrapped in a nor'easter"[3] which produced a storm more than 1,000 miles across with a super powerful punch. Paul's job in October 2012 was to hold things together, as best he could, keeping food and fuel flowing not just to Department of Defense bases, but playing his part orchestrating restoration of energy and water services up and down the eastern seaboard. At the NARUC meeting, drawing from lessons from San-

---

3   https://patch.com/new-jersey/tomsriver/not-just-hurricane-what-made-sandy-superstorm

dy, Paul addressed disaster preparedness and the implications of extended power outages. Called "black sky" events, these are outages lasting a month or more that affect multiple states. They have the potential to turn natural or human induced disasters into catastrophes. No matter their cause—weather, cyberattack or terrorism—no one wants to have experience a black sky event, but they must prepare nevertheless. In a supporting document he added:

> Commissioners also face the risk of outages lasting even longer and covering a wider area than those caused by Sandy. A range of natural and manmade hazards could create "worse than Sandy" events. Federal and State emergency management agencies are treating preparedness for such catastrophes as a rapidly growing priority. These extraordinary and hazardous events will pose special risks to the resilience of electric utilities. Accordingly, State Commissions may wish to proactively consider assessment frameworks for investments in resilience that are structured to account not only for Sandy-scale major outage events, but also for black sky days.[4]

And indeed, most infrastructure defenders would admit that the longer duration events Stockton spoke of in 2014 are, if anything, even more likely ten years hence.

Another type of darkness we'd prefer not to encounter is the oft-referenced *Black Swan* event. A book on response strategies and the psychology of disaster preparedness by Nassim Nicholas Taleb, addresses rare outlier events having catastrophic impact. Central to his thesis is the perspective that we should not attempt to predict Black Swan events, but rather to build robustness and resilience regardless of this type of extreme event or its timing—sounds at first blush like resilience to all hazards.

Taleb's guidance syncs well with the left of boom-right of boom construct developed in the context of improvised explosive devices (IEDs) in Iraq that wreaked havoc on U.S. soldiers. The "boom" referred to the explosion. Efforts developed to detect roadside bombs and to disrupt the insurgents before they armed and planted them became known as left of boom activities.[5] On the other side, a variety of specialized skills were formulated to make progress on "IED Defeat." The technicians and soldiers who devised those techniques, married expertise from a range of disciplines, including explosives, chemistry, communications, cybersecurity, and physics. The challenge demanded mental agility and flexibility in evaluating candidate approaches.

---

4   https://pubs.naruc.org/pub.cfm?id=536F42EE-2354-D714-518F-EC79033665CD
5   https://leftofboomconference.com/

Critical Function Assurance: Finding the Hidden Vulnerabilities Left of Boom

Developed at Idaho National Laboratory (INL) in collaboration with partners, while initially intended for cybersecurity risks from top-tier adversaries, Critical Function Assurance (CFA) is a proactive and purposefully cross-discipline strategy. It identifies an organization's vulnerabilities and mitigates them before they become liabilities. In some important respects, CFA is the art of finding an organization's Achilles Heel, and then doing something about it before Paris' arrow strikes. It seeks to prioritize risk based squarely on impact, not probability. That is accomplished by determining how an organization's most critical, mission-supporting functions are delivered. In so doing, it reinforces a focus on what matters most and illuminates overlooked sources of risk. As the INL team defines it:

> CFA is an approach to prioritize and address risk based on impact and is rooted in a holistic understanding of how critical functions are delivered. It provides rapid focus to what matters most and illuminates elements and areas of risk that otherwise are often overlooked. This focus enables effective application of available security resources to the most vital areas of a business/mission/entity and provides the foundation for optimizing greater security strategy and policy efforts.[6]

Today we increasingly rely on digitization and cloud services to increase efficiency, but this reliance also creates complex technological dependencies. Consider the supply chain disruptions that have recently roiled manufacturing operations, and the present and increasingly disruptive impacts of climate change—each presents its own constellation of challenges. Whether it's a ransomware attack compromising a firm's financial system, extended heatwaves affecting data centers, or malign actors targeting a nation's electrical grid, critical infrastructure defenders must anticipate a growing volume of significant threats and prepare for them well in advance.

Digitization and cloud services are making companies more efficient but at the cost of making them more dependent on other organizations and increasingly complex technologies. These factors will compound by orders of magnitude when AI technologies permeate operations. At the same time, climate change is driving rapid onset extreme weather events like heatwaves, wildfires, floods and freezes, as well as slower moving droughts, melting permafrost, and coastal inundation from sea level rise.

---

6   Gellner, J., et al. 2023.

Staying One or More Steps Ahead of Disaster

From the perspective of an individual organization, it is difficult-bordering-on-impossible to know in what form disaster will strike, but here are some candidates:

- Ransomware bricks a billing system and it turns out that back-up files didn't include the necessary configuration information. And paying off the attackers didn't work when they took the money and disappeared.

- A two week-long heat dome that shutters a primary data center(s) neutralizes the ability to serve on-line customers which account for 80 percent of sales

- The same extreme heat event melts runways so that air carriers have to reroute for weeks

- A company that owns hundreds of data centers projects that the water they depend on for cooling will become scarce due to drought in several operating regions

- A region's electric grid and many of the larger generation plants and key substations have been immobilized by coordinated physical and cyber attacks.

While these situations may sound hopeless, and others marginally manageable, the main point about CFA is that it aims to make conditions "less bad" in the face of a crisis. As former DHS executive and presidential advisor Juliette Kayyem says in *The Devil Never Sleeps: Learning to Live in the Age of Disasters*:

> "Every institution has the capacity to assess its single points of failure, to assume that the last line of defense is not that, and then focus on avoiding losses that are not inevitable."[7]

She forcefully makes the case for a broadened perspective among all infrastructure defenders:

> Despite best efforts, the "boom" will arrive. The boom may be a crack, a surge, an electric fizzle, a howl, a deadly quiet. They are all booms: disaster management is about being ready for any boom in any shape, for whatever the devil brings. This concept, known as *all hazards* planning, does not focus on one specific hazard but instead on all of them. Some specialized threats may need specialized reactions—a fire is, in fact, different from a cyber-attack—but fewer specialized reactions than we may think. Accepting both the commonality and the frequency of disasters on the few key skills needed to manage them rather than highly specialized measures

---

7   Kayyem, J. *The Devil Never Sleeps*. 2022. P. 108.

that belong to limited environments. Beings can be slow or fast, wet or dry, hot or cold, silent or loud, visible or invisible. It does not, it should not, matter. It will come. So, we must focus on the right-of-boom activities, which are all those things we do to respond, recover, and build more resilience once the devil has arrived, again.[8]

Thus, another dimension of CFA is not about absolute prevention but is more attuned to enhancing an organization's crisis response. As Kayyem concludes, every entity (though few do comprehensively) can identify its most profound vulnerabilities, eschew over-reliance on final defenses, and strive to prevent avoidable losses.

Exploring the Cyber and Physical Climate Interface in Polycrises

Defenders need to open their risk apertures. Based on the foregoing, regardless of where we sit on critical infrastructure defense continuum, we all need to get into the Mission Assurance space. We would then be Mission Assurors—determined, and equipped to confront any and all hazards, proactively and reactively. This necessitates leveraging our primary areas of expertise, but also extending our capabilities well beyond the threats we were first trained on.

A clear-eyed approach that enables all mission assurers to expand the breadth of their situational awareness and proficiencies is required. For example, infrastructure defenders in the OT Cyber space and those primarily concerned with climate risk should consider enhanced communication and collaboration. From a different vantage point, in an age of simultaneous, interwoven crises, it is advantageous for infrastructure defenders to think beyond their traditional domains.

In order to examine this topic and to facilitate productive collaboration, an exploratory typology is presented in Figure 1. It is intended to reveal areas where selected defender skills and capabilities may be transferable to other threat categories.

Two infrastructure defense domains that have much in common are OT cybersecurity and climate physical risk, via resilience (asset hardening) and process adaptation strategies. While these initially may seem to be so different in kind as to render any comparison unproductive, the types of knowledge and skills defenders require for success are substantially similar. Perhaps the two most important resources that can be brought to bear against both threat types are a deep understanding of the characteristics of the system(s) being defended, as well as experience gained from defending similar threats in the past. There are additional areas of overlap, however, where defender capabilities in cyber scenarios might be cross-applied to climate physical risks, and vice versa.

---

8 Kayyem, J. *The Devil Never Sleeps*. 2022. P. 11.

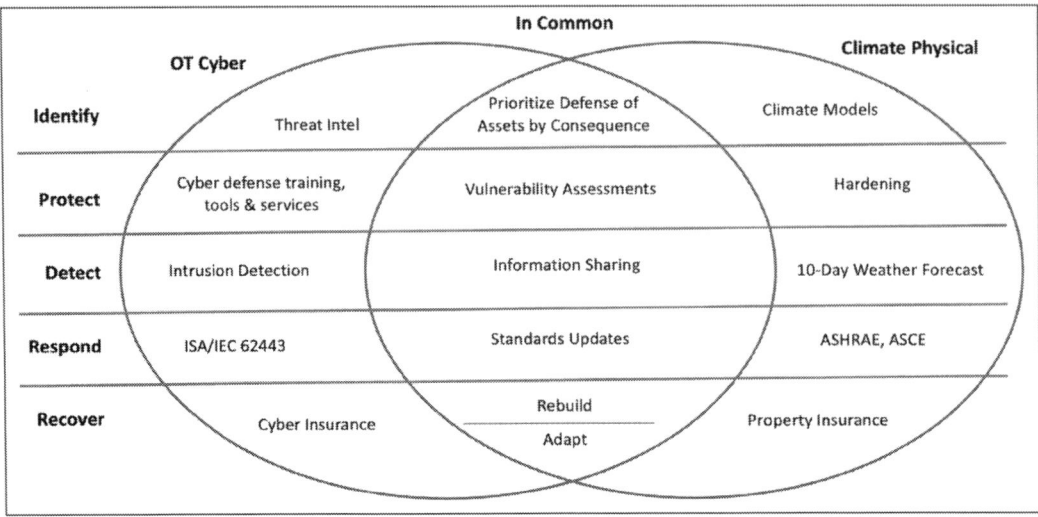

Figure 1: OT Cyber/Climate Physical Venn Diagram

Figure 1 draws its structure from the original NIST Framework[9] for cyber defense in the left-most column breaking the challenge into five, roughly discreet, roughly sequential tasks: identify, protect, detect, respond, and recover. Of course, the activities required to successfully defend against cyber attacks conducted by human actors are quite different than those necessary to thwart the physical forces generated by a warming atmosphere and ocean. Yet they do share some similarities that may be leveraged to good effect:

Identify

What mission are you trying to protect? What are the critical functions that must not be allowed to fail and what, in terms of people, process and technology, enable them?

Protect

What defensive strategies can be deployed to make the adversary's job more difficult in the case of cyber, or to ensure that infrastructure elements can withstand and continue to operate in the face of more-extreme natural conditions? In the case of the former, some basics like closing unused ports, segmenting networks, employing robust access controls, and granting least privilege authentication rights are significantly helpful.

For physical climate risks like floods, fires, freezes and extreme heat events, an assortment of engineered "hardening" strategies available like elevating equipment in flood-prone areas, undergrounding or fireproofing equipment in loca-

---

9   https://www.nist.gov/system/files/documents/cyberframework/cybersecurity-framework-021214.pdf

tions with above average wildfire potential, and winterizing systems to operate reliably at temperatures below or far below previous lows.

Detect

Is it possible to see the threat coming before it actually arrives, as in threat intelligence for cyber and downscaled climate model projections for physical climate risk? The answer to both is yes, with varying degrees of certainty and time to prepare. In the case of cyber, it could be as long as years once a particular attack type or vulnerability exploitation surfaces in the wild, or as brief as just a few seconds. On the other hand, methods for determining the likely arrival date of more damaging climate forces is a problem being worked at science labs around the world. Here the timeframes can be measured in decades, though any particular event (e.g., severe storm, flood, heat dome, etc.) may arrive with only a few days warning by meteorologists.

Respond[10]

There are a number of actions that can be conducted in the event of imminent or near-imminent cyber or climate threats. The concept of "conversative operations"[11] prompts organizations to prioritize resilience even at the expense of efficiency, profit maximization, and even full-services delivery if the threat is perceived to be significant enough to warrant such actions. In cyber this may mean isolating and/or greatly reducing access to the most critical systems. Physical climate risks can be met in ways as familiar as the boarding up of windows on a residential scale, to de-energizing power lines deemed likely to blow over during high wind events in areas with where they might trigger wildfires. In both cases, communicating the inbound threat to governmental and private sector support organizations is crucial.[12]

Recover

Depending on the degree of damage incurred, this phase includes both the restoration of services as quickly as possible, plus taking time to learn from the event to then apply lessons learned to strengthen activities conducted and capabilities achieved in the framework's earlier phases.

---

10 The term "respond" obscures the proactive intent of this framework element. It's more about implementing the last lines of defense—potentially operationally limiting actions that bring a higher degree of confidence that an organization will "weather the storm" even if in a degraded fashion, and hasten the return to normal operations.

11 https://www.jhuapl.edu/sites/default/files/2022-12/PostCyberAttack.pdf

12 For example, in the energy sector, the Electricity Information Sharing and Analysis Center, or E-ISAC is one such communication and coordination hub, and there are other sector-specific ISACs.

Conclusions

While domain-specific skills are required to prepare for and conduct defensive operations for the two threat types discussed, there are also opportunities for collaboration across specialized defender communities. Since that is the case, then perhaps defenders against other threat types may find similar benefit in coordinating and drawing support in times of need from still other domains. Examples might be found within an organization, as technical SMEs address an imminent or ongoing cyber attack by reducing automation, others might shift to perform those functions in a mode closer to manual operations. This could be the case when other hazards arise, such as earthquakes, solar storms, or as Ukraine has demonstrated, even when critical infrastructure is subjected to continuous kinetic attack, as evidenced by its electric grid's resilience under bombardment.

Author Capsule Bio

Andrew Bochman is Senior Grid Strategist for Idaho National Laboratory's (INL) National and Homeland Security directorate. Mr. Bochman provides strategic guidance on topics at the intersection of grid security, the Energy Transition, and infrastructure climate resilience and adaption to senior U.S. and international government and industry leaders. A Non-Resident Senior Fellow at the Atlantic Council's Global Energy Center, in 2021 he published *Countering Cyber Sabotage: Introducing Consequence-based Cyber-Informed Engineering*. He began his career as a communications officer in the U.S. Air Force, and, prior to joining INL, was a Senior Advisor at the Chertoff Group and the Energy Security Lead at IBM. Mr. Bochman received a BS from the U.S. Air Force Academy and an MA from Har-vard University.

He is currently working on a second book prospectively titled *Defending Civilization: Stories from the Fronts Lines of Critical Function Assurance*. It applies the Critical Function Assurance risk reduction approach to four distinct but overlap-ping digital and physical threat types to critical infrastructure: Cyber, AI, Climate, and Kinetic, with the latter emphasizing lessons from Ukraine. These include how to design, build and operate electric grids and similar infrastructure components under bombardment. Infrastructure operators and defenders and multiple stake-holder types will find lessons for application with as much alacrity as possible. Publication is anticipated in late 2024 or early 2025 by Taylor & Francis / CRC Press.

New SEC Cybersecurity Disclosure Protocols: Enhanced Transparency, Short Deadlines

Brian Walker[1]

[1] Founder, The CAP Group, Brian@TheCAP.Group

Abstract

The Securities and Exchange Commission (SEC) issued its final rule on Cybersecurity Risk Management, Strategy, Governance, and Incident Response on July 26, 2023. This mandates that SEC-regulated companies disclose both significant cybersecurity incidents and their cyber risk management processes. These public disclosures will be made via existing SEC reporting channels. They are intended to provide investors with enhanced transparency into the cyber risks and mitigation strategies employed by SEC-regulated corporations.

This landmark decision marks the culmination of an 18-month intensive rulemaking process that commenced in March 2022. The process was anything but smooth. The interval from the SEC's original announcement to the finalization of the rules was marked by fervent debate, heated public discourse, and diverging viewpoints.

Adapting to the new regulations will vary among companies. Established firms with robust practices will find the transition smoother, primarily focusing on initial disclosures for the year's 10-k report. In contrast, companies with less structured cyber risk approaches and reliant on reactive measures, will grapple with substantial challenges. Central to this transition is the collaboration between boards and executives in defining "material" cyber incidents. While no fixed formula exists to gauge impact, it is crucial for leadership to holistically understand and swiftly assess potential repercussions—spanning operational costs, legal ramifications, brand implications, and revenue loss—during emergent cyber situations.

Introduction

The continuing surge of cybercrime in the U.S. has led to colossal financial losses, estimated in the hundreds of billions of dollars, posing not only a significant economic threat but also jeopardizing public safety.[1] In a pivotal move to address this concern, on July 26, 2023, the SEC issued its final rules for companies disclosing key information regarding cyber risk.[2] The landmark decision marked the culmination of an 18-month intensive rulemaking process that commenced in March 2022.

The process was characterized by passionate public debate and discussion and a wide spectrum of perspectives. While a segment argued about the tangible benefits of such reporting, others questioned the SEC's jurisdiction in mandating the new disclosures. Furthermore, the discourse was rife with intricate discussions on defining terms and assigning responsibilities pertaining to cyber risks. Despite divergent opinions, the SEC addressed the majority of the concerns, culminating in finalization of the rules. As a result, companies are expected to align with these compliance norms starting December 2023.

Annual Cyber Risk Disclosures

The rules as finalized in July are focused on the public disclosure of cyber risk information. There are two disclosure time horizons: annual and incident driven. On an annual basis, companies are required to incorporate new cyber-specific information in their SEC Form 10-k that addresses two general areas:

Cyber Risk Management

This incorporates the strategies and processes used by the company in monitoring and managing cyber risk overall. This area is broadly focused on providing clarity into how a company thinks about cyber risk at-large and how it frames risks that originate in the cyber domain. They exist in the context of numerous other enterprise risks such as competition, regulation, financial/currency exposures, physical plant operations risks, etc.

Cyber Risk Governance

These involve the professional backgrounds, roles, and responsibilities of those involved in monitoring and managing cyber risk. This area is focused on understanding the mechanics of how cyber risk is governed across the company. The governance focus includes both the board of directors and the executive leadership team. The original draft rules in 2022 included a requirement to reveal the names and biographies of key directors and officers who are viewed by a company

---

[1] "The U.S. Is Less Prepared to Fight Cybercrime Than It Could Be," General Accounting Office, WatchBlog, August 29, 2023.

[2] SEC Adopts Rules on Cybersecurity Risk Management, Strategy, Governance, and Incident Disclosure by Public Companies, U.S. Securities and Exchange Commission, Press Release, July 26, 2023.

as having credible cyber risk expertise. While the 2023 finalized rules omitted the board of directors from this mandate, it retained the emphasis on key executives. This move underscores the importance of leaders actively involved in cyber risk comprehension and mitigation.

These data are slated for release as a component of the traditional 10-k disclosure mechanism. The inaugural set of disclosures will be requisite for organizations scheduled to publicize their 10-k post-mid-December 2023. Note that the SEC did not provide detailed guidance on how to provide these disclosures. They did not mandate specific elements for inclusion, provided no lexicon/framework, and remained silent on the granularity of detail sought. The SEC's primary focus is transparency at-large—leaving the particulars to the discretion of each company's leadership.

Incident Disclosures: A Closer Look

Beyond annual declarations, the SEC has decreed that enterprises disclose significant cyber-related incidents. Aligning with its stance on yearly revelations, the SEC refrained from outlining the criteria defining a material cyber incident. The notion of public disclosure of material incidents is not new, so the SEC will rely on existing case law and precedents for gauging the materiality of cyber incidents, just as companies have to evaluate the materiality of other business incidents such as natural disasters, currency fluctuations, factory fires, etc.

There is one nuance in incident disclosure where the SEC issued a prescriptive requirement—the timeliness of such disclosures. As per the SEC rules, companies must disclose material incidents within four business days of reaching the determination of materiality. Note that this is not four days from when the incident occurred or was discovered, but four days from when the determination of materiality has been completed. This is in alignment with other material non-cyber disclosures as the SEC seeks to treat cyber risks in similar fashion to all other business risks.

Navigating Adoption Hurdles

The degree of difficulty in adopting these new rules will vary widely, based on a company's current level of sophistication in managing cyber risk. For large, sophisticated organizations with highly-developed cyber risk management capabilities, this adoption will require only modest effort—likely focused primarily on the initial release of information for inclusion in the first year's 10-k.

Companies with less structured cyber risk management practices are poised to encounter substantial adoption challenges. Historically, many of these firms have relied on a reactive, improvisational strategy, where the ingenuity and adaptability of their leadership play pivotal roles during cyber events. Those informal and reactive methods are rarely documented in clear, concise terms, with unambiguous processes and roles that would give transparency and comfort to investors. For these firms, the fourth quarter of 2023 could require an intense first-time documentation of such practices with sufficient clarity—and legal approval—to be ready for formal disclosure in an SEC 10-k.

In addition to the mechanics of risk management and governance, there are key strategic decisions that must be made requiring the alignment of the board and the executive team. One key alignment is the definition of materiality. As part of an organization's risk management process, there needs to be agreement on the parameters of cyber risk that will be considered when evaluating a cyber incident. Typical considerations include the costs associated with technical resumption of operations, costs associated with litigation and fines, loss of brand goodwill, and unrecoverable lost revenue. Each incident may involve different portions of these and many other considerations, and an exact formula isn't feasible. However, it is feasible—and expected—that directors and officers understand the potential mix of impacts in determining materiality and that they align on the mechanics of rapidly evaluating these as a fast-moving cyber incident is unfolding.

Crucial Areas of Focus

Compliance with the SEC rules will be based on key foundational capabilities that are not new but will be more visible given the transparency requirements. In parallel with drafting the materials for annual disclosure, it will be important to ensure that the underlying processes, tools, and capabilities are sufficiently robust to enable actual cyber defense and response to incidents.

Some of these key focus areas include:

Incident Classification

There should exist a well-understood, pre-defined methodology for classifying cyber incidents, especially those that are ultimately defined as material. A clear lexicon of terms as well as roles and responsibilities for detecting and making key decisions on a timely basis will be fundamental.

Incident Response

There should exist a well-structured and efficient process for managing the remediation and recovery of any incident, regardless of materiality. This will include clear identification of roles such as Incident Commander and other key technical support roles.

Crisis Response Plans

The capabilities for managing external communications need to be well-established in advance and it is important that this exist as a separate, specialized capability in the communications organization. This is often mistakenly presumed to be included as part of an Incident Response Process, which is more appropriately a technology and operations role with different functions and skills needed for communication with media, regulators, and shareholders.

Regular Testing

Given the necessity for swift materiality assessments and disclosures, operational efficiency is key. Regular drills and simulations, complemented by post-action analyses, can be instrumental in refining processes and roles, ensuring everyone is aligned and any gaps are promptly addressed.

Critical Infrastructure Considerations

The SEC's new cybersecurity rules are designed to enhance investor understanding and trust regarding cyber risk. More specific and frequent disclosures will likely advance this aim significantly, while at the same time creating several key challenges that operators of critical infrastructure will need to grapple with:

Pay Now or Pay Later

Additional demands on already-strapped experts could be material in companies who are relatively low in their cyber risk management maturities. It will be important to recognize the incremental demands on those resources and budget accordingly with appropriate staffing and enabling technologies. Adopting the new requirements won't "just happen"—specific accountabilities and priorities need to be defined and funded.

Regulator Bingo

The SEC is one of many key regulators that the cyber risk program must account for. In parallel with the SEC reporting requirements, the Cybersecurity & Infrastructure Security Agency (CISA) is finalizing its own incident reporting requirements that will likely be more technical and detailed in nature. Both will seek information on the most relevant, "material" incidents and companies will need to ensure which—or both—regulator requires reporting on which incidents. Key sectors like the electricity industry are already intimately familiar with NERC-CIP requirements that must simultaneously be addressed—and that is just in the United States—similar regulators exist in many other key geographies. Companies need to have an integrated, holistic strategy for harmonizing and synchronizing all these existing regulatory requirements and start building capacity for the inevitable addition of others.

Materiality Beyond First-Party

In addition to the traditional litmus test of materiality as it affects a company's shareholders, critical infrastructure companies can have material impact on stakeholders beyond shareholders. Imagine energy refineries that suffer a hack to industrial control systems that result in physical damage of assets and the release of toxic chemicals, explosions, or fires. Traditional first-party risk management processes will account for the materiality of such incidents to shareholders, the knock-on effect to adjacent communities and the broader commercial ecosystem will also need to be planned for and managed.

Author Capsule Bio

Brian Walker is Founder of the CAP Group, based in Dallas, Texas. The firm pro-vides cyber risk advice to directors and officers of clients ranging in size from global Fortune 500 to regional G2000. He is a frequent writer and speaker on cyber risk strategy—regularly appearing at NACD, PDA, GARP, and others. He has spe-cialized in the formulation of strategies to mature defensive capabilities for criti-cal infrastructure, including both information technology (IT) and operational technology (OT) / industrial control systems (ICS). His assignments have in-cluded global clients, as well as regional clients in North America, Japan, Europe, and Asia. He has led maturation-in-place initiatives as well as provided interim CIO/CISO roles in support of turnaround/urgent situations. He has managed the launch of information security and privacy subcommittees (ISPS), including definition of policy frameworks and all associated policies and standards. Opera-tional responsibilities have included adherence to regulators including SEC, FIN-RA, OCC, NERC, FERC, TSA and DHS. In addition, he has created and matured technology partner ecosystems including cybersecurity, infrastructure operations, cloud services, applications management, and bundled As-A-Service capabilities.

National Infrastructure Bank: A Permanent Solution and Timely Budget Work-Around

Stanley Forczyk[*]

[*]President, Advisory Board, Coalition for National Infrastructure Bank

Abstract

The passage of time, chronic underinvestment, and climate change have left America's public infrastructure dangerously overstretched and vulnerable. The bipartisan Infrastructure Investment and Jobs Act (IIJA) of 2021 provided billions of dollars in new Federal spending for infrastructure. While a significant start, the IIJA addressed only a small fraction of the nation's current, unfunded needs. A $5 trillion National Infrastructure Bank, as proposed in HR4052, would fill that gap, provide technical/regulatory assistance, and turbocharge the American economy, with no need for added spending, taxes, or increases to the National Debt.[1]

Introduction

In the landscape of industrialized economies, the United States stands as a testament to the critical role of robust infrastructure in driving economic vitality. The intricate network of transportation, digital communications, energy grids, and water systems forms the backbone of the nation's economic engine, catalyzing growth and enhancing the quality of life.

Investment in public infrastructure is not merely a matter of maintenance or upgrade; it is a strategic imperative for economic expansion and social progress. Conversely, the failure to adequately invest in and modernize public infrastructure can have dire consequences. Stagnation in infrastructure development can serve as a precursor to broader economic malaise. Outdated or inadequate infrastructure hampers efficiency, stifles innovation, and can create obstacles that impede economic activity. The ramifications may extend beyond mere economic metrics; they can erode the fabric of communities, as deteriorating infrastructure disproportionately affects disadvantaged populations.

Businesses, particularly those reliant on efficient supply chains and logistics, encounter escalating operational costs as they navigate the repercussions of neglected infrastructure. The resulting inefficiencies not only diminish the competitive edge of businesses but also contribute to increased costs for consumers.

---

1   HR4052 text here: https://www.congress.gov/118/bills/hr4052/BILLS-118hr4052ih.pdf

And competitor countries that heavily invest in critical infrastructure have a distinct advantage in economic efficiencies, bringing products to market, and growing their industrial base.

Thus, the imperative for continuous investment in public infrastructure is clear. It is a critical lever for economic stability and social equity, ensuring that both businesses and families not only survive but thrive. As we chart the course for future economic policy, prioritizing infrastructure investment is a commitment to the United State's collective prosperity and well-being.

In its 2021 Report Card, the American Society of Civil Engineers (ASCE) estimated that $6.1 trillion over ten years will be needed just to bring the nation's infrastructure up to a state of good repair (ASCE, 2021). Of that total, $2.6 trillion remains unfunded for roads, bridges, freight corridors, and mass transit; electric grids; schools; dams, levees, waterways, and ports; airports; rail; drinking water and wastewater; public parks and recreation; and hazardous waste (ASCE 2023; see Table 1 below). In addition to these categories, the United States needs:

- Intercity High-Speed Rail linked to improved urban transit networks (USHSR)

- Complete Broadband access (FCC)

- Affordable Housing (NLHC)

- A Renewable Energy Super-Grid (Behr)

- Major Water Management Projects to supply water to America's driest regions (CBS News)

All of these investments require a steady source of long-term funding, strategic planning, and the latest smart technologies for optimal return on investment and minimal environmental impact.

Despite these pressing needs, however, vital improvements have not been adequately financed by the Federal budget, nor by state and local budgets, nor by private capital markets for that matter. In fact, Federal money for infrastructure as a percent of Federal spending has fallen sharply since the 1980s, and now state/local dollars and borrowing pay for the bulk of infrastructure projects (McNichol). At present, the U.S. faces a budget constraint, with mounting national debt (Ritcher), fast-rising interest payments on the debt (Reuters, Oct 2023) and more military spending (Stein, 2023). A politically divided Congress can't agree on a budget, while one faction is demanding broad spending cuts, including for infrastructure legislation that has already been enacted. Therefore, it is unlikely that adequate financing to cover the substantial infrastructure funding gap will come from the Federal budget.

Table 1

Table 1. Comparison of the National Infrastructure Bank (NIB) and Bi-Partisan Infrastructure Bill Cumulative Infrastructure Needs over Ten Years: 2020-2029

(In billions of 2019-dollars)

Infrastructure Categories	NIB Total Lending Amount	2021 Bipartisan Infrastructure Law (BIL, or IIJA) Over 5 Years 12/
Total	**$5,000**	**$550**
ASCE 2021 Report Card 1/	Funding Gap 2/ 3/ 4/	New Money
Subtotal for 16 Categories	**$2,626**	**$436**
Surface Transportation Including:	**$1,205**	
Roads & Bridges	$785	$110
Transit	$250	$39
Passenger Rail	$45	$66
Half the amount for Schools	$125	
Electric Vehicles		$15
Safety / Reconnecting Neighborhoods		$12
Water Infrastructure Including:	**$1,089**	
Drinking Water, Wastewater, and Stormwater 5/	$801	$55
Dams, Levees	$85	$3
Public Parks	$78	
Half the amount for Schools	$125	
Power Infrastructure 6/	**$197**	**$73**
Aviation	**$111**	**$25**
Inland Waterways & Ports	**$25**	**$17**
Hazardous 7/ & Solid Waste	**$0**	**$21**
Infrastructure Resiliency		$50
Additional Mega Projects Including:	**$2,374**	
Affordable Housing 8/	$720	
High Speed Rail 9/	$1,074	
Broadband Complete Access 10/	$100	$65
Renewable Energy Super-Grid Overlay 11/	$80	
Large Water Management Projects	$400	

1/ See 2021 Report Card: https://infrastructurereportcard.org/wp-content/uploads/2020/12/National_IRC_2021-report.pdf .
2/ See Failure to Act, Table 2 at https://infrastructurereportcard.org/the-impact/failure-to-act-report/ . May not add due to rounding.
3/ Already funded means: Baseline Federal grants and loans appropriated through the Federal budget; and state, local, utility, transit and port and airport authorities' spending financed by: local government revenues, special taxes, user fees, and borrowed money.
4/ Funding gap excludes money already funded. The National Infrastructure Bank will cover all of the funding gap, plus additional for mega projects.
5/ **Comprises $434 B for drinking and wastewater, $286 B to meet the EPA Copper and Lead Rule, to remove all lead service lines, and $81 B for stormwater repairs.**
6/ Excludes $3 trillion estimated as governments cost to electrify vehicles and move all generation and distribution off of fossil fuels.
   See DOT Study: https://www.ourenergypolicy.org/resources/mobilizing-for-a-zero-carbon-america-jobs-jobs-jobs-and-more-jobs/
7/ 2021 Report Card states there are 35 shovel ready projects in the Superfund that have not received Federal funding, but gives no dollar amount.
8/ Estimated 7.3 million affordable housing units needed (https://nlihc.org) times $100,000 per unit.
9/ High Speed Rail Alliance estimate for 100% of Federal Railroad Administration's 11 High Speed Rail Corridors covering 8965 miles.
10/ Federal Communications Commission 2016 Broadband Progress Report. Jim Clyburn Broadband Bill proposes $94 billion.
11/ US 2019 DOE estimate, see: https://www.eenews.net/stories/1061403455 . Also see 2021 estimate of $50 billion at:
    https://theconversation.com/the-us-needs-a-macrogrid-to-move-electricity-from-areas-that-make-it-to-areas-that-need-it-155938 .
12/ What's in the $1.2 trillion Senate infrastructure package. By Heather Long, Aug. 10, 2021.

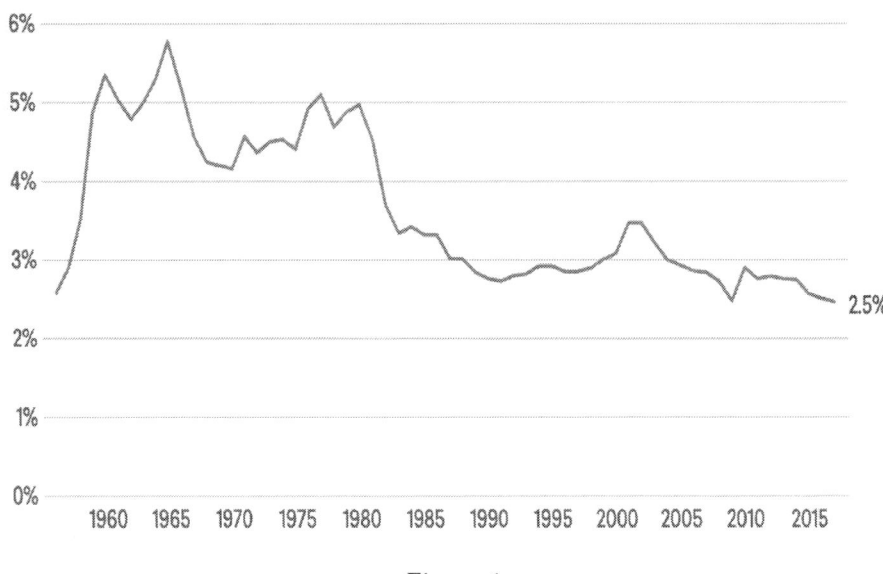

Figure 1

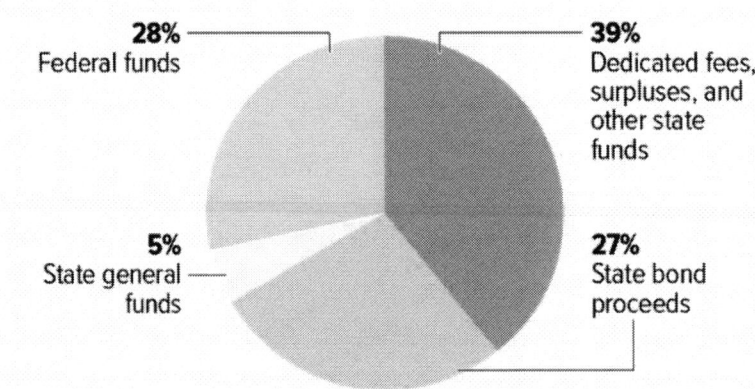

Figure 2

Legislation in Congress to Create a National Infrastructure Bank

As the United States grapples with the challenge of rebuilding its aging infrastructure, policy analysts agree that traditional methods may no longer suffice. The Council on Foreign Relations underscores this urgency, noting that despite the IIJA and related legislation, experts believe much more funding is required to overcome the country's infrastructure deficit. Similarly, the National Governors Association has made a strong appeal to Congress for increased investment in water infrastructure, highlighting the critical needs for modernizing drinking and stormwater systems. This raises a pivotal question: if the combined resources of federal and state budgets, along with private capital (as identified by CNIB in 2022), fall short, what alternative financing solutions can be tapped? As previously noted, addressing this gap is not just a matter of prudent policy but a crucial step towards ensuring sustainable and resilient infrastructure for future generations

Congress is currently considering a groundbreaking legislative proposal (HR4052, as detailed on Congress.gov), aimed at revolutionizing America's approach to infrastructure financing. This bill introduces the concept of a $5 trillion National Infrastructure Bank (NIB). Unlike traditional funding sources, the NIB, which would operate outside the national budget, represents an innovative solution to bypass the limitations of Federal and local budgets. As a federally incorporated entity (as per Wikipedia, Oct. 2023), the NIB would be uniquely capitalized by swapping existing private sector Treasuries for equity in the Bank.

This model isn't new to American economic history. It mirrors successful precedents, such as the First Bank of the United States, established in 1791 by Treasury Secretary Alexander Hamilton (referenced in Wikipedia, Nov. 2023), and the Reconstruction Finance Corporation initiated under FDR (Butchiewicz). Like a commercial bank, the NIB would offer low-cost loans for specific infrastructure projects to entities in control of public infrastructure.

The operating costs of the NIB would be minimal, requiring only a small initial appropriation from Congress (CNIB, 2021). This self-sustaining model would not only avoid adding to national deficits or debt but could provide an annual dividend payment to the government. This unique financial structure is designed to garner bipartisan support, reflecting the long-standing consensus that infrastructure development is a cross-party priority. As David Leonhardt (Leonhardt, 2023) has pointed out, such a national infrastructure investment program would unleash numerous synergies, significantly advancing the nation's economic and structural resilience.

Fully Complements Federal Programs

The NIB is a pivotal initiative designed to bridge crucial financing gaps in America's infrastructure landscape. Uniquely positioned to complement, not duplicate, existing Federal programs like the IIJA and the Inflation Reduction Act, the NIB would be a game-changer for multiple critical infrastructure sectors. It would provide essential funding where it is most needed —in areas like U.S. transportation for both passengers and freight, the power grid, water systems, and housing. For instance, imagine a scenario where the NIB steps in to finance a critical section of a high-speed rail network, connecting communities previously underserved by public transportation. This approach not only raises U.S. productivity but also ensures that tax dollars are utilized more effectively. The creation of the NIB marks a significant stride towards a more organized, efficient, and forward-thinking infrastructure system. This bold step would change the face of American infrastructure from one reliant on legacy systems to modern, future-oriented systems rivaling our most formidable competitors.

Sectors and projects requiring immediate attention include:

Water infrastructure and water management. ASCE estimates that $801 billion is needed over 10 years to update drinking water (Greenfield), wastewater, and stormwater systems (Rubenstein), and to replace all lead water supply lines (Pittman). However, the IIJA only provides $55 billion. Similarly, $110 billion is needed to re-build ports and inland waterways— locks (Thomas), dams (Klemm), and levees—but the IIJA appropriates only $20 billion. And there is no provision in current legislation (including the next 5-year Farm Bill) to provide new water resources for the drought-stricken Southwest where 50% of our nation's farm-to-table food. The NIB will make strategic, sustainable investments in all of these areas, including by formulating a national plan for water management.

Transportation. As depicted in HB4052, the NIB would finance all of the roads and bridges where IIJA financing is slated to be insufficient ($785 billion needed vs. $110 billion provided). Beyond that, the bank would orchestrate a fundamental shift, by financing projects that move more passengers and express freight onto rail, so as to relieve congestion on roads and at airports and better save on CO_2 emissions (Mineta). Accordingly, the NIB incorporates $1.1 trillion to build a fully electric high speed rail network across America (Jones), as well as $406 billion in added financing for transit, passenger rail, and airports to rationalize and speed transportation systems. Projects would include critical improvements along the busy Northeast Corridor as well as completion of the NY-NJ Gateway Project (Forczek).

Electricity and Broadband. Although they are mostly privately-owned, these two sectors are struggling to deliver new capacity where it is most needed. The nation's electric grid is vulnerable to weather events, cyberattacks, and problems of peak demand, and is not ready for a shift to renewable energy (Englund). This includes accommodation of electric vehicles (cars, trucks buses, etc.). The NIB will specifically finance a power grid overlay to transport renewable generation around the country that is not financed in the IRA (Behr). And it will build a more resilient grid to protect against escalating problems associated with climate change (Biesecker). Moreover, the NIB will fill in holes where privately financed telecommunications companies have failed to deliver broadband services because it is not initially profitable to do so.

Affordable Housing. Although not normally thought of as infrastructure, affordable housing is in crisis, and efforts to increase supply through the Federal budget have fallen woefully short (GAO). Currently, two million Americans are unhoused, while 40 million live below the poverty line (Lee) and are just a paycheck away from being evicted from their homes. The National Low Income Housing Coalition estimates that the U.S. faces a shortage of **more than 7.3 million homes** which are affordable and available for renters with the lowest incomes, a shortage that worsened during the COVID pandemic (NLHC). The NIB could provide $720 billion over ten years to build or refurbish units for these lowest income earners, and would employ best practices for social housing to ensure that units remain sustainably affordable (Gowan).

Building Resiliency. Over the past two decades, storms, floods, heatwaves, droughts, and wildfires have taken lives and destroyed property, with global warming making events more frequent and severe. New data indicate that two thirds of this damage is due to storms (Carrington), while at the same time sea levels are rising. Meanwhile, costs for remediation to protect infrastructure and property from climate-induced damage do not yet appear to be fully factored into total financing needs, even those estimated by ASCE. For example, Houston requires a dyke to protect its port and oil facilities estimated to cost $34 billion (Drane), plus enhanced drainage to fight property damage arising from bigger storms (Borenstein). New Orleans needs billions of dollars and planning to rebuild wetlands to protect its Port and surrounds (USGBC and Mooney Aug. 2023). Florida has yet to devise a plan to protect cities like Pensacola from rising sea levels that contribute to tropical storm intensity (Mooney, 2023). The NIB would make strategic, sustainable investments in all of these geographic areas, and support U.S. Army Corps of Engineers programs which remain chronically underfunded in the Federal budget (Helwig).

Reaching Rural America. Rural communities face a critical infrastructure funding gap, an issue increasingly acknowledged by local legislators and supported by insights from Rebuild Rural. The funds allocated through the IIJA are disproportionately missing these areas, and private capital investment is similarly lacking. The consequences are starkly evident: a dramatic decline in small business formation in non-metropolitan areas over the past decade, as highlighted by Meyerson's research, and a concerning trend of rural populations migrating in search of better employment opportunities, as noted by Johnson.

Addressing this imbalance is where proposed NIB financing will come into play. Crucially, the Bank's mandate includes a requirement for appropriate geographic distribution of funds, ensuring that rural areas are not overlooked in the national push for infrastructure revitalization. In partnership with the U.S. Department of Agriculture, the NIB would enhance community development programs that have been historically underfunded. Moreover, it would provide vital engineering and technical assistance, empowering local municipalities in rural America to effectively manage and execute infrastructure projects. This comprehensive approach promises to not only to bridge the current urban-rural divide in infrastructure development but also to foster more resilient economies across the country.

Turbocharges the Economy, Productivity, and Worker Pay

NIB's launch is set to significantly benefit the American economy, reminiscent of the transformative impact of historical infrastructure initiatives. Key among these benefits is the creation of approximately 25 million new jobs, as defined by the Bureau of Labor Statistics standards, offering union-level "Davis-Bacon" wages. This is expected to catalyze economic growth and enhance productivity, mirroring the achievements during the era of the Reconstruction Finance Corporation (RFC) from 1933 to 1957. During that period, the economy experienced an average growth of 5.5% per year (as indicated by FRED data), with Total Factor Productivity peaking at 3.4% annually in the 1940s, alongside a significant rise in unskilled wages (Williamson) and Federal income tax receipts.

In today's economic context, even with near-full employment, similar outcomes are achievable. A 2014 study by the University of Maryland commissioned by the National Association of Manufacturers projected that increased infrastructure spending could accelerate annual economic growth to 2.9 percent and raise real disposable income by 3.4 percent, compared to the stagnant growth average of 1.8 percent per year (Werling). This is critical, as the ASCE's 2021 Report Card on America's Infrastructure presages severe economic repercussions if the infrastructure investment gap remains unaddressed. The NIB, therefore, stands not just as a financial institution, but as a catalyst for sustainable economic growth and prosperity in the United States. By 2039, a continued underinvestment would cost an estimated:

- $10 trillion in cumulative lost GDP,

- More than 3 million jobs in year 2039, and

- $2.24 trillion in exports over the next 20 years.

Meanwhile, well-targeted investments will help to control inflation because, for every dollar borrowed and spent on infrastructure, three new dollars in economic output will be created: a greater supply of goods means lower prices (Werling). Moreover, NIB-financed spending will provide a steady demand for manufactured goods made in America, which grows that sector and adds more high-paying jobs. Spending can also be accelerated to offset the effects of any potential future.

Restores International Competitiveness

For anyone traveling abroad, it's obvious that the United States lags behind other developed countries including China in terms of infrastructure quality and competitiveness. The disparities can be traced back to lower levels of infrastructure investment (see chart below), less integrated national planning, and more costly construction compared to many international peers (Ziegler).

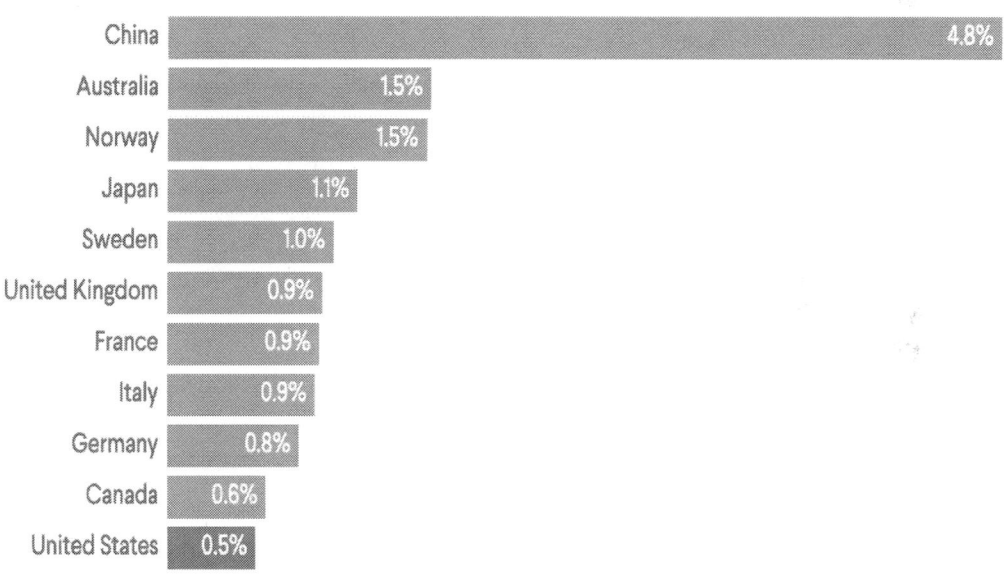

Figure 3

Source: Organization for Economic Cooperation and Development

It should come as no surprise to learn that Europe, Japan, Canada, India, and China all employ national or international development banks to finance their infrastructure projects and better plan to meet ongoing development needs. In fact, many countries copied the "American System" after sending delegations to America in the mid-1800s to study it (Wikipedia, Sep. 2023). They understood that the economic and environmental benefits of such banks were substantial. China, for example, has relied on three state-owned "policy banks" to finance high speed rail that is unrivaled anywhere on earth. Built in just over just 12 years, China's HSR has linked rural populations with urban centers, enabled the buildup of new manufacturing centers, helped to lift 800 million people out of poverty, and paved the way for China's global trade supremacy (Whitney). Added to that, China's banks financed a nation-wide water grid that tamed rivers, diverted water supplies to where they were needed, produced electricity, and greened parched farmlands to ensure adequate food supplies for a growing population (Brown). America needs a comparable set of projects if we are to compete, prosper and succeed.

Conclusion

The stark reality highlighted in the 2014 "60 Minutes" documentary, *America's Crumbling Infrastructure*, remains a pressing issue. Despite the clear and present danger posed by deteriorating infrastructure—from blocked ports and unstable bridges to regular electric outages and a critical housing shortage—effective solutions have been elusive. The IIJA and other recent outlays will have significant impact in this arena but does not contain sufficient financing to fundamentally improve the full range of inadequate or deteriorating infrastructures.

At this juncture, it is vital to ask: How can we finance comprehensive infrastructure that not only reach every American but also buttress our economy? Traditional approaches, limited by stretched Federal and state budgets—as well as insufficient interest from private capital markets—fall short. The answer may lie in innovative legislative solutions like HR4052, which proposes the establishment of a $5 trillion National Infrastructure Bank. This initiative is ambitious in scope and capable of addressing the entire financing gap. Moreover, it has a historical precedent, having been successfully implemented four times in U.S. history and emulated by other nations.

The National Infrastructure Bank promises to extend its reach to every corner of the country, bolstering local economies and creating high-paying jobs without burdening the federal budget. With 19 Congressional co-sponsors and a growing chorus of support from state and local legislators, this legislation stands as a beacon of hope. It represents a tangible, proven solution to a problem that has long plagued the country. The time for decisive action is now—to rebuild, revitalize, and future-proof America's infrastructure for generations to come

Author Capsule Bio

Stanley Forczek serves as the Advisory Board President for the Coalition for a National Infrastructure Bank. He is a diversified infrastructure expert with a comprehensive background in transportation and energy management. His career spans over four decades, including significant roles with Amtrak. At Amtrak, he served as the first Director of Finance for the Northeast Corridor and the initial Director for Strategic Planning. His responsibilities at Amtrak also involved managing a substantial energy budget and playing a key role in the economic dispatch of a 1,200-mile electric transmission network and power pool.

He has a notable history of involvement with electric regulatory bodies, such as PJM, NY-ISO, ISO-NE, FERC, and several State Commissions. His work has covered areas including market development, transmission utilization, transmission overbuild, and generation development. In the realm of energy management, he has overseen the procurement of approximately 900 megawatts of electricity and over 750,000 dekatherms of natural gas. His strategic procurement initiatives led to significant Amtrak cost savings. His expertise also extends to integrating traction/transit operations with energy management and planning.

Outside of Amtrak, he has managed energy procurements for various large-scale institutional users. His experience covers the entire range of processes, from presentation and negotiation to the execution and management of procurement contracts. This work has spanned across the U.S., with a particular focus on the mid-Atlantic and New England regions.

He runs his own consulting firm in the New Jersey/Pennsylvania region, offering services to clients, including Goldman Sachs, Exelon, and Concord Engineering. He holds an Executive MBA from the University of Virginia, Darden School of Business, and a BS in Accounting from Fairleigh Dickinson University. He has also completed coursework at the University of Illinois, focusing on Energy Engineering Business Strategies.

References

"60 Minutes." *America's Crumbling Infrastructure.* Archive, 2014, re-cast Feb. 2023. https://www.youtube.com/watch?v=xoYYxs9OSUg.

American Society of Civil Engineers (ASCE). "Failure to Act: Economic Impacts of Status Quo Investment Across Infrastructure Systems." 2021. https://infrastructurereportcard.org/the-impact/failure-to-act-report/.

American Society of Civil Engineers (ASCE). "Assessing America's Infrastructure Gap." Updated 2023. https://infrastructurereportcard.org/resources/investment-gap-2020-2029/.

Behr, Peter. "Details emerge about DOE 'super-grid' renewable study." E&E News, October 29, 2019. https://subscriber.politicopro.com/article/eenews/1061403455.

Biesecker, Michael, Bernard Condon, and Jennifer McDermott. "Videos put scrutiny on downed power lines as possible cause of deadly Maui wildfires." AP News, August 16, 2023. https://apnews.com/article/hawaii-wildfires-maui-electricity-power-utilities-c46a106db3c5019ac835ddcb01fde25f.

Borenstein, Seth, and Frank Bajak. "Houston drainage grid 'so obsolete' it's just unbelievable." Chicago Tribune, August 29, 2017. https://www.chicagotribune.com/nation-world/ct-houston-drainage-grid-obsolete-20170829-story.html.

Brown, Ellen. "How to Green Our Parched Farmlands and Finance Critical Infrastructure." ScheerPost, September 1, 2022. https://scheerpost.com/2022/09/01/ellen-brown-how-to-green-our-parched-farmlands-and-finance-critical-infrastructure/.

Butkiewicz, James. "Reconstruction Finance Corporation." Economic History Association. https://eh.net/encyclopedia/reconstruction-finance-corporation/.

Carrington, Damian. "Climate crisis costing $16m an hour in extreme weather damage, study estimates." *The Guardian*, October 9, 2023. https://www.theguardian.com/environment/2023/oct/09/climate-crisis-cost-extreme-weather-damage-study.

CBS News. "Mega-drought takes dramatic toll on Colorado River system that provides water to 40 million people." June 9, 2021. https://www.cbsnews.com/amp/news/mega-drought-colorado-river-system-water-system/?__twitter_impression=true&s=09.

Coalition for a National Infrastructure Bank (CNIB). "National Infrastructure Banks are Proven Superior to Public-Private Partnerships." Updated August 20, 2022. https://www.nibcoalition.com/national-infrastructure-banks-are-proven-superior-to-public-private-partnerships.

"How the National Infrastructure Bank (NIB) Creates and Makes Money." Updated June 30, 2021. https://www.nibcoalition.com/how-the-nib-creates-and-makes-money.

Congress.gov. "The National Infrastructure Bank Act of 2023." Sponsor Danny K. Davis with 18 Co-sponsors. https://www.congress.gov/bill/118th-congress/house-bill/4052.

Drane, Amanda. "Ike Dike gates won't allow for large ships to use Houston Ship Channel, study says." *Houston Chronicle*, February 9, 2023. https://www.houstonchronicle.com/business/energy/article/houston-port-channel-ike-dike-expansion-17771423.php.

Englund, Will. "Plug-in cars are the future. The grid isn't ready." *The Washington Post*, October 16, 2021. https://www.washingtonpost.com/business/2021/10/13/electric-vehicles-grid-upgrade/.

Federal Reserve Bank of St. Louis (FRED). "Real Gross Domestic Product." 1933–57. https://fred.stlouisfed.org/series/GDPC1.

Federal Trade Commission (FCC). "Broadband Progress Report." 2016. https://www.fcc.gov/reports-research/reports/broadband-progress-reports/2016-broadband-progress-report.

Forczek, Stan. "National Infrastructure Bank – A Hamiltonian Solution to Today's Infrastructure Crisis." New Jersey League of Municipalities, May 2019, pg. 28. https://www.njlm.org/Archive.aspx?ADID=1618.

Government Accountability Office (GAO). "The Affordable Housing Crisis Grows While Efforts to Increase Supply Fall Short." October 12, 2023. https://www.gao.gov/blog/affordable-housing-crisis-grows-while-efforts-increase-supply-fall-short.

Gowan, Saoirse, and Ryan Cooper. "A Plan to Solve the Housing Crisis Through Social Housing." People's Policy Project, April 5, 2018. https://www.peoplespolicyproject.org/project/a-plan-to-solve-the-housing-crisis-through-social-housing/.

Greenfield, Nicole. "America's Failing Drinking Water System." NRDC, October 5, 2023. https://www.nrdc.org/stories/americas-failing-drinking-water-system.

Helwig, David. "$227 million lock replacement could start this year." *SooToday*, March 30, 2002. https://www.sootoday.com/local-news/227-million-lock-replacement-could-start-this-year-87075.

Johnson, Calvin. "Rural America Lost Population Over the Past Decade for the First Time in History." Carsey School of Public Policy at the University of New Hampshire, February 22, 2022. https://carsey.unh.edu/publication-rural-ameri

ca-lost-population-over-past-decade-for-first-time-in-history.

Jones, Ben. "High speed trains are racing across the world. But not in America." CNN Travel, April 18, 2023. https://www.cnn.com/travel/article/high-speed-rail-us/index.html.

Klemm, Josh, and Isabella Winkler. "Which of the World's Hundreds of Thousands of Aging Dams Will Be the Next to Burst?" *The New York Times*, September 17, 2023. https://www.nytimes.com/2023/09/17/opinion/libya-floods-dams.html.

Lee, Juhohn. "37.9 million Americans are living in poverty, according to the U.S. Census. But the problem could be far worse." CNBC, March 7 2023. https://www.cnbc.com/2023/03/07/why-poverty-might-be-far-worse-in-the-us-than-its-reported.html.

Leonhardt, David. "Longer Commutes, Shorter Lives: The Costs of Not Investing in America." *The New York Times Magazine*, October 17, 2023. https://www.nytimes.com/2023/10/17/magazine/us-public-investment.html.

McBride, James, Noah Berman, and Anshu Siripurapu. "The State of U.S. Infrastructure." Council on Foreign Relations (CFR), Updated September 20, 2023. https://www.cfr.org/backgrounder/state-us-infrastructure.

McNichol, Elizabeth. "It's Time for States to Invest in Infrastructure." Center on Budget and Policy Priorities, March 19, 2019. https://www.cbpp.org/research/its-time-for-states-to-invest-in-infrastructure.

Meyerson, Harold. "Investing in Disinvested America." *The American Prospect*, October 12, 2023. https://prospect.org/economy/2023-10-12-investing-in-disinvested-america/.

Mineta Transportation Institute. "The Economic and Environmental Potential of High-Speed Rail." October 2023. https://transweb.sjsu.edu/research/2367-Economic-Environmental-Potential-High-Speed-Rail.

Mooney, Chris, and Brady Dennis. "Seas have drastically risen along southern U.S. coast in past decade." *The Washington Post*, April 10, 2023. https://www.washingtonpost.com/climate-environment/2023/04/10/sea-level-rise-southern-us/.

Mooney, Chris, Zoeann Murphy, Ricky Carioti, and John Muyskens. "Facing the surge." *The Washington Post*, August 7, 2023. https://www.washingtonpost.com/climate-environment/interactive/2023/new-orleans-sea-level-hurricane-wetlands/.

National Low Income Housing Coalition (NLHC). "No State Has an Adequate Supply of Affordable Rental Housing for the Lowest Income Renters." 2023. https://nlihc.org/gap.

National Governors Association (NGA). "Governors Urge Congress to Address Water Infrastructure Funding Cuts." September 14, 2023. https://www.nga.org/advocacy-communications/letters-nga/governors-urge-congress-to-address-water-infrastructure-funding/.

Pittman, Craig. "Surprise! Florida leads the nation in lead pipes carrying water supply." *Florida Phoenix*, April 13, 2023. https://floridaphoenix.com/2023/04/13/surprise-florida-leads-the-nation-in-lead-pipes-carrying-water-supply/.

Rebuild Rural. "Federal funding often is limited for rural projects." https://rebuildrural.com/#page2.

Reuters. "Torrential rains bring flooding to New York." September 29, 2023. https://www.reuters.com/pictures/torrential-rains-bring-flooding-new-york-2023-09-29/.

"U.S. Budget Gap Soars to $1.7 Trillion, Largest Outside COVID Era." U.S. News & World Report, October 20, 2023. https://money.usnews.com/investing/news/articles/2023-10-20/u-s-budget-deficit-jumps-23-to-nearly-1-7-trillion-as-social-security-health-costs-rise.

Ritcher, Wolf. "Congrats, America We Made it! Government Debt Spikes past $33 Trillion: +$1.6 Trillion since Debt Ceiling, +$2.2 Trillion from Year Ago." *Wolf Street*, September 18, 2023. https://wolfstreet.com/2023/09/18/congrats-america-%f0%9f%a5%82we-made-it-government-debt-spikes-past-33-trillion-1-6-trillion-since-debt-ceiling-2-2-trillion-from-year-ago/.

Rubenstein, Dana. "Was New York City Unprepared to Handle Last Week's Extreme Rainfall?" *The New York Times*, October 5, 2023. https://www.nytimes.com/2023/10/05/nyregion/adams-flood-nyc.html.

Stein, Jeff, Nick Miroff, and Jacob Bogage. "What's in Biden's $106 billion funding request for Israel, Ukraine." *The Washington Post*, October 20, 2023. https://www.washingtonpost.com/business/2023/10/20/biden-ukraine-israel-package/.

Thomas, Ken. "U.S. Races to Expand Michigan Locks and Secure the Supply Chain." *The Wall Street Journal*, October 15, 2023. https://www.wsj.com/us-news/u-s-races-to-expand-michigan-locksand-secure-the-supply-chain-1a13bcca?mod=djem10point.

U.S. High Speed Rail Association (USHSR). "High Speed Rail Policy." 2023. http://www.ushsr.com/policy/.

U.S. Green Building Council (USGBC). "Dutch dialogues: New Orleans talks resiliency with the Netherlands." October 6, 2014. https://www.usgbc.org/articles/dutch-dialogues-new-orleans-talks-resiliency-netherlands.

Werling, Jeffrey, and Ronald Horst. "Catching Up: Greater Focus Needed to Achieve a More Competitive Infrastructure." National Association of Manufacturers, September 1, 2014. https://www.ourenergypolicy.org/resources/catching-up-greater-focus-needed-to-achieve-a-more-competitive-infrastructure/.

Whitney, Mike. "The One Chart That Explains Everything." *The Truthseeker*, July 14, 2023. https://www.thetruthseeker.co.uk/?p=271060.

Wikipedia. "American System (economic plan)." Last accessed September 2023. https://en.wikipedia.org/wiki/American_System_(economic_plan).

Wikipedia. "State-owned enterprises of the United States." Last accessed October 2023. https://en.wikipedia.org/wiki/State-owned_enterprises_of_the_United_States.

Wikipedia. "First Bank of the United States." Last accessed November 2023. https://en.wikipedia.org/wiki/First_Bank_of_the_United_States.

Williamson, Samuel, Prof. "Unskilled wage index, U.S." 1933–57. https://eh.net/database/unskilled-wage-index-u-s/.

Ziegler, Bart. "Why Is U.S. Infrastructure So Costly—and What Can We Do About It?" *The Wall Street Journal*, July 24, 2022. https://www.wsj.com/articles/infrastructure-us-costly-explained-solutions-11658263884.

Archival Section Overview

Richard M. Krieg

This archival section is a curated revisit to some of the pioneering articles that have helped shape *JCIP*'s trajectory to date. These seminal works offer a retrospective on selected topics—among many—that we've explored in past years. They reflect our commitment to underscoring critical aspects of infrastructure resilience and policy-relevant discourse.

    These cornerstone articles also embody *JCIP*'s dedication to an interdisciplinary platform that addresses complex issues with analytical depth. They are a collective narrative that present scholarly achievements but also set the stage for future exploration and policy refinement. Together, they embody the Journal's mission to inform, influence, and inspire the critical infrastructure community in shaping more resilient and secure systems.

    It is hoped that the Journal will continue to help illuminate the path forward, guiding researchers, practitioners, and policymakers in their vital quest to safeguard the infrastructural underpinnings of modern societies.

Article Selection

The difficulty of selecting any sample of articles from a corpus collectively authored by over a hundred individual contributors was daunting. To do so, we relied on the following criteria:

Relevance to Evolving CI Complexity

Articles were chosen for their deep analysis of CI as complex adaptive systems, highlighting the interconnectivity and the potential cascading effects of failures across sectors.

Insight into Post-9/11 Security Developments

Selected works offer critical perspectives on the changes in national security post-9/11, particularly the advancements and ongoing vulnerabilities within CI in the face of modern threats.

Responses to Natural and Human-Made Disasters

Priority was given to articles that address the burgeoning risks posed by such disasters, showcasing the imperative for resilience and adaptability in CI planning and response.

Contribution to CI Policy Discourse

The articles illuminate the intricate layers of CI policy, contributing to a field that requires a nuanced understanding of the interplay between technical risk assessment, governance, and the crafting of responsive strategies.

Innovative Solutions and Strategies

Works that propose innovative solutions or strategies to enhance CI resilience and adaptability were particularly sought after, reflecting the journal's focus on forward-looking, actionable research.

Cross-Sector Impact Analysis

We favored articles that examine the implications of CI vulnerabilities and resilience across various sectors, providing insights that transcend individual industries or fields.

Interdisciplinary Approach

Articles that employ an interdisciplinary approach, integrating perspectives from engineering, policy studies, economics, and social sciences, were selected for their holistic view of CI challenges.

The Articles

"Progress toward Resilient Infrastructures: Are we falling behind the pace of events and changing threats?" by **David Woods and David Alderson** opened the discourse by dissecting the Strategic Agility Gap. This analytical work probed the dichotomy between the rapid evolution of infrastructural threats and the comparatively sluggish pace of adaptive organizational strategies. The authors brought to light the myriad unforeseen breakdowns and the pressing need for a strategic pivot toward resilience-focused strategies. Through a detailed examination of recent infrastructural failures, the authors call for a reevaluation of current methodologies and the adoption of innovative approaches that embrace scientific advancements to enhance strategic agility across various critical infrastructure sectors.

My Editor's Interview with **Maria Korsnick** ("Small Nuclear Reactors Essential to the U.S. Energy & Climate Change Future") offered a deep dive into the transformative potential of nuclear energy in the context of climate change. Korsnick articulates a strategic vision where Small Modular Reactors (SMRs) and microreactors emerge as game-changers in the decarbonization of the nation's energy sources. This conversation provided a thorough examination of the dual objectives of economic feasibility and enhanced safety protocols. The interview illuminated the complexities of integrating advanced nuclear technologies into our energy matrix and points to the broader implications for policy, industry, and environmental sustainability.

In "Energy Supply Chains and Change," **Diane Graziano, Elisa Alonso, Fletcher Fields and Diana Bauer** presented a comprehensive model for understanding the global energy markets, with a particular focus on the critical role of large gas turbines in electricity production. Their article delved into the intricate dynamics of energy supply chains, offering an analytical framework that considers the multifaceted interactions of market forces, technology production, and anticipated trends. This piece stood out for its systematic approach to dissecting the complexities of the energy sector and its supply chain dependencies, providing a critical tool for policymakers and industry stakeholders.

George Baker's exploration of the resilience of the United States' critical infrastructure against electromagnetic pulses provided an in-depth analysis of the nation's electric grid vulnerabilities. In "Electromagnetic Pulse Resilience of United States Critical Infrastructure: Progress and Prognostics," he meticulously outlines the strategies needed to shield the grid against both natural and adversarial electromagnetic threats, drawing on a rich body of research and strategic defense insights. It presented a comprehensive overview of operational vulnerabilities and proposed a suite of strategies aimed at safeguarding critical infrastructure, thereby contributing to the national dialogue on grid security and resilience.

"The 2021 Texas Electric Grid Failure: Causes, Consequences, and Cures" by **Thomas Popik and Richard Humphreys** delivered a critical post-mortem on one of the most significant infrastructural failures in recent history. The authors provide a granular analysis of the technical failures and policy oversights that led to widespread blackouts. Their findings advocated for systemic reforms, including market model adjustments, to prevent future infrastructural failures. This piece continues to serve as a pivotal resource for understanding the vulnerabilities in our energy infrastructure and the necessary steps to enhance grid reliability and resilience.

Daniel Shea's "Nuclear Policy in the States: A National Review" provided an exhaustive review of the legislative landscape influencing the advancement of nuclear energy at the state level. The article maps out the legislative momentum and its substantial impact on the nuclear industry's trajectory, elucidating the complex interplay of policy development, federalism, and industry dynamics. It stands as a comprehensive source of information on the nuances of nuclear energy policy and its implications for the broader energy policy discussions.

"Incentivizing Good Governance Beyond Regulatory Minimums: The Civil Nuclear Sector" by **Debra Decker and Kathryn Rauhut** introduced a novel "Good Governance Template" to the discourse on critical infrastructure security. The article examines how market incentives can be strategically employed to encourage enhanced security practices beyond regulatory requirements. This piece continues to contribute to the conversation on innovative policy solutions, highlighting the role of market mechanisms in achieving security objectives and the potential for such frameworks to transform security practices across critical infrastructure sectors.

Finally, "Evolution and Trends of Industrial Control System Cyber Incidents Since 2017" by **Robert Grubbs, Jeremiah Stoddard, Sarah Freeman, and Ron Fisher** addressed the growing cyber threat to industrial control systems. The article provides a thorough analysis of the vulnerabilities and incidents that have marked the landscape in recent years. By advocating for a proactive policy framework, the authors underlined the critical need for robust cybersecurity measures to protect the operational technology environments that are vital to national and economic security.

Strategic Perspectives

Progress toward Resilient Infrastructures: Are we falling behind the pace of events and changing threats?

David D. Woods[1] and David L. Alderson[2]

[1] Professor Emeritus, Dept of Integrated Systems Engineering, Ohio State University, woods.2@osu.edu

[2] Professor, Operations Research Dept, Naval Postgraduate School, dlalders@nps.edu

[*see Author Capsule Bios below*]

Abstract

The current strategy for achieving resilient infrastructures is making progress too slowly to keep up with the pace of change as evidenced by a continuing stream of "shock" events. How do we better anticipate changing threats and recognize emerging new vulnerabilities in an increasingly interconnected world? We are facing a Strategic Agility Gap that requires us to revise our current perspective and processes if we are to make meaningful progress.

Introduction: The Critical Infrastructure Challenge

For over a decade, societies across the globe have realized the need to make critical infrastructure systems more resilient in the face of threats from natural disasters, risks from technological change, and adversarial actions (e.g., Flynn 2007). In the opening pages of this journal, Krieg (2020, p. 1) restated the challenge of resilient infrastructure: Critical infrastructures "are highly complex, interconnected and sometimes unplanned—and they are evolving at exponential rates. Impairment in one sector can cascade into multiple sector shutdowns leading to serious societal consequences. Each sector encompasses an array of physical assets, organizations and people as well as important cyberspace components. These factors can present unforeseen built-in vulnerabilities, and accidents are likely to be experienced as systems become more complex, opaque and interactive."

In response to this challenge, there has been major investment over more than a decade on the part of universities, national laboratories, and funding agencies in *modeling and simulation* as a means

- to describe and predict system behavior within lifeline infrastructures so as to find vulnerabilities (holes);

- for identifying dependencies across infrastructure sectors to project lines of propagation of events to minimize loss of valued services when infrastructures are threatened; and

- to fill holes and/or block propagation to contain consequences.

The basic strategy is invest to build up modeling tools that represent specific infrastructures in specific jurisdictions to capture the interconnections across these lifeline infrastructures. The investment in modeling tools tailored for lifeline infrastructures is intended to provide a base—a modeling "infrastructure" so to speak—that can be used to address new cases or re-examine changes to previous cases. Using the base of modeling capabilities to analyze infrastructures will support identification, assessment, and prioritization of vulnerabilities and associated consequences so stakeholders can the select most important ones for mitigation given limited resources. Continued investment will expand the capability for modeling and, over time, will lead to sufficiently detailed and thorough models of critical lifeline infrastructures and interconnections to support timely, practical decision making. These decisions can be assessed in terms of improved robustness relative to the vulnerabilities identified in the modeling and simulation runs. The modeling and simulation over different types of failure and attack will show which interventions produce measurable gains in either how well systems can withstand threats or how quickly systems will recover normal services.

However, the current strategy has scientific, technical, and practical limits that are revealed when we look at the continuing stream of disruptive events given the growth of complexities (Carlson and Doyle, 2000; Alderson and Doyle, 2010). These limits make the current strategy less responsive than events demand, leaving organizations stranded in the Strategic Agility Gap (Woods, 2020; Figure 1). For example, the current strategy rests on the assumption that modeling can uncover holes and map interdependencies rather completely—whereas work on the fundamentals that give rise to complexity penalties has revealed that, inevitably, past models will miss important aspects as processes of change, improvement, and adaptation continue. One of the new findings is that resilience depends on timely model updating and revision (Woods, 2018).

Falling Behind: The Strategic Agility Gap

Since the critical infrastructure challenge was recognized, the world has not stood still—growth occurred as new technology and opportunities arose, complexities grew, and new threats emerged as other parties hijacked valued capabilities for their own purposes. The pace of change continues to accelerate leading to expanded scales of operation, dramatic new capabilities, extensive and hidden interdependencies, intensified pressures, new vulnerabilities, and puzzling failures with far reaching consequences. Society and organizations face the challenge of how to adapt to the increasing pace of change, scale, capability, risk, and threats, all in more complex, interconnected worlds.

Experience across industries, regions, and societies indicates organizations are *slow and stale* to adapt to new threats, as well as to seize new opportunities to build resilience. The result is a *Strategic Agility Gap* evidenced by the regular occurrence of surprising failures at organizational, regional, national scales—breakdowns that trigger or threaten widespread service outages with large financial and human costs (Woods, 2020). The Strategic Agility Gap is the difference between the *rate* at which an organization can *adapt to change* and the rise of new unexpected challenges at a larger industry or society scale. It is a *mismatch in velocities of change and velocities of adaptation* (Figure 1). Can organizations learn how to offset changing risks before failures occur as growth continues? Can organizations build capabilities to be poised to adapt to keep pace with and stay ahead of the trajectory of growing complexity and the penalties that arise as a result?

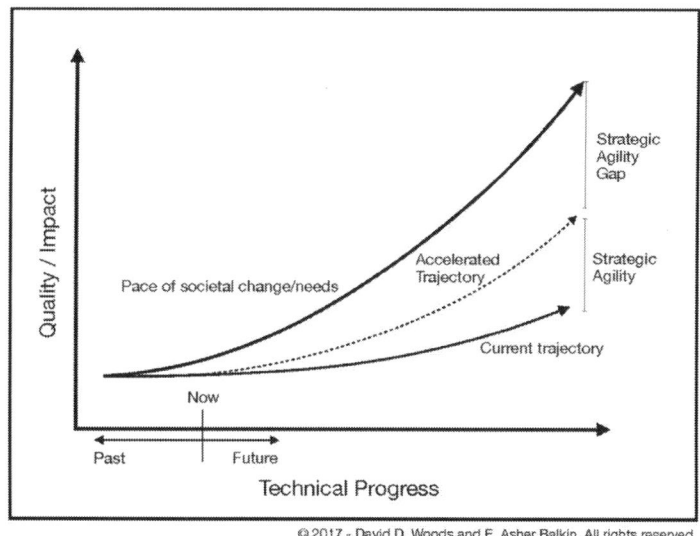

Figure 1. The Strategic Agility Gap. Reproduced from Woods (2020)

Resilience is a verb in the future tense

Starting as early as 2000, the idea emerged that complex systems, as distributed, layered networks with extensive tangles of interdependencies, are fundamentally brittle. But adaptive systems possess capabilities for resilience, as a basic adaptive capacity, to offset the complexity penalties that arise as growth and change go on (Hollnagel et al., 2006; Alderson and Doyle, 2010; Woods, 2019).

The basic signature of complexity penalties is the surprising sudden collapse of function against backdrop of continuous improvement and injection of new capabilities. Carlson and Doyle captured the basic finding as (2000, p. 2529): systems/layered networks "which are robust to perturbations they were *designed to handle*, yet fragile to *unexpected perturbations* and *design flaws*." The core result is that the pursuit of new capabilities under pressure to achieve new levels of productivity, efficiencies, and financial returns inevitably increases the risk of brittle collapse. Worse yet, each case of brittle collapse tends to be cryptic, in the sense that ambiguities about the multiple contributors that produced the breakdown make learning difficult, given the system has a record of past success and improvement. The difficulties are magnified because learning requires revision of past models based on a new understanding of the emergent properties that cut across critical infrastructures and all of the interacting systems, roles, and organizations.

Fortunately, the initial work on resilience also began to derive lessons from biological, human, and human-technology systems that have adapted to flourish in the face of the risk of brittle collapse. The lessons emphasized how these successful systems were *poised to adapt* to keep pace with change. The new work shifts the focus from why a failure occurred. Instead, adaptive capacity was revealed by looking at the challenges that occurred (much more often than stakeholders realized), but were managed by resilient performances (e.g., how does emergency medicine adapt to handle beyond-surge-capacity events successfully despite the threat of overload and bottlenecks).

The critical definition turned out to be "what is adaptive capacity?":

> Definition: *Adaptive capacity* is a system's readiness or potential to change how a system currently works—its models, plans, processes, behaviors, relationships—to continue to fit changing situations, anomalies, and surprises.

All adaptive systems, at all scales, possess the capacity to stretch or extend performance when events challenge their normal competence for handling situations. Without this capability for extensibility, brittle collapse would occur much more often than it is observed (Woods, 2018; Sharkey et al., 2020).

Three of the critical capabilities that support adaptive capacity as extensibility are:
- the ability to *revise* previous models and methods to recognize emerging new vulnerabilities as interconnections change;
- the ability to *synchronize* activities over multiple roles and layers of a network to scale responses to the scope of challenges; and
- the ability to *anticipate* challenges ahead to recognize of emerging new challenges, vulnerabilities and threats before capabilities are overloaded or oversubscribed.

Note these capabilities are *verbs*—actions that contribute to resilient performances—and not nouns or states. Even more surprising, adaptive capacity is future oriented. Adaptive capacity consists of readiness to respond and readiness to revise in advance of events that challenge the system's design. These properties are quite evident in studies of resilient performance in emergency medicine when challenged by beyond-surge-capacity events (Chuang et al., 2021).

Hence, the phrase "resilience is a verb in the future tense" provides a compact distillation of the findings. Thinking about the critical infrastructure challenge in terms of these new science results leads to new modeling approaches that complement the current strategy (e.g., Sharkey et al., 2020). Thinking of the capacity for resilient performance in this way represents a shift in how we can meet the goal of resilient critical infrastructures in a complex, changing, limited resource world.

Surprising failures and service outages continue to be regular occurrences

The continuing stream of shock events should remind stakeholders that they do not possess the adaptive capacity to match the trajectory of change and challenge as shown in Figure 1. As a result, the goal of resilient infrastructure remains an aspiration for the future.

New advances on the fundamental science of adaptation and complexity in distributed, tangled layered networks in the last few years have revealed basic patterns, findings, and laws that transcend particular triggering events, lines of interdependencies, and physical parts of infrastructure systems that are involved in any particular failure.

These general patterns are evident in multiple shock events that occurred in 2021. The shock events reveal general constraints that apply to future events as well. We refer to these events as shocks not because of the consequence, but rather because the events reveal gaps and holes in our models of how these systems work, the threats they face and the necessary countermeasures.

In challenge events

a. there is an expanding, but previously hidden, tangle of interdependencies that cross infrastructures and impact valued services;

b. the triggering event produces *effects at a distance* as impacts spread over the tangled lines of dependencies;

c. the effects increase tempos of activity over a wide set of roles across diverse organizations, challenging all to up their pace of activity and coordinate these activities in synchrony with other roles and levels;

d. the scale of effects expands across more organizational and jurisdictional boundaries with regional, societal wide, and even global reverberations;

e. the growing disruptions that flow from the triggering event put greater pressures on each stakeholder and increase the challenges each faces for their own scope of responsibility and for how their activity within their scope supports or hinders other related stakeholder activities; and

f. forces for fragmentation come to the fore and undermine the ability to synchronize actions over layers and roles to scale responses to match spreading disruptions and challenges.

These and many other kinds of emergent system patterns arise regardless of the whether the trigger/driver of the shock comes from extreme weather events (and longer-term climate volatility), the fragilities that accompany growth of capabilities, or new paths for adversarial conflict.

For example, extreme weather triggered the Texas energy crisis in February 2021 with at a minimum 151 deaths (with some estimates running several hundred higher) and at least $200 billion in financial loses. A previous widespread cold snap in 2010 foreshadowed the 2021 crisis, but lessons from the precursor energy system breakdown were weak and led to little or ineffectual remedies (large scale and duration cold snaps did not produce system wide energy system failures prior to 2010). Changes to economic incentive structures in pursuit of efficiencies based on models of deregulation and decentralized markets made the energy system remarkably brittle as spreading disruptions undermined the ability of other resources to come to bear to mitigate the consequences. The economic losses spread beyond Texas to affect ratepayers in distant states. Changes in the energy mix since the last extreme cold weather event had strong implications for how the system would respond to the next event, but modeling did not provide timely reassessments to recognize the potential for new risks and associated costs.

The framework of modeling did not include the general phenomenon of brittle collapse and any notions of resilience were primitive, disconnected from the growing base of general findings about complexity and adaptation. Instead, the distributed, layered network of human and organizational roles struggled to react to the spreading disruptions in local and fragmented ways compounding the consequences. As after the previous cold snap induced energy crisis in 2010, stakeholders continue to struggle to learn and implement systemic changes to build robustness and resilience.

Digital infrastructure—that underpins many valued services including all other lifeline infrastructures—represent another important example. Consider just three of the outages of valued digital services that occurred in 2021: the Fastly outage on June 8, 2021; a Facebook outage on October 4, 2021; and the AWS (Amazon) cloud services outage on December 7, 2021. These events demonstrate how the growth of capabilities produces hidden interdependencies, expands the scale of disruptions, and increases the difficulties of diagnosis and mitigation. In the AWS outage, computer engineers were hampered by a common problem, namely the tools used to diagnosis problems in the software infrastructure also are software-based and were degraded by the very outage the engineers needed to diagnose via these tools (Woods and Allspaw, 2019). The engineers in this case, and in ones that exhibit the same general pattern, had to develop ways to adapt around the bottleneck while disruptions spread and potential for consequences grew.

These digital infrastructure outages reveal important lessons. In all three of these outages, interdependencies occurred over multiple levels of software services across multiple organizational boundaries. Currently, these interactions are very difficult to recognize until loss of service is threatened. For example, Fastly is one major supplier of a specialized software service (CDN or Content Delivery Network) that operates invisibly in the background to improve responsiveness and load management. This service is valuable to nearly all internet-facing companies. One surprise was how a small unremarkable change by one of their customers revealed a dependency that disrupted their geographically distributed fleet of servers. Rebooting the fleet to restore the functionality meant customers' servers would try to repopulate their data *all at the same time* to regain the valued functionality.

In software engineering this is a "cache stampede" problem which degraded widespread services across multiple organizations. The problem in this case/infrastructure is an instance of a more general pattern in complex systems where common resources become oversubscribed when multiple parties begin to respond to disruptions in ways that overload some resources. Note another general pattern in this event: the story of the outage involved a surprisingly large number of organizations (a) in the genesis of the disruption, (b) those engaged in responding to spreading disruptions, and (c) those who had to cope with widespread secondary service disruptions. Also, note that two of these events began with leading service providers who operate with significant technical, financial, and expert human resources. These events are reminders—no organization is immune from complexity penalties.

One reaction to these incidents is: "but these are not the kind of 'critical' services we refer to when addressing 'critical infrastructures.'" However, the patterns are the same, such as "effects at a distance" which make diagnosis more difficult. In addition, losing valued services is critical to those who depend on them. For example, the Facebook outage affected WhatsApp, but in some parts of the world many critical human and business activities have adapted to take advantage of WhatsApp capabilities and to work around various local constraints. As a result, an outage that undermines this service disrupts a wide range of societal activities in these regions for a time. This pattern is observed often: new capabilities start as non-essential improvements, but as they provide value, the capabilities migrate to undergird primary activities until they become essential to those activities. Inevitably, as new capabilities provide services valuable to human roles, people adapt to take advantage of that value so that outages become crises or even safety threats.

In addition, all of the patterns evident in the three software outages above appear in recent adversarial threats such as Colonial Pipeline (May 7, 2021), emergence of new tactics in ransomware, Solar Winds (2020), and the Log4j Shell server vulnerability (late 2021). There are interesting overlaps of the Log4j Shell server vulnerability story with non-adversarial software incidents (Allspaw and Cook, 2018).

The trajectory of ransomware threats over time illustrates how our capabilities also need to adapt over time to match the pace of change. The emergence of cryptocurrencies triggered significant growth of ransomware threats which have continued to evolve tactics, frequency, and scale of impact. The continuing story of ransomware is but one illustration of the need to recognize and redress the strategic agility gap.

Finally, a combination of the three classes of triggering events is eminently possible. Adversarial intrusions can hijack or disable services needed when extreme weather events increase criticality and degrade services themselves. Again, the patterns are generic and not simply about the details of any particular trigger event, targeting any particular set of infrastructure systems.

The point of reviewing a sample of visible recent outages isn't about the outages that resulted. From a resilience perspective, the information needed to build and sustain adaptive capacity does not lie in *why* a particular outage happened, but rather, in how other challenges have been occurring yet are dealt with successfully before visible outages resulted (Woods and Allspaw, 2019). Ironically, resilience as a verb in the future tense is most visible in the incidents that do not progress to tangible failures with losses for stakeholders (Hollnagel et al., 2006).

Are We Doomed to be Stuck in the Gap?

The recurrence of increasingly disruptive events in these systems, despite recent investments to avoid or mitigate them, provides evidence of technical and practical limits to the current strategy for building resilient infrastructure.

The most obvious problem is one of scale. The current strategy of building and deploying tools to model specific systems in specific jurisdictions is never going to address the entire problem. There are too many systems and too many interdependencies that continue to evolve. *We are never going to have a complete view of critical infrastructure such that we can close all the holes; such a vantage point does not exist.* Moreover, the current piecemeal approach prevents sharing details and/or insights about our infrastructure systems (often for valid security reasons) that are slowing our collective learning (Alderson, 2019).

Modeling individual critical infrastructures remains necessary and important because it forces a closer look at how systems actually work, which is often misunderstood. Operational models of specific infrastructures are incredibly helpful as decision support tools (Alderson et al. 2015). Many modern critical infrastructure systems, such as the electric grid, are so complicated that it is near impossible to operate them without the support of modeling and simulation tools. But it is important to recognize "the model" of any particular infrastructure system is never complete because the system is not static. Rather, the system continues to evolve as new opportunities are explored and new vulnerabilities exploited.

Confident that the complex world will continue to throw novel challenges at us, we need to expand our current perspective and processes if we are really going to build resilient infrastructure.

Pivoting to Increase Strategic Agility

New fundamental findings provide opportunities to pivot from the current approach, enhance our tempo of progress, and reduce the strategic agility gap. These new insights have revealed general patterns and laws about complexity and adaptation (e.g., Chiang et al., 2007; Woods, 2018; Nakahira et al., 2021). These lawful patterns play out in particular settings as new capabilities are deployed, as processes of adaptation transform these improvements in unexpected ways, and as competitors/adversaries hijack new capabilities to pursue their own ends. In this paper we have illustrated just a small portion of these patterns using recent infrastructure outages arising from external events (extreme weather), fragilities that accompany growth (complexity penalties) and adversarial intrusions to degrade valued services.

One of the fundamentals about adaptive capacity is the ability to revise—building our models and tools in ways that make updating, revising, reframing and reconceptualizing straightforward. This requires an ability to recognize the significance of early, often "weak" signals that change is afoot in ways that might matter. Rather than discount such signals, resilient performance depends on seeing discrepancies as unexpected anomalies that trigger re-examination of previous beliefs. For example, the most common statement in after-action reviews of incidents that threaten loss of service in critical digital infrastructure is "I didn't know it worked that way" (e.g., Woods, 2017).

When organizations adopt processes to discover hidden interdependencies—rather than assume all are well-mapped and well-guarded—learning, updating, and revising models of how a system works is facilitated. The organization introduces probes, generally in non-risky periods or situations, in order to challenge and update its understanding of the challenges it faces and the processes it uses to handle challenges. This approach has become widespread in critical digital services as part of continuous development and deployment processes (Rosenthal and Jones, 2020).

In one common technique (which software reliability engineers call chaos engineering), system operators conduct frequent experiments by injecting small disruptions into their system as a means to uncover/discover how it actually responds to various disruptions. As complexity increases, this technique quicky shows how the system is more vulnerable than previously understood. The insights guide interventions that increase system robustness to the specific previously 'hidden' vulnerabilities. The probes also provide insights about what factors contribute to resilient performances in many different kinds of anomalous situations could occur that were not part of the test event (Allspaw and Cook, 2018; Woods and Allspaw, 2019). Techniques like this enhance the ability of the entire cyber-physical-human system to adapt to novel challenges—a boost in adaptive capacity and resilient performance.

Underlying these efforts is a recognition that the abstract capabilities of the organization are more important than the physical assets (Finkel, 2011). In addition, emergency response plans, no matter the efforts at pre-planning, cannot be sufficiently robust in themselves when events call them into action (this has turned out to be a fundamental constraint; e.g., Alderson and Doyle, 2010; Woods, 2018; Rosenthal & Jones, 2020). Thus, it is important to study the way organizations can mobilize and generate additional adaptive capacity when non-routine events threaten to overload (saturate) initially deployable responses as breakdowns spiral into accidents or disasters (Mendonça at al., 2007; Chuang et al., 2021). Recent studies investigating the resilience of organizations in response to 2011 Superstorm Sandy (Zhang and Mendonça, 2021) and the 2015 refugee influx to Sweden (Degerman, 2021) are promising steps in the right direction. Moreover, there is a need to continue investment in training and exercises for developing adaptive capacity at upper echelons of organizations and how these layers synchronize with other organizational layers (e.g., Bergström et al., 2011; Alderson et al., 2022).

Conclusion

In this paper we pose a simple question: despite investments and progress in the development of critical infrastructure systems, *are societies, especially our own, falling behind the pace of events and changing threats?* The current strategy to develop resilient infrastructure, while a necessary part of the portfolio for progress, has been running into scientific, technical, and practical limits leaving progress stalled in the strategic agility gap. Increasing the tempo of progress requires a strategic course adjustment synchronizing efforts across stakeholders, disciplines, and agencies in new ways. Ironically, the guide for a shift in course—as researchers, managers, operators, funders—is to apply the results on adaptive capacity and resilient performance to ourselves to keep pace with changes, growth, interdependencies.

The advances in the underlying science create a timely opportunity now. The next step is for all the stakeholders to come together to pivot from how they cooperate today. This is an invitation to the operational, research, and management communities to chart an expanded course of action and take advantage of the new advances to build strategic agility.

Acknowledgments

David Woods was supported by funding from the SNAFU Catchers Consortium. David Alderson was supported by the Office of Secretary of Defense Strategic Environmental Research and Development Program (SERDP) Project #RC21-1233.

Author Capsule Bios

David Woods, Professor Emeritus in Department of Integrated Systems Engineering at the Ohio State University and Principal at Adaptive Capacity Labs (PhD, Purdue University) has worked to improve systems safety in high-risk complex settings for 40+ years. He began developing Resilience Engineering on the dangers of brittle systems and the need to invest in sustaining sources of resilience beginning in 2000–2003 as part of the response to several NASA accidents (see the 2006 book Resilience Engineering and many subsequent works available at ResearchGate). He developed the first comprehensive theory on how systems can build the potential for resilient performance despite complexity. The results of this work on how complex human-machine systems succeed and sometimes fail has been cited over 39K times (H-index > 92).

He is Past-President of the Resilience Engineering Association. He has received many awards; for example, the Laurels Award from Aviation Week and Space Technology (1995). He has carried out accident investigations in aviation, nuclear power, critical care medicine, crisis response, military operations, and space operations (advisor to the Columbia Accident Investigation Board). He is frequently asked for advice by many government agencies, and companies, both domestically and abroad (e.g., DoD, NASA, FAA; ir France, TNO, IBM; UK MOD, NHS, Haute Authorité de Santé).

David Alderson is a Professor in the Operations Research Department and serves as Founding Director for the Center for Infrastructure Defense at the Naval Postgraduate School in Monterey, CA. His research focuses on the function and operation of critical infrastructures, with particular emphasis on how to invest limited resources to ensure efficient and resilient performance in the face of accidents, failures, natural disasters, or deliberate attacks. His research explores tradeoffs between efficiency, complexity, and fragility in a wide variety of public and private cyber-physical systems. Dr. Alderson has been the Principal Investigator of sponsored research projects for the Navy, Army, Air Force, Marine Corps, and Coast Guard.

He received his doctorate from Stanford University and his undergraduate degree from Princeton University. He has held research positions at the California Institute of Technology (Caltech), the University of California Los Angeles, the Xerox Palo Alto Research Center (PARC), and the Santa Fe Institute. He has extensive industry experience and has worked for several venture-back startup companies. His early career was spent developing technology at Goldman Sachs & Co. in New York City.

References

Alderson, D.L., (2019). Overcoming Barriers to Greater Scientific Understanding of Critical Infrastructure Resilience. In M. Ruth and S. G. Reisemann (Eds)., *Handbook on Resilience of Socio-Technical Systems*. Edward Elgar Publishing, pp. 66-88.

Alderson, D.L., Brown, G., and Carlyle, W.M. (2015). "Operational Models of Infrastructure Resilience," *Risk Analysis* 35(4): 562-586.

Alderson, D.L., Darken, D.P., Eisenberg, D.A., and Seager, T.P. (2022). Surprise is inevitable: How do we train and prepare to make our critical infrastructure more resilient? *International Journal of Disaster Risk Reduction*, forthcoming.

Alderson, D.L., and Doyle, J.C. (2010). Contrasting Views of Complexity and Their Implications for Network-Centric Infrastructures. *IEEE Transactions on Systems, Man, and Cybernetics-Part A*, 40(4): 839-852.

Allspaw, J., Cook, R. I. (2018). SRE cognitive work. In *Seeking SRE: Conversations About Running Production Systems at Scale*, ed. D. Blank-Edelman, 441-465. O'Reilly Media.

Bergström, J., Dahlström, N., Dekker, S., Petersen, K., (2011). Training organisational resilience in escalating situations, in: E. Hollnagel, Paries, J., Woods, D.D., and Wreathall, J., Eds., *Resilience engineering in practice*. Ashgate, pp. 45–57.

Carlson, J. M., & Doyle, J. (2000). Highly optimized tolerance: Robustness and design in complex systems. *Physical Review Letters*, 84(11), 2529.

Chiang, M., Low, S. H., Calderbank, A. R., & Doyle, J. C. (2007). Layering as optimization decomposition: A mathematical theory of network architectures. *Proceedings of the IEEE, 95*(1), 255-312.

Chuang, S.-W., Woods, D. D., Reynolds, M., Ting, H-W., Balkin, E. A. and Hsu, C-H. (2021). Rethinking preparedness planning in disaster emergency care: Lessons from a beyond-surge-capacity event. *World Journal of Emergency Surgery.* https://doi.org/10.1186/s13017-021-00403-x

Degerman, H. (2021). Barriers towards Resilient Performance among Public Critical Infrastructure Organizations: The Refugee Influx Case of 2015 in Sweden. *Infrastructures, 6*(8), 106.

Finkel, M. (2011). On flexibility: recovery from technological and doctrinal surprise on the battlefield. Stanford University Press.

Flynn, S.E. (2007). *The Edge of Disaster: Rebuilding a Resilient Nation.*

Hollnagel, E., Woods, D. D., & Leveson, N. (Eds.). (2006). *Resilience engineering: Concepts and precepts.* Ashgate Publishing, Ltd.

Krieg, R.M. (2020). Editor's Letter, *Journal of Critical Infrastructure Policy,* 1, 1 Spring/Summer 2020.

Mendonça, D., Jefferson, T., and Harrald, J. (2007). Collaborative adhocracies and mix-and-match technologies in emergency management. *Communications of the ACM, 50*(3), 44-49.

Nakahira, Y., Liu, Q., Sejnowski, T. J., & Doyle, J. C. (2021). Diversity-enabled sweet spots in layered architectures and speed–accuracy trade-offs in sensorimotor control. *Proceedings of the National Academy of Sciences, 118*(22):e1916367118. doi: 10.1073/pnas.1916367118.

Rosenthal, C., & Jones, N. (2020). Chaos engineering: System resiliency in practice. O'Reilly Media.

Sharkey T.C., Nurre Pinkley S.G., Eisenberg D.A., Alderson D.L. (2020). In search of network resilience: An optimization-based view, *Networks,* 1-30. https://doi.org/10.1002/net.21996

Woods, D. D. & Branlat, M. (2011). How Adaptive Systems Fail. In Hollnagel, E., Paries, J., Woods, D.D., & Wreathall, J. (Eds.), Resilience Engineering in Prac3ce (pp. 127-143). Aldershot, UK: Ashgate.

Woods, D. D., ed, (2017). SNAFUcatchers Workshop on Coping with Complexity. *Brooklyn NY, March 14-16, 2017 Download from stella.report*

Woods, D. D. (2018). The Theory of Graceful Extensibility: Basic rules that govern adaptive systems. *Environment Systems and Decisions, 38*(4), 433-457.

Woods, D.D. (2019). Essentials of Resilience, Revisited. In M. Ruth and S. G. Reisemann (Eds)., *Handbook on Resilience of Socio-Technical Systems*. Edward Elgar Publishing, pp. 52-65.

Woods, D.D. (2020). The Strategic Agility Gap: How Organizations are Slow and Stale to Adapt in a Turbulent World. In Journé, B., Laroche, H., Bieder, C. and Gilbert, C. (Eds.), *Human and Organizational Factors: Practices and Strategies for a Changing World*. Springer Open & the Foundation for Industrial Safety Culture, Springer Briefs in Safety Management, Toulouse France, pp. 95-104 https://doi.org/10.1007/978-3-030-25639-5

Woods, D. D. and Allspaw, J., Eds., (2019). Revealing the Critical Role of Human Performance in Software. Special Issue, *ACM Queue*, 17(6), November-December, 2019.

Zhang, X. and Mendonça, D., (2021), Co-evolution of work structure and process in organizations: improvisation in post-disaster debris removal operations. *Cognition, Technology & Work* 23: 343–352.

Energy Supply Chains and Change

Diane J. Graziano,[1] Elisa Alonso,[2] Fletcher Fields,[3] Diana Bauer[4]

[1] Corresponding author: Argonne National Laboratory, graziano@anl.org
[2] Oak Ridge National Laboratory
[3] Formerly, U.S. Department of Energy
[4] U.S. Department of Energy

Abstract

The energy sector's critical importance to the economy and national security on the one hand and its association with potential environmental impacts on the other subject it to competing and sometimes oscillating forces in policymaking and corporate decision-making that can affect both supply and demand. As such, energy supply chains need to be resilient in order to meet the economy's dynamic demand for energy services, adapt to policy actions, respond effectively to natural and manmade disasters, foster transitions to emergent technologies, and serve long-lived infrastructure. This paper presents a framework that guides systematic analysis of energy supply chains subject to ongoing change. While the framework is qualitative, it is strengthened by quantitative data. A case study of the utility-scale gas turbine supply chain illustrates the framework.

Keywords: critical infrastructure, energy, energy policy, supply chain, gas turbine

Introduction

Energy resource and technology supply chains (herein called "energy supply chains"[1]) directly comprise a small fraction of a nation's gross domestic product. However, they are foundational for the broader economy, societal welfare, security, and the environment. These supply chains produce energy technologies that power farm equipment for modern-day agriculture; factories producing food and goods; utilities providing drinking water, lighting, and temperature control essential to shelter and health; mobility for safety and commerce; and information tech-

---

1 Abbreviations used in this article: CT = combustion turbine; CCGT = combined-cycle gas turbine; DHS = US Department of Homeland Security; EIA = Energy Information Administration; GE = General Electric; MHI = Mitsubishi Heavy Industries; MHPS = Mitsubishi Hitachi Power Systems; NG = natural gas; OEM = original equipment manufacturer; PPIFUA = Power Plant and Industrial Fuel Use Act; R&D = research and development.

nologies fostering communication and economic growth. As such, energy supply chains are critically important to the economies and national security postures of both developed and developing countries. Not only is energy infrastructure considered a "critical infrastructure sector," it also underlies a number of other critical infrastructure sectors, ranging from water and wastewater to transportation to communications to critical manufacturing (DHS n.d.).

The energy sector's importance to the economy and national security on the one hand and its association with potential environmental impacts on the other subject it to competing and sometimes oscillating forces in policymaking and corporate decision-making that can affect both its supply and demand (Nyman 2018, 118-145; Wirth, Gray, and Podesta 2003, 132-155). Because of their importance, energy supply chains need to be resilient in order to meet an economy's dynamic demand for energy services, adapt to policy actions, respond effectively to natural and manmade disasters, foster transitions to emergent technologies, and serve long-lived infrastructure (Araújo 2014, 112-121). The large number of forces and responses at different spatial scales over different time horizons can be difficult to untangle. Nevertheless, obtaining a deep understanding of the dynamic forces and responses is valuable because energy supply chains are so important across society and are sensitive to the broader context.

While there are many studies that address supply chains, studies focused on supply chain dynamics that comprehensively consider the conflicting forces and complexity affecting energy technology markets are sparse. Published studies of energy supply chains commonly focus on the production, processing, and delivery of fuels, such as NG, petroleum, and biofuels. Many of these studies address the important issues of energy security and resilience (Månsson, Johansson, and Nilsson 2014, 1-14; Urciuoli et al. 2014, 46-63; Winzer 2012, 26-48; Yergin 2006, 69-82). Energy supply chains, however, also include those that produce, deliver, and maintain technologies that generate and transmit electricity (e.g., nuclear reactors, wind turbines) and use energy (e.g., industrial motors, lighting, and vehicle power-trains). The concepts of industrial dynamics (Bonaccorsi and Giuri 2000, 847-870, 2001, 1053-1083; Jacobsson and Bergek 2004, 815-849; Klepper 1997, 147-182), innovation (Gravier and Swartz 2009, 87-102; Lee and Lee 2013, 415-432; Malerba 2007, 675-699), and sociotechnical transitions (Geels 2010, 495-510; Markard, Raven, and Truffer 2012, 955-067; Smith and Stirling 2010) are important for studying change in these supply chains. In fact, developing a rich understanding of the effect of change on energy supply chains requires consideration of all of these concepts.

We present a framework that guides systematic conceptual analysis of energy supply chains subject to ongoing change. While the framework is qualitative, it is strengthened by quantitative data. The framework guides the analyst in identifying and assessing change experienced by the supply chain.

Methods—Framework

In the framework, shown in Figure 1, change vectors—including industrial dynamics, policy, innovation, and resources—lead to changes in market conditions in which the energy supply chain operates. These changes include demand growth and shrinkage, technology shift, resource undersupply, and supply disruption. In turn, these market condition changes lead the supply chain to respond—in various ways and across time frames—to meet demand for its energy products. The supply chain's characteristics are likewise dynamic and affected by change vectors, changing market conditions, and how the supply chain responds to change.

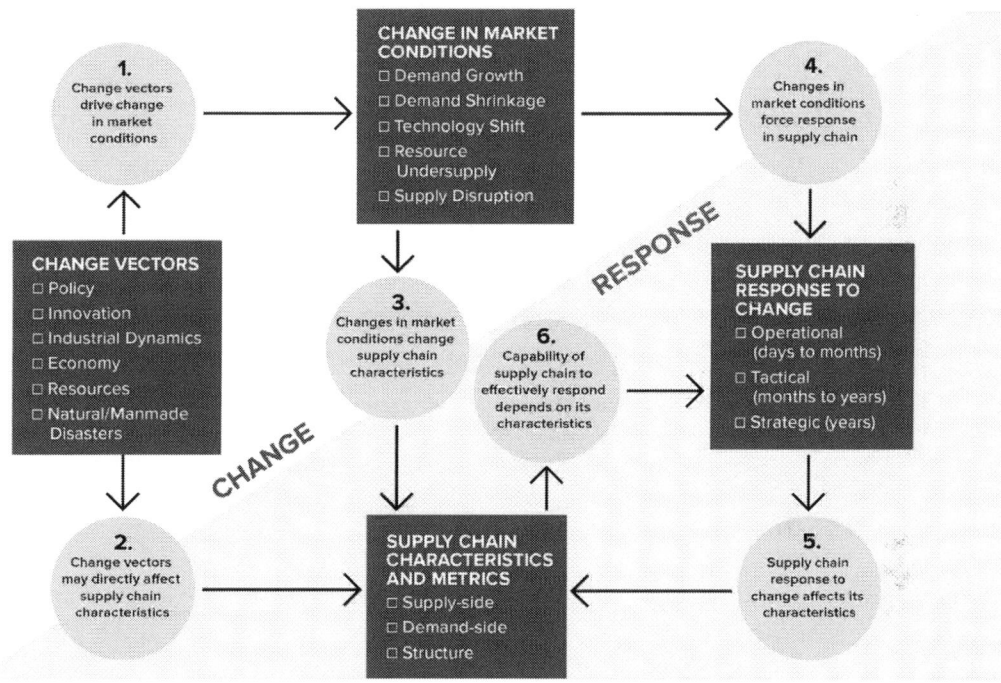

Figure 1. Framework for envisioning change in energy supply chains

The framework also describes how supply chains respond to change. Understanding how the network of companies that manufacture energy technologies can deploy their resources to respond to changes and meet demand is important. Focusing attention on the supply chains, however, can be constrained by a lack of visibility of their capacity to meet demand under changing conditions. The framework presented here is a structured conceptual approach that takes advantage of available data to assess plausible supply chain responses to forces of change, where:

1. Supply chains need to respond to change in different time frames: operational, tactical, and strategic.

2. Their capacity to respond, in turn, is dependent on their intrinsic supply-side, demand-side, and structure characteristics and associated metrics (Wagner and Neshat 2010).

The operational, tactical, and strategic time frames are related to the length of time in which an effective supply chain response can be implemented and the complexity of the required response. Regarding the latter, the strategic time frame is distinguished from the tactical time frame by the complexity and innovation required of the response. For example, adjusting inventories can be achieved in an operational time frame (days to months) to resolve a temporary shortfall in supply. If the supply shortfall extends to months or years, tactical or strategic responses are necessary: tactical if adding supply capacity is feasible, strategic if novel changes in the product design and its manufacture are required.

The "characteristics" considered in the framework describe different aspects of the supply chain, including those that pertain to the production chain (supply-side), the product technology and end-use market (demand-side), and the types and organization of firms (structure). "Metrics" are observable, measurable, and useful for quantitatively or comparatively assessing their associated characteristics. The intrinsic capability of a supply chain to respond (its robustness and resilience) can be described by these characteristics and associated metrics.

In the following section, we illustrate how the framework can inform thinking of supply chain dynamics using a case study of the gas turbine global supply chain. The next section reviews change vectors and market condition changes historically experienced by the supply chain—the "change" elements of the framework. The last section applies the framework to explore the "response" elements of the framework, namely, the supply chain's responses and capacity to respond to ongoing market changes. While the discussion presented here examines historical phenomena, the framework can be applied to explore current scenarios and future change.

Results—Case Study

Gas turbines are marketed in different sizes ranging from 50–600 MW capacity, where smaller units are deployed in mechanical drive and industrial applications and larger ones are deployed in utility-scale electricity generation (Frost and Sullivan 2014). We focus the case study analysis on the latter, including the production and sales of gas turbines for CT and CCGT power plants. In 2017, approximately 23 percent of world electricity use was generated by natural gas (International Energy Agency [IEA] 2018). This market is particularly important for climate goals, supporting the switch from coal to gas, and providing flexibility for the integration of renewables (IEA 2019).

Figure 2 shows the major components of large gas turbines. The global gas turbine supply chain includes four main production stages. It begins with (1) raw materials suppliers, followed by (2) the refining and processing of materials, (3) fabrication and subcomponent supply, and (4) final turbine assembly (Court 2008). Figure 3 shows these major production steps and the selected materials, additives, and parts manufactured in each step. Many different plants and companies source intermediate products with varying levels of market concentration. For example, the thermal barrier coatings contain yttrium, a rare-earth element of which more than 85 percent of mined supply over the past decade has originated from a single country: China (Van Gosen al. 2017). As one example of the complexity of the gas turbine supply chain, a Siemens turbine blade reportedly required as many as seven global supply chain steps, including both in-house and external production (Capgemini 2008). By another account, gas turbines contain more than 1,000 precision parts cast from a range of metal alloys (Moss et al. 2013). At the final assembly stage, only a few large OEMs remain, of which GE, Siemens, and MHI control the majority of the global market (Crooks 2018). Note that MHI's gas turbine business is currently operated through MHPS, which is a joint venture formed in 2014 between MHI and Hitachi, Ltd.

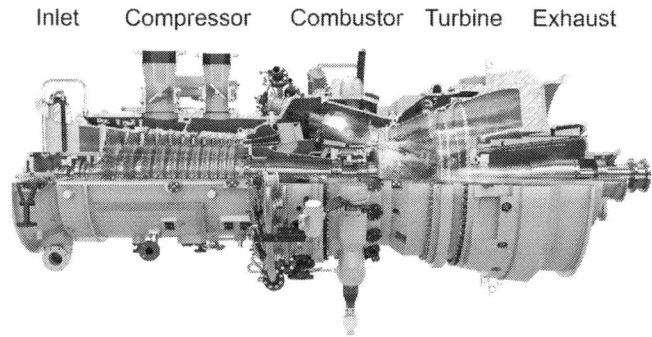

Figure 2. Diagram showing gas turbine components
(Source: Siemens 2017a, copyright Siemens AG, Munich/Berlin)

SELECT COMPONENTS	PROCESS STEPS				
	MINING AND CONCENTRATION →	REFINING, PROCESSING AND ALLOYING →	FABRICATION →	FINAL ASSEMBLY →	TURBINE DEMAND
COMPRESSOR AND COMBUSTER	Iron, chromium, titanium, molybdenum, aluminum, tin, zirconium	Creep-resistant martensitic steel, low alloy steels, titanium alloys	Rotor and stator blades, discs, casings, burners	Original Equipment Manufacturers (OEMs)	Electric power plants
TURBINE	Nickel, chromium, cobalt, aluminum, molybdenum, titanium, rhenium, tungsten, tantalum and hafnium, iron	Nickel-based superalloys, steels	Blades, discs, rotor shafts, bolted joints, casing		
COATINGS AND SEALS	Yttrium, zirconium, cerium, aluminum oxide	Yttrium-Stabilized Zirconia (standard Thermal Barrier Coating), Alumina and Ceria (additive)	Plasma spray, vapor deposition, honeycomb seals		

Figure 3. Major production and demand stages of the industrial gas turbine supply chain.

For our case study and with reference to the systems analysis framework shown in Figure 1, we define the gas turbine supply chain to encompass both turbine production and demand from owner/operators of electric power plants. To reflect this definition, turbine demand is included in the far right column of Figure 3. In the following sections and in the context of the gas turbine supply chain, we examine the change elements of the framework ("change vectors" and "change in market conditions") and response elements ("supply chain response to change" and "supply chain characteristics and metrics").

Systems Analysis Framework Illustration: Change

From the time that gas turbines first entered the electricity generation market in the 1950s, change vectors have affected the supply chain's market conditions. Figure 4 highlights examples of policy, innovation, resources, and industrial dynamics/economy change vectors that have created change in US market conditions over time. In the text that follows, we describe examples of US and global market changes (specifically, demand growth and shrinkage, technology shift, and resource undersupply) caused by various change vectors. Importantly, change vectors have led to market condition changes in both the production of and demand for utility-scale gas turbines. We consider both in our analysis. Further, we describe a few examples of how change vectors and market conditions have affected gas turbine supply chain characteristics (Figure 1 circles labeled 2 and 3, respectively).

Demand Growth and Shrinkage

As Figure 5 (EIA 2017) shows, US demand for gas-fueled power plants has experienced periods of both growth and shrinkage. US demand originally grew in response to the Great Northeast Blackout in 1965 and then fluctuated in response to policy and economic changes affecting natural gas prices and electricity demand (Unger and Herzog 1998). One such policy that led to demand shrinkage was the 1978 PPIFUA, which prohibited the burning of natural gas in new power plants. Rescission of this policy in 1987 fostered growth in US gas turbine demand in the 1990s. In the late 1990s, a confluence of factors led to a "dash for gas" in the United States, which by far led to the largest surge in gas turbine installations. Contributing factors to the surge included natural gas and electricity deregulations, improved gas turbine efficiency, and increasing cost competitiveness of natural gas compared to other power plant fuels.

Other nations experienced their own versions of a dash for gas with similar timing. Kern (2012) identifies several change vectors enabling rapid adoption of CCGTs in the United Kingdom in the 1990s, including the economy, favorable policy, innovation, and industrial dynamics. The economy driver was the availability of inexpensive gas to fuel new power plants. Influential policies included those that fostered electricity sector competition and environmental regulations that increased the costs of coal-fired electricity.

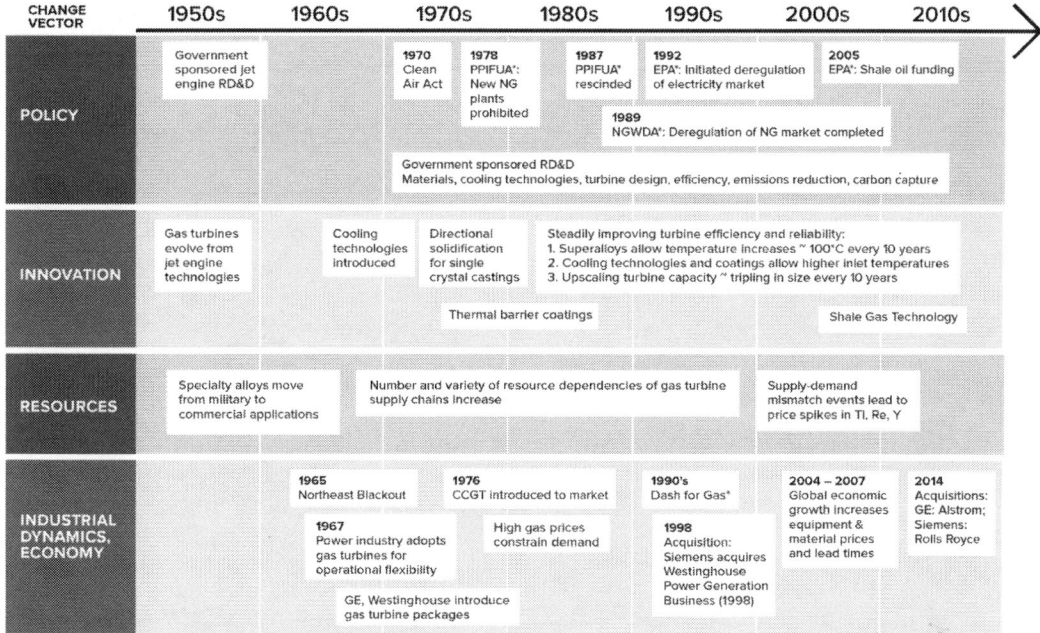

Figure 4. Change vectors affecting U.S. demand for utility-scale gas turbines since their introduction to the market. * Change fostering the U.S. "Dash for Gas" included electricity market restructuring (policy), technology improvements (innovation), and cost competitiveness of natural gas compared to other energy sources (economy). Abbreviations: EPA = Energy Policy Act; NGWDA = Natural Gas Wellhead Decontrol Act; PPIFUA = Power Plant and Industrial Fuel Use Act; RD&D = research, development, and demonstration.

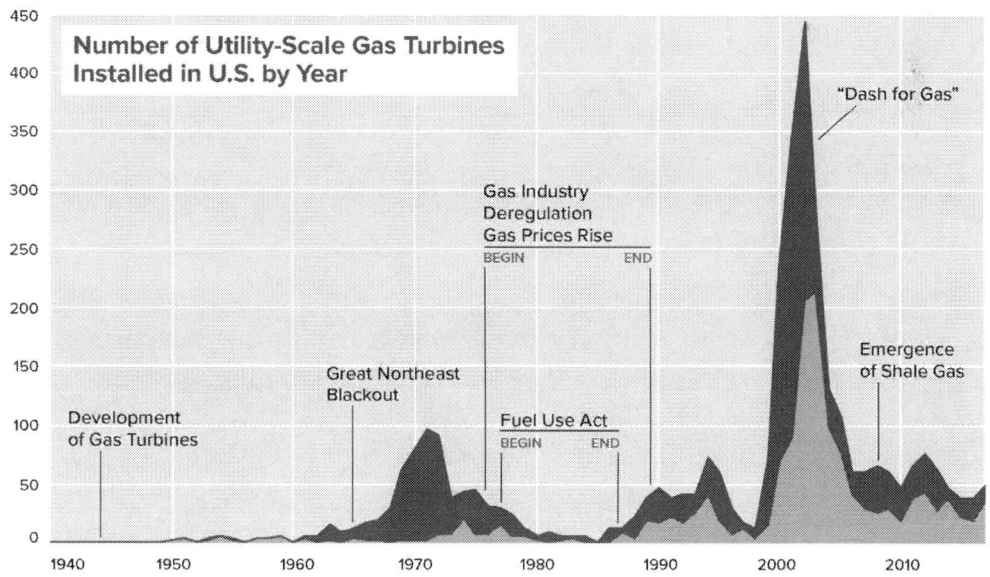

Figure 5. Number of utility-scale gas turbines installed in the United States by year of first operation (Source: EIA 2017). Key: blue = combustion turbine (CT), yellow = combine cycle gas turbine (CCGT).

After the dash for gas, US demand shrank dramatically in the mid-2000s as a result of market saturation. Escalating costs for materials (e.g., steel, concrete), heavy equipment manufacturing, and labor in the 2004–2007 period may also have deterred new construction (Pauschert 2009). After the precipitous decline, US demand steadied due to low-cost shale gas, enabled by the innovations of horizontal drilling and hydraulic fracturing, which vastly increased US gas reserves. In the mid-2010s, the gas turbine market faced headwinds from change vectors including climate change policies and innovation, which increase the cost competitiveness of renewable energy and energy storage technology. These change vectors are leading to demand shrinkage in both the domestic and global markets for utility-scale gas turbines, as the overall energy supply chain is facing fierce competition introduced by renewable energy sources, energy storage, and demand response.

Technology Shift

Technology shifts are often spawned by the innovation change vector. A first technology shift in the gas turbine supply chain occurred after World War II with a public-private partnership that translated jet engine technology to industrial gas turbines (Unger and Herzog 1998). Another major shift was the introduction of larger and more efficient gas turbines designed specifically for CCGT power plants in the 1990s (Chase 2001). Since the 1990s, decades of public R&D investment in jet engine technology and sustained R&D investment by equipment manufacturers have improved the cost competitiveness of gas relative to coal power plants (Kern 2012). Elements of this technology shift include advances in turbine blade coatings and methods for coating application, blade metallurgy, blade designs for enhanced cooling, and combustion systems (Willis 2002). One formative innovation was directionally solidified and single-crystal superalloys for blades and vanes, allowing higher operating temperatures and associated higher efficiencies (Seth 2000, 3-12).

Resource Undersupply

Innovation in specialized superalloys and thermal barrier coatings fostered the capacity of gas turbines to operate at increasingly higher firing temperatures and thereby achieve higher efficiencies (Sims 1984). These coatings and alloys, however, contain specialized materials, introducing the possibility of resource undersupply, beginning in the 2000s. These materials include titanium alloys used in the compressor, rhenium used in superalloys (John et al. 2017), and yttrium used in thermal barrier coatings (Van Gosen et al. 2017). These metals have experienced volatile price periods indicative of resource supply shortages—titanium in the early 2000s (Seong, Younossi, and Goldsmith 2009), rhenium in 2005–2009 (Desai 2007), and yttrium in 2010–2011 (Humphries 2012). Reviews of production, markets, and approaches to mitigating the undersupply of rhenium can be found in Kesieme, Chrysanthou, and Catulli (2019, 150-158) and for yttrium in Zhang, Kleit, and Nieto (2017, 899-015).

Change Vectors Directly Affecting Supply Chain Characteristics (Figure 1, Circle 2)

Kern (2012) identifies change vectors during the British "dash for gas" that directly affected supply chain characteristics. For example, the production capacity increased, unit cost decreased, and the supply chain structure changed when the four mature OEMs (GE, Westinghouse, Siemens, and ABB) pursued takeovers and new licensing deals with other manufacturers. The industrial dynamic vector in this case imparted change in the supply chain's supply-side (production capacity and costs) and structure (supply network) characteristics.

Market Conditions Directly Affecting Supply Chain Characteristics (Figure 1, Circle 3)

The gas turbine supply chain's technology shifts caused changes in supply chain characteristics; for example, increasing turbine performance efficacy with larger capacities and increased thermal efficiency from 5MW and less than 20 percent efficiency in the 1950s to greater than 570MW and nearly 65 percent efficiency in 2018. One consequence of these efficacy advances is the increased technological complexity of gas turbines; for example, intricate air-cooled turbine blade designs have been developed using high performance computing.

Whereas this section has focused on historical changes affecting the gas turbine supply chain, the next section shifts focus to supply chain responses to a recent change in the gas turbine market: namely, demand shrinkage.

Systems Analysis Framework Illustration: Response

We use the systems analysis framework to explore how the utility-scale gas turbine supply chain's supply-side (production chain), demand-side (product technology and end-use market), and structure (types and organization of firms) characteristics affect its capacity to respond to recent demand shrinkage in the operational (days-months), tactical (months-years), and strategic (years) time frames. As noted previously, the strategic responses are distinguished from tactical responses by their complexity and degree of innovation. Table 1 lists example supply chain characteristics and associated metrics that may affect a supply chain's responses in these three time frames.

For the analysis, we rely heavily on OEMs' annual reports (GE, Siemens, and MHI), corporate press releases, market reports, journal articles, and government reports, websites, and datasets. The majority of publicly available data applies to the final assembly and demand supply chain stages as shown in Figure 3. The

OEMs' outlooks for the large gas turbine market reported in their 2013 annual reports were relatively bullish. Starting in 2014, annual reports noted a downturn in demand and a shift in demand to smaller, more flexible power generation for decentralized energy supply and supplementary power for renewable energy. In the text that follows, information pulled directly from annual reports does not include a separate citation.

Table 1. Example supply chain characteristics and associated metrics that affect supply chain's responses to change.

Response Time Frame	Characteristics and Metrics		
	Supply-Side	*Demand-Side*	*Structure Side*
Operational	*Supply responsiveness* • Lead time • Capacity utilization • Manufacturing flexibility	*Inventory management performance* • Working inventory • Storage costs *Market attractiveness* • Profit margins	*Network architecture* • Sourcing flexibility
Tactical	*Barrier to entry* • Entry cost and time • Technology complexity *Efficiency of supply* • Unit production cost • Materials and energy efficiency	*Demand predictability* • Demand stability • Demand visibility	*Network architecture* • Supplier diversity • Vertical integration
Strategic	*Resource supply* • Resource basic availability	*Technology attractiveness* • Performance efficacy • Product customization *Market attractiveness* • R&D expenditures	*Market structure* • Market size

Operational Time Frame (Days to Months)

Operational responses focus on meeting existing demand and managing supply chain logistics. Supply and demand may be volatile, and supply chains must be able to dampen this volatility in such a way that they are still able to meet demand profitably. Operational responses to demand shrinkage may include decreasing capacity utilization, reducing inventories, adjusting profit margins, or deploying alternative suppliers. In the operational time frame, the effectiveness of a supply chain's response to change will depend on its readily available resources and capacities. As detailed in this section, the gas turbine OEMs responded to demand shrinkage by decreasing capacity utilization and reducing profit margins. These responses, in turn, affect these supply chain characteristics, challenging future operational responses. The capability of the OEMs to deploy alternative suppliers, however, was constrained.

Supply-Side Responses

Capacity utilization among the major OEMs has been on a decline since 2014. In 2017, Siemens reported expected future demand of 110 turbines per year, while its global manufacturing capacity could produce about 400 turbines annually (Heller 2017).

Long lead times limit operational responses to demand shrinkage. Pauschert (2009) finds that gas turbine lead times increased from about 12 months to 16–18 months when global economic growth and competition for manufacturing capacity escalated after 2004 and remained high until the global recession in 2008. Lead times for the commissioning of gas power plants are even longer and include allowing for engineering, procuring, constructing, and the actual commissioning. Overton (2015) reported such lead times of 28–30 months with aggressive scheduling. MHI Group provided contract announcement dates and delivery months for a few major projects in their annual reports; see Table 2. These data indicate that lead times for delivery of gas turbines exceed the operational time frame.

Table 2. Lead times between contract announcement and delivery for individual gas turbine plants as reported in MHI Annual Reports 2014, 2015, and 2016. (Lead time ranges are estimated from the month of the reported contract announcement and the delivery year.)

Contract Announcement	Delivery	Lead Time Range (derived)
January 2016	2020	48–59 months
October 2015	2018	27–39 months
January 2015	2018	36–47 months
May 2014	2016	19–31 months
March 2014	2016	21–33 months

Demand-Side Responses

Evidence exists that OEMs have been responding to shrinking demand and overcapacity by reducing prices, hence lowering profit margins. Since 2015, Siemens has reportedly reduced large turbine prices by 40 percent (Goodall 2018).

Structure Responses

In general, OEMs facing demand shrinkage may seek to reduce costs by switching suppliers. Structure metrics that indicate the capability for such operational responses include sourcing flexibility, import reliance, and geographic concentration. However, in the manufacture of gas turbines, engaging available alternative suppliers may not be feasible for highly specialized parts and components or for parts that require certification.

Tactical Time Frame (Months to Years)

Tactical responses rely on the supply chain's capacity to respond to emerging market conditions and signals without certainty of future markets. In the tactical time frame, the effectiveness of a supply chain's response to change will depend on its alignment with current trends and its capacity to improve its operational and marketing performance. OEMs' tactical responses to demand shrinkage may include reducing capacity, minimizing production costs, expanding revenue sources, and restructuring their supply chains. We find that while high barriers to entry limit tactical responses, the OEMs responded to recent demand shrinkage by decreasing production costs, improving manufacturing efficiency and cost-effectiveness, differentiating product offerings to retain or capture greater market share, and restructuring operations and supply chains.

Supply-Side Responses

Barrier to entry is a key supply-side characteristic that is relevant to the tactical time frame. While perhaps obvious for periods of growing demand, this characteristic has relevance to periods of shrinking demand as well. The barrier to entry of companies as OEMs to the utility-scale gas turbine market is significant due to high capital and operating costs, the complexity of gas turbine technologies, existing patents, and the regulatory framework. Given these barriers, decisions to temporarily or permanently curtail or shut down capacity carry significant financial and opportunity risks should demand rebound.

In 2014, GE reported a focus on reducing production costs, with a goal to reduce its H-Class gas turbine costs by 25 percent. Among its proposed responses were increasing automation, using new manufacturing tools, insourcing, and accelerating its suppliers' learning curves. MHI reported a goal to increase the profitability of ongoing projects by increasing power plant construction efficiency.

In tactical response to demand shrinkage, OEMs have been restructuring their businesses, shutting down capacity, and reducing staff to reduce unit production costs. GE took actions to reduce costs by $3.5 billion in 2017 and 2018, including a layoff of 12,000 employees, or 20 percent of its turbine business staff (GE 2017). In November 2017, Siemens announced the elimination of 6,900 jobs

(Larson 2018), although it reduced the cuts after reconciliation (Siemens 2017b). The company has reportedly floated the idea of selling its gas turbine business in the face of declining demand (Sachgau and Henning 2018).

Demand-Side Responses

OEMs manage their markets through contracts to make demand more predictable, services to expand business revenue areas, and expansion of their global marketing. Gas turbine demand predictability and visibility are relatively high since orders involve major cost input and contracts. In response to expected shrinkage in gas turbine demand, OEMs have increased revenue through a focus on maintenance and digitalization services to expand their markets. To improve profitability, MHI is pursuing funded opportunities to increase efficiency and reduce carbon emissions of existing power generation facilities, among other initiatives. MHI also notes opportunity space in demand from emerging countries.

Structure Responses

Over the past several years, OEMs have restructured their global supply chains and addressed market competition through a variety of acquisitions. In 2014, GE initiated acquisition of Alstom with expected benefits to include $5 billion in revenues from replacing external with internal suppliers, improved project management capability, and increased global market access. According to Frost & Sullivan (2014), Alstom held the fourth-largest share of gas turbine sales (by MW) in 2013, with 3.6 percent of the market. As a condition of their approval, European Union regulators required GE to sell some of Alstom's heavy-duty gas turbine assets to Ansaldo Energia. In 2016, GE acquired Metem Corporation, a turbine superalloy component manufacturer, with the objective of insourcing cooling hole drilling and other advanced manufacturing technologies.

Siemens has also actively acquired gas turbine capabilities, including the aero-derivative gas turbine business from Rolls-Royce Energy in 2014. One product that has emerged from this acquisition is a mobile, aero-derivative gas turbine designed for the fast power market, which is reportedly capable of reaching full power from a cold start in nine minutes (Siemens 2017c). With this acquisition, Siemens' intent is to become more competitive in the emerging market for flexible power production.

Strategic Time Frame (Years)

Strategic responses require foresight, planning, and resources that foster sustainability and innovation. In the strategic time frame, companies envision and pursue their future markets. Supply chains need the ability to respond to forecasted market changes by transforming production processes, technologies, resource use, and supply chain structure. Other strategies include diversifying product lines and customers. In the strategic time frame, we see evidence that OEMs have responded to demand shrinkage by investing in novel manufacturing technologies and adapting products to meet evolving customer needs.

Supply-Side Responses

Strategic responses focused on the supply side may include developing alternative resources for scarce materials or novel manufacturing technologies to sustain or improve products and business performance. Such responses are intended to retain market competitiveness in the long term. GE and Siemens have invested in the additive manufacturing of turbine components, capitalizing on the capacity for innovative designs and rapid prototyping. As reported by Prandi (2018), Siemens has been using additive manufacturing for more than ten different gas turbine parts, including a gas burner. In 2016, it acquired Materials Solutions, a leading additive manufacturing company. GE has improved fuel and air premixing with more efficient geometries enabled by additive manufacturing (Proctor 2018).

Demand-Side Responses

Strategic responses focused on demand include adapting energy technologies to changing customer expectations and investing in R&D to create new technologies and new markets. R&D expenditure is a key supply chain metric enabling strategic response. While OEMs do not report R&D investment by product line, Table 3 shows their reported R&D expenditures relative to revenues or net sales. For comparison, Table 3 includes data on 2015 global R&D expenditures as a percentage of global sales for US companies in select industries related to the gas turbine supply chain.

The gas turbine market demands high efficiency, reliability, and flexibility. In response, OEMs and governments have invested in R&D to achieve aggressive performance goals. For example, the US Department of Energy (DOE) sponsors R&D on advanced turbines with the expressed goal to "achieve greater than 65 percent combined cycle efficiency" and "support load following capabilities to meet the demand of a modern grid" (National Energy Technology Laboratory 2016). Over time, gas turbine efficiencies have steadily improved from increased firing temperatures enabled by specialty materials and coatings, advanced cooling technologies and blade designs, and other design improvements.

Larson (2018) reports OEMs' progress in reaching 65 percent combined cycle efficiency:

- MHPS: M501JAC gas turbine = 575 MW, 64% efficiency, 99.5% reliability
- GE: 9HA.02 gas turbine = 826 MW, exceeded 64% efficiency
- Siemens: HL-class turbine = 63% efficiency

Table 3. Gas turbine OEMs' R&D expenditures as a percentage of annual revenues (MHI = percent of net sales) and R&D expenditures for US companies by select industrial sectors reported as a percentage of global sales in 2015 (Source: NSF 2018).

Year	GE (%)	Siemens (%)	MHI (%)
2018		6.7	
2017	4.6	6.2	4.3
2016	4.4	5.9	4.1
2015	4.5	5.9	3.7
2014	4.5	5.7	3.4
2013	4.8	5.7	4.1

2015 R&D Expenditures for U.S. Companies by Sector	(% of Global Sales)
Engines, turbines, and power transmission equipment	3.5
Aircraft, aircraft engines, and aircraft parts	9.8
Semiconductors and other electronic components	12.5
Fabricated metal parts	1.3
Primary metals	0.7
Paints, coatings, adhesive, and other chemicals	3.54

Keywords: energy supply chain, change, resilience

GE's innovations include advances in cooling and sealing, emissions reductions via fuel staging, improved aerodynamics, and high-temperature materials and coatings (Vandervort, Leach, and Scholz 2016, 121-129). In the race to 65 percent efficiency, MHI is using supercomputers to design turbine blade castings and internal passageways for cooling them while in service (Browning 2017).

With the objective to increase their market size, all three major gas turbine OEMs invest in digital solutions to improve gas turbine design and performance and in the flexibility, control, and maintenance of operating gas power plants. The GE 2015 Annual Report, titled "Digital Industry," announced the formation of "GE Digital." The Siemens 2014 Annual Report introduced the Digital Factory Division (reorganized to the Smart Infrastructure and Digital Industries Division in 2018) and a new mission statement: "We make real what matters by setting the benchmark in the way we electrify, automate and digitalize the world around us." In 2017, MHPS began providing internet-of-things and artificial intelligence technologies for thermal power generation facilities.

Structure Responses

The OEMs' physical and digital innovations impart consequent changes to the structure characteristics of their supply chains. While we do not have visibility into their external supply chains, we note that the OEMs are acquiring hardware and software companies, thereby insourcing supply and strengthening their digital product offerings. Examples include Siemens's acquisition of Mendix in 2018 and GE's acquisition of ServiceMax in 2016.

Discussion

Understanding energy supply chains is essential because of how fundamental energy resources and technologies are to the US economy, national security, social welfare, and the environment. Nevertheless, untangling the forces and factors that affect and are affected by change can be difficult. To that end, the framework we have developed for envisioning change in energy supply chains provides a systems perspective and structure to guide conceptual analysis informed by quantitative data. The framework features broad change vectors, including policy, innovation, industrial dynamics, and resources. These change vectors drive change in market conditions, such as demand growth and shrinkage, technology shift, and resource undersupply. OEMs and other actors in the supply chain must interpret, anticipate, and respond operationally, tactically, and strategically to such changes in market conditions. Their capacity to adapt to change, in turn, depends on their supply chain characteristics as measured through metrics. In addition, change vectors, market conditions, and OEM actions directly affect supply chain characteristics. The framework provides a tool for exploring the possible effects of future change, whether they are planned (as in the case of policy actions), anticipated (such as technology maturity or demand shrinkage), or uncertain (such as economic downturns).

Our case study illustrates how the framework can be used, exploring the dynamics of gas turbine supply chains, with a focus on OEMs. The dominant change vectors evolved over time, shifting among industrial dynamics, policy, innovation, and resources. Historical change in market conditions was dramatically shown by annual installations of utility-scale gas turbines in the United States: there was a spike in installation demand in the early 2000s that was primarily caused by policy-driven natural gas and electricity market restructuring, with technical innovations also playing a role.

The framework also guided our analysis of OEM responses to changes in the gas turbine supply chain from 2013 through the present. Resilient supply chains are poised to respond operationally to market dynamics in the short term, while interpreting market signals to inform longer-term tactics and strategies. Although there has been some volatility in the market, including some resource constraints, the dominant recent signal has been of shrinking demand. OEMs have been responding to this shrinking demand in a variety of ways, including by reducing costs through improving efficiency of production, by delivering more flexible and efficient turbines, and by restructuring their supply chains.

Use of the framework also informs systematic thinking on the interactions of various supply chain characteristics across multiple time horizons. For example, actions in the tactical time horizon (e.g., reduction of production capacity in response to demand shrinkage) can affect the ability of the supply chain to respond to changes in the operational time horizon (e.g., by increasing the capacity utilization). In general, for the supply chain characteristics, there is a tension between supply chain characteristics that enable flexible response in the operational time horizon, those that underlie efficiency in the tactical time horizon, and innovation in the strategic horizon.

The framework supports systematic thinking with limited data, yet also helps to prioritize the gathering of additional data to deepen insight. For example, to further explore current strategic responses to demand shrinkage, additional quantitative data could be assembled on supply chain characteristics in operational, tactical, and strategic time frames (e.g., vertical integration, performance efficacy, market size, demand predictability) and how they have changed over the past decade.

The authors recognize the difficulty in collecting data on energy supply chains, particularly for intermediate manufacturing stages. OEMs' annual reports, corporate press releases, online industry journals, and government reports, websites, and datasets, which are accessible via the internet, provide information primarily for the final product: gas turbines in our case study. Government websites with particularly relevant data include: (1) the US EIA (https://www.eia.gov/) and (2) the US Census Bureau (https://www.census.gov/data.html). Other supply chain information can be found in market reports and the scientific literature, both of which may need to be purchased. Although outside the scope of this study, discussions with or surveys of subject matter experts and practitioners within the supply chain would strengthen the analysis.

Conclusions

Overall, the case study illustrates how this framework can be applied to evaluate the potential consequences and effects of change (including policy change) on energy supply chains over different time scales. The framework can be used with existing data to deliver insights on change in supply chains while also highlighting important data gaps that, if filled, would help in understanding additional dynamic phenomena.

Application of the framework can inform structured thinking of how a policy option might affect the associated energy supply chains in the context of ongoing change and responsiveness. Policy (including R&D investment, electricity market restructuring, natural gas market regulation, and environmental policy) is explicitly considered as a change vector that acts on energy supply chains in a variety of ways and elicits responses necessary for the supply chains to meet demand. The process of mapping change can illuminate the vulnerabilities of the supply chains in achieving these responses and meeting demand on various time scales associated with specific supply chain characteristics. In turn, certain supply chain characteristics and associated metrics are directly affected by existing or proposed policy. Moreover, the framework enables systematic thinking of interactions among different types of policies as experienced by supply chains that could inform conceptual policy design.

The framework can also guide analysts in identifying energy supply chain metrics to consider as focal points in policy development. By focusing on influential metrics, costly data collection and analysis could be minimized. In summary, the framework provides a systematic approach for considering the implications of policy over time in the context of energy supply chains that are continually evolving. This approach may be particularly useful in determining how a policy action directed at an emerging energy technology could be adapted over time to ensure its effectiveness as the technology and supply chain mature.

Acknowledgments

The submitted manuscript has been created by UChicago Argonne, LLC, Operator of Argonne National Laboratory (Argonne). Argonne National Laboratory's work was supported by the US Department of Energy, Office of Energy Policy and Systems Analysis, under contract DE-AC02-06CH11357. The US Government retains for itself, and others acting on its behalf, a paid-up nonexclusive, irrevocable worldwide license in said article to reproduce, prepare derivative works, distribute copies to the public, and perform publicly and display publicly, by or on behalf of the Government. The Department of Energy will provide public access to these results of federally sponsored research in accordance with its Public Access Plan (http://energy.gov/downloads/doe-public-accessplan).

References

Araújo, Kathleen. 2014. "The Emerging Field of Energy Transitions: Progress, Challenges, and Opportunities." *Energy Research & Social Science* 1: 112–21.

Bonaccorsi, Andrea and Paola Giuri. 2000. "When shakeout doesn't occur: the evolution of the turboprop engine industry." *Research Policy* 29 (7-8): 847–70.

———. 2001. "The Long-Term Evolution of Vertically-Related Industries." *International Journal of Industrial Organization* 19 (7): 1053-83.

Browning, Paul. 2017. "The Race to 65% Efficiency." *MHI Spectra*. https://spectra.mhi.com/the-race-to-65percent?msclkid=f1e92a4a782215c14c69719874aec75

3&utm_source=bing&utm_medium=cpc&utm_campaign=*NA%20%7C%20 USA%20%7C%20EN%20%7C%20Non-Brand%20%7C%20Energy%20%7C%20 MBM.&utm_term=%2Bgas%20%2Bturbines&utm_content=Turbines.

Capgemini. 2008. *Transforming the Business and IT in Gas Turbine Manufacturing*. https://www.capgemini.com/no-no/resources/siemens_pg/.

Chase, David L. 2001. "Combined-Cycle Development Evolution and Future." *GE Power Systems GER-4206* (04/01). https://www.ge.com/content/dam/gepower-pg-dp/global/en_US/documents/technical/ger/ger-4206-combined-cycle-development-evolution-future.pdf.

Court, Stephen A. 2008. *The Mapping of Materials Supply Chains in the UK's Power Generation Sector*. Materials UK Energy Review and National Metals Technology Center (NAMTEC).

Crooks, Ed. 2018. "Gas Turbine Competition Heats up." *Financial Times*, August 16, 2018.

Desai, Pratima. 2007. "Analysis–Wonder Metal Rhenium Rockets as Deficit Grows." *Reuters*, July 19, 2007.

Energy Information Administration. 2017. "EIA-860 Detailed Data Table." 3_1_Generator_Y2017.xls.

Frost & Sullivan. 2014. *Global Gas and Steam Turbine Markets Conventional Thermal Power Expansion Driven by Emerging Markets and Rising Natural Gas Availability. Market report: M96C-14*. June.

General Electric. 2017. "GE Power Announces Global Headcount Reduction of 12,000 Jobs as Part of Plan to Take out $1 Billion in Structural Costs." Press release. December 7, 2017.

Geels, Frank W. 2010. "Ontologies, Socio-Technical Transitions (to Sustainability), and the Multi-Level Perspective." *Research Policy* 39 (4): 495–510.

Gravier, Michael J. and Stephen M. Swartz. 2009. "The Dark Side of Innovation: Exploring Obsolescence and Supply Chain Evolution for Sustainment-Dominated Systems." *The Journal of High Technology Management Research* 20, no. 2: 87–102.

Goodall, David. 2018. "'Burning to the Ground': The Carbon Bubble in Gas Turbines." *Carbon Commentary*. January 26, 2018.

Heller, Matthew. 2017. "Siemens job cuts target gas turbine business." *CFO Magazine*. November 16, 2017.

Humphries, Marc. 2013. "Rare Earth Elements: The Global Supply Chain." *Congressional Research Service Report for Congress*, June 8.

International Energy Agency. 2019. *Tracking Clean Energy Progress—Natural Gas-Fired Power*. https://www.iea.org/tcep/power/naturalgas/. Accessed July 22, 2019.

———. 2018. *Electricity Information 2018: Overview*. https://webstore.iea.org/electricity-information-2018-overview. Accessed July 22, 2019.

Jacobsson, Staffan and Anna Bergek. 2004. "Transforming the Energy Sector: The Evolution of Technological Systems in Renewable Energy Technology." *Industrial and Corporate Change* 13 (5): 815–49.

John, David A., Robert R. Seal II, and Désirée E. Polyak. 2017. *Rhenium*. No. 1802-P. US Geological Survey, 2017, *Critical Mineral Resources of the United States—Economic and Environmental Geology and Prospects for Future Supply, U.S. Geological Survey Professional Paper 1802*, P1–P49. Edited by K.J. Schulz, J.H. DeYoung, Jr., R.R. Seal, II, and D.C. Bradley. doi:10.3133/pp1802P

Kern, Florian. 2012. "The Development of the CCGT and the 'Dash for Gas' in the UK Power Industry (1987–2000)." *Final Case Study Report as Part of Work Package 2 of the UKERC Project: 'CCS–Realising the potential*.

Kesieme, Uchenna, Andreas Chrysanthou, and Maurizio Catulli. 2019. "Assessment of Supply Interruption of Rhenium, Recycling, Processing Sources and Technologies." *International Journal of Refractory Metals and Hard Materials* 82: 150–58.

Klepper, Steven. 1997. "Industry Life Cycles." *Industrial and Corporate Change* 6 (1): 145–82.

Larson, Aaron. 2018. "Gas Power Generation Thrives, Turbine Manufacturers Struggle." *POWER*, Jan. 3, 2018.

Lee, Kyungpyo and Sungjoo Lee. 2013. "Patterns of Technological Innovation and Evolution in the Energy Sector: A Patent-Based Approach." *Energy Policy* 59: 415–32.

Malerba, Franco. 2007. "Innovation and the Dynamics and Evolution of Industries: Progress and Challenges." *International Journal of Industrial Organization* 25 (4): 675–99.

Månsson, André, Bengt Johansson, and Lars J. Nilsson. 2014. "Assessing Energy Security: An Overview of Commonly Used Methodologies." *Energy* 73: 1–14.

Markard, Jochen, Rob Raven, and Bernhard Truffer. 2012. "Sustainability Transitions: An Emerging Field of Research and its Prospects." *Research Policy* 41 (6): 955–67.

Moss, Ray, L., Evangelos Tzimas, Peter Willis, Josie Arendor, Paul Thompson, Adrian Chapman, Nick Morley, Edward Sims, Ruth Bryson, and James Pearson et al. 2013. "Critical Metals in the Path towards the Decarbonisation of the EU Energy Sector." *Assessing Rare Metals as Supply-Chain Bottlenecks in Low-Carbon Energy Technologies. JRC Report EUR* 25994.

National Energy Technology Laboratory. 2016. *Advanced Turbines*. https://www.netl.doe.gov/sites/default/files/2017-11/Program-108.pdf.

National Science Foundation. 2018. "Business Research and Development and Innovation: 2015." *Detailed Statistical Tables, NSF 18-318*. August 30, 2018.

Nyman, Jonna. 2018. "Rethinking Energy, Climate and Security: A Critical Analysis of Energy Security in the US." *Journal of International Relations and Development* 21 (1): 118–45.

Overton, Thomas W. 2015. "Controlling Schedule, Quality, and Costs for New Gas-Fired Plants." *Power*, September 1, 2015.

Pauschert, Dirk. 2009. "Study of Equipment Prices in the Power Sector." *Energy Sector Management Assistance Program Technical Paper 122/09*.

Prandi, Roberta. 2018. "New HL-class gas turbines grow in the market." *Diesel & Gas Turbine Worldwide*. August 27, 2018.

Proctor, Darell. 2018. "Efficiency Improvements Mark Advances in Gas Turbines." *Power*. January 3, 2018.

Sachgau, Oliver and Eyk Henning, E., 2018. Siemens said to mull sale of flagship gas turbine business. *Bloomberg*. June 13, 2018.

Seong, Somi, Obaid Younossi, and Benjamin W. Goldsmith. 2009. *Titanium: Industrial Base, Price Trends, and Technology Initiatives*. Rand Corporation.

Seth, Brij B. 2000. "Superalloys: the utility gas turbine perspective." *Superalloys 2000*: 3–12.

Siemens. 2017a. Siemens Press pictures, im2017010300pg_300dpi_original gas turbine picture.

———. 2017b. *Agreement at Siemens on Measures to Boost Competitiveness.* October 24, 2017.

———. 2017c. *A Dependable Power Supply.* March 21, 2017.

Sims, Chester T. 1984. "A History of Superalloy Metallurgy for Superalloy Metallurgists." *Superalloys* 1984: 399–419.

Smith, Adrian and Andy Stirling. 2010. "The Politics of Social-Ecological Resilience and Sustainable Socio-Technical Transitions." *Ecology and Society* 15 (1).

Unger, Darren P. and Howard J. Herzog. 1998. *Comparative Study on Energy R & D Performance: Gas Turbine Case Study.* Energy Laboratory, Massachusetts Institute of Technology.

Urciuoli, Luca, Sangeeta Mohanty, Juha Hintsa, and Else Gerine Boekesteijn. 2014. "The Resilience of Energy Supply Chains: A Multiple Case Study Approach on Oil and Gas Supply Chains to Europe." *Supply Chain Management: An International Journal* 19 (1): 46–63.

US Department of Homeland Security. (n.d.) *Critical Infrastructure Sectors, Energy Sector.*

Van Gosen, Bradley S., Philip L. Verplanck, Robert R. Seal II, Keith R. Long, and Joseph Gambogi. 2017. *Rare-Earth Elements. US Geological Survey Professional Paper 1802, O1–O31.* doi:10.3133/pp1802O.

Vandervort, Christian, David Leach, and Marcus Scholz. 2016. "Advancements in H Class Gas Turbines for Combined Cycle Power Plants for High Efficiency, Enhanced Operational Capability and Broad Fuel Flexibility." In *The Future of Gas Turbine Technology, 8th International Gas Turbine Congress.*

Wagner, Stephan M., and Nikrouz Neshat. 2010. "Assessing the Vulnerability of Supply Chains using Graph Theory." *International Journal of Production Economics* 126 (1): 121–29.

Willis. 2002. *Gas Turbines in the Modern Power Industry: Technical Report.* December 2002.

Winzer, Christian. 2012. "Conceptualizing Energy Security." *Energy Policy* 46: 36–48.

Wirth, Timothy E., C. Boyden Gray, and John D. Podesta. 2003. "The future of energy policy." *Foreign Affairs*: 132–55.

Yergin, Daniel. 2006. "Ensuring energy security." *Foreign Affairs*: 69-82.

Zhang, Kuangyuan, Andrew N. Kleit, and Antonio Nieto. 2017. "An Economics Strategy for Criticality–Application to Rare Earth Element Yttrium in New Lighting Technology and its Sustainable Availability." *Renewable and Sustainable Energy Reviews* 77: 899–915.

# Electromagnetic Pulse Resilience of United States Critical Infrastructure: Progress and Prognostics

George H. Baker[1]

[1]Professor Emeritus, James Madison University, bakergh@jmu.edu

Thanks largely to Presidential Executive Order 13865,[1] national electromagnetic security vis-à-vis the nuclear electromagnetic pulse (EMP[2]) and solar geomagnetic disturbances (GMD) has received substantial attention at the highest levels of the U.S. national policy and technical establishments. Despite diversion of national security efforts to Covid-19 pandemic response, there is notable progress on the electromagnetic security front since the executive order's debut in March 2019. Executive order activities have provided important insights into priority system identification, interdependency, EMP susceptibility, protection requirements, hardening methods (including some new technologies), and protection costs. EMP environment benchmarks for critical national infrastructure have been established and published.[3] NOAA and USGS are continuing efforts to map U.S. and Canadian geoelectric properties and developed improved models of electric power EMP/GMD response. A pilot demonstration program at Joint Base San Antonio has been especially helpful by successfully establishing federal/state/local/industry public-private partnerships for the expressed purpose of implementing EMP resilience including electric power, communication/control systems, emergency services, fuel supply, and water supply infrastructures. The executive order has invigorated Department of Defense (DOD), Department of Homeland Security (DHS), and Department of Energy (DOE) efforts and cooperation in addressing the significant challenges associated with national EMP preparedness. It is important to note that EO 13865 requirements are also mirrored in the FY2020 National Defense Authorization Act (NDAA) passed by the Senate in December 2019.[4]

This paper primarily focuses on civilian infrastructure preparedness. DOD's past and ongoing success in assessing, prioritizing, and protecting military systems from EMP threats has paved the way for the civilian critical infrastructure resilience programs spurred by the Executive Order. The military has a 50-year head start on the civilian sector in achieving EMP resilience.

---

1. Coordinating National Resilience to Electromagnetic Pulses, Executive Order 13865, Presidential Documents, Federal Register Vol. 94, No. 61, p. 12041-12046, 29 March 2019.
2. The EMP acronym as used here refers to EMP produced by a high-altitude nuclear burst.
3. D. Brouillette, Physical Characteristics of HEMP Waveform Benchmarks for Use in Assessing Susceptibilities of the Power Grid, Electrical Infrastructures, and Other Critical Infrastructure to HEMP Insults, U.S. Secretary of Energy Memorandum, January 2021
4. https://www.hsgac.senate.gov/media/majority-media/sen-johnson-statement-on-bipartisan-hsgac-emp-gmd-legislation-in-ndaa

The large geographic areas exposed by EMP and GMD events, the ubiquity of systems affected, and hardening costs, require careful discretion in downselecting the systems and facilities to protect. Priority system identification requires locating critical life-support services (e.g., electric power, water plants, fuel supply, communications network operation centers, transportation hubs) and national security facilities (strategic bases, war headquarters, national essential function (NEF) sites, etc.). Risk assessment based on combined function and fault tree analysis of life and security critical services will be important to identify priority infrastructure systems. Assigning a "recovery time objective (RTO)" in hours, days, or weeks will help in ranking systems to protect. Some systems must be able to "operate through" an EMP/GMD contingency, while others have lower time urgency and can be allowed to fail if provision is made for repairing the systems and restoring their electric power and communication/control connectivity within their specified RTO.

DHS leads the priority system identification process and has initially placed the electric power and communications sectors at the top of their list vis-à-vis EMP protection. These infrastructures exhibit the highest electromagnetic susceptibility due to the large EMP/GMD coupling cross-sections of their long mission-essential connecting lines. DHS is expanding their priority list by identifying the additional infrastructures supporting the operation of electric power and communications.

Thanks to DOD's attention to EMP effects and hardening since the 1960s, including the development of handbooks and standards, protection engineering solutions are known, tried, and true.[5] DOD's success in producing peer-reviewed techniques and guidelines have enabled us to begin protecting priority infrastructure without delay. Electromagnetically simple systems with a contiguous shield and a limited number of protected penetrations will survive EMP. The governing engineering principles are straightforward. These include minimizing the volume of the space occupied by mission-critical electronics, enclosing this equipment in a single continuous shield (use of multiple shielding layers significantly complicates the hardness surveillance and maintenance processes), limiting the number of electromagnetic penetrations through the shield, and protecting all remaining penetrations. The engineering approach also includes certifying the hardness of protected systems via shielding effectiveness measurements and current injection tests of cable penetrations, plus periodically retesting system shielding and penetration protection to ensure continuing hardness integrity. Numerous systems, both military and civilian, have successfully implemented the military standard approach in an affordable manner. EMP mitigation measures are becoming part of the industrial and public consumer culture. Thanks in large measure to DOD,

---

5 G. Baker, Evolution and Rationale for United States Department of Defense Electromagnetic Pulse Protection Standard, *Insight Magazine*, Vol. 19, Issue 4, December 2016.

EMP protection hardware is now readily available as well as protection installation and testing by turn-key full system EMP protection contractors for communications and data processing systems and facilities as well as emergency backup power systems.

As noted, DHS has initially designated electric power and communications as the top priority infrastructure categories. These infrastructures are not only the glue supporting and interconnecting all other infrastructures during normal situations, but they must also operate early in crisis situations to provide situational awareness and to enable emergency responder efforts to restore other infrastructures. The President's National Security Telecommunications Advisory Council (NSTAC) has also identified these two infrastructures[6] as essential in preventing long term national disasters.[7] It is essential to also identify, include, and protect other infrastructures in our priority list that are necessary for the operation of power and communications. Down-selection of the power and communication sites to harden must take into account national security and lifeline infrastructures in all sectors to ensure that their energy and communication requirements are met.

Electric Power Grid Resilience

The electric power grid and its supporting infrastructures are at the forefront of present national "electromagnetic security" efforts. The electric power grid is arguably the most critical infrastructure, but lamentably it is also the infrastructure most vulnerable to EMP/GMD.[8] Achieving EMP/GMD resilience of the national grid must incorporate both a top-down effort to protect our bulk electric generation and transmission system, and a bottom-up effort to protect electric distribution system and electric power CI customers.[9]

The top-down approach focuses on protecting the bulk-power electric system (BES). In order to ensure the situational awareness that is necessary to avert and respond to outages, system operators' central control facilities and communication-data networks must be the top priority. Protection of the power generation and transmission elements of the BES begins with blackstart and nuclear generation stations. Blackstart and islanding processes must be developed and exercised

---

[6] Report to the President on Telecommunications and Electric Power Interdependencies: The Implications of Long-Term Outages, National Security Telecommunications Advisory Council, December 2006.

[7] NSTAC identified the phenomenon of a "Long-Term Outage" (LTO), which it defined as "an interruption of communications and/or electricity for a period long enough, and within a large enough geographic region, to hamper providing communications and electric power by even alternative means." LTOs are also commonly referred to as "black sky events."

[8] G. Baker, "EMP Knots Untied: Some Common Misconceptions about Nuclear EMP," Proceedings, Dupont Summit, Carnegie Institute, Washington, D.C., 2013.

[9] G. Baker, Written Testimony before the Senate Committee on Homeland Security and Governmental Affairs, February 27, 2019.

over regions up to and including CONUS-wide. A previous Federal Energy Regulatory Commission (FERC) effort to identify and prioritize U.S. electric power facilities will significantly reduce the costs to protect the BES.

The bottom-up EMP protection approach involves protecting the distribution grid and life-supporting services, under the jurisdiction of State and local governments. Since communities are likely to be on their own for extended periods in a wide-area blackout, local community awareness is essential. EMP preparedness programs should identify and address a thin line of life-support infrastructures including local backup power generation systems, emergency services (law enforcement, fire, EMS, and their communication systems), water supply/treatment, hospitals, and the necessary logistics tail (food, fuel, and transportation). The San Antonio Electromagnetic Defense Initiative and the Carolinas' Lake Wylie project provide models for completing a bottom-up EMP/GMD assessment and protection program for a minimum set of essential systems.

The federal government will play an important role in coordinating the interface between the top-down and bottom-up electric power protection efforts. The interface demark occurs at substations where the bulk power high voltage transmission grid meets the lower voltage (< ~100 KV) distribution grid supplying local public and industry user services.[10] FERC has jurisdiction over the higher voltage BES, while States have jurisdiction over the lower voltage distribution systems.

To protect the higher voltage systems that generate, transmit, and distribute electricity, overvoltage protection and low pass filtering techniques have been applied successfully to limit the fast EMP pulse (E1).[11] Solutions for the slow EMP/E3 and solar GMD pulses have been developed and partially demonstrated. Neutral blocking devices offer promise,[12] but require further beta testing at additional grid locations, especially generator step-up transformers (GSUs). We know that large transformers are susceptible to damage from quasi-DC GMD and EMP-E3 surges. There is limited evidence that BES generators are also susceptible to damage.[13] Proposed E3/GMD grid system fail-safe disconnection and islanding solutions also need to be tested on larger scales. The EMP (E1, E2, and E3/GMD) threat-level laboratory test data base for large transformers and BES generators is lacking such that prevalent assertions concerning vulnerability or invulnerability cannot be substantiated at present. It is encouraging that the Idaho National Laboratory and Savannah River National Laboratory have developed detailed propos-

---

10 G. Baker, Senate Testimony, op. cit.

11 For a brief tutorial on E1 and E3 see https://works.bepress.com/george_h_baker/32/

12 F. Faxvog, G. Fuchs, W. Jensen, D. Wojtczak, M. Marz, S. Dahman, "HV Power Transformer Neutral Blocking Device Operating Experience in Wisconsin," MIPSYNCON, November 2017.

13 L. Marti, A. Rezaei-Zare, Generator Thermal Stress during a Geomagnetic Disturbance, IEEE 978-1-4799-1303-9/13, Toronto, Canada, 2013.

als to develop the necessary test beds. The Interagency should expedite funding for test-bed development and threat-level transformer and EMP/GMD protection hardware testing.

EMP Executive Order activities have promoted the development and demonstration of innovations in grid EMP protection technology including lower-cost shielding materials, modular EMP-hardened substation control buildings and containers, EMP-E3/GMD ground current blocking devices, dual-use EMP/lightning surge arrestors, and high voltage transmission line E1 limiters.

Important milestones remain in the U.S. electric grid's "electromagnetic security" challenge. As previously mentioned, we have not developed the necessary EMP threat-level effects test data base on large transformers and generation stations. Threat level EMP testing of transformers has been limited to small distribution units. Threat level testing of generation stations has only just begun. There have been several analytical studies and low-level tests with optimistic survivability prognostics, but experience dictates that conclusions about system EMP immunity based on analysis and low-level testing are not reliable.[14] Unfortunately, some senior officials in government and industry have accepted and openly endorsed these inconclusive and tenuous analytical results. The DOD program test statistics demonstrate that analytical studies of system EMP effects without follow-on threat-level system testing have a very high likelihood of erroneous conclusions. If analytical studies that predict transformer EMP immunity prove to be incorrect, because of considerable replacement transformer procurement lead times, national recovery periods would be extended from an estimated 30-day minimum to in excess of one year.

Microgrids as an Electric Power EMP Resilience Tool

Recent major power outages in Puerto Rico, California, and Texas have contributed to a large increase in microgrid installations. EMP-hardened microgrids are a helpful tool as part of the previously mentioned bottom-up effort to protect time-urgent high-risk lifeline and national security infrastructure sites. Microgrids offer many advantages that are accelerating their incorporation as primary local power sources. The main benefit is the elimination of unacceptably high risks of extended grid outages by incorporating organic power sources independent of the BES and local electric distribution systems. An important microgrid attribute, in relation to improved grid survivability and recovery, is their inherent islanding (ability to function disconnected from the rest of the grid) capability. If properly designed and installed, microgrid islands continue to function independent of the larger grid during blackout contingencies. In addition to sustaining critical

---

14 Electromagnetic Effects Comparison Test and Reliability Assessment (ELECTRA) Program, Executive Summary of the ELECTRA Technical Review Group, Defense Nuclear Agency, 1995.

services, they can be helpful in blackstarting the larger electric grid.[15] As a bonus, when completely isolated from the larger grid, microgrids' small footprint makes them immune to EMP-E3 and GMD effects.

However, without intentional protection, microgrids are far from a silver bullet solution to threats and hazards associated with the larger electric power "macrogrid." Because of their organic digital monitoring and control systems, microgrid networks are highly susceptible to EMP and cyberattacks. Furthermore, integration of microgrids into the larger existing electric power grid, without attention to protection engineering, actually increases the vulnerability of the larger grid composite by exacerbating the "vulnerability of complexity."[16] Because microgrid control systems interface with control systems for the larger grid, microgrids provide attack paths into the generation, transmission, and distribution sectors of the larger national grid.[17] Microgrid installations to date have not incorporated protection engineering. Without attention to protection engineering, the proliferation of microgrids makes our composite electricity supply system more vulnerable to EMP and cyber threats. Designed-in protection represents a single digit percentage cost differential. DOD experience indicates that retrofit protection costs run an order of magnitude higher than designed-in protection.

Communications, Data Systems, and Network Resiliency

Telecommunications infrastructure continues to undergo significant transformation. Packet-based internet protocol networks have largely subsumed circuit-switched networks enabling broadband, diverse, scalable packet-based networks, now in the 4th generation and transitioning to 5th generation (5G) technology. There is a continuing dramatic growth in wireless services and applications including the proliferation of base stations and radio-cell tower infrastructure throughout wireless provider service areas.

Dependency on digital mobile phones, Internet communications, and wireless local-area networks support a growing internet of things (IOT) comprising a host of new controlled physical infrastructures including the smart grid, smart buildings and smart homes. This expansion will increase the consequences of EMP/GMD-caused power outages and electronics failures. The rapid proliferation and integration of telecommunications and computer systems and networks have connected infrastructures to one another in a complex network of interdependence. Higher bandwidth wired and wireless systems have increased the capabilities and use of digital automation of life-line infrastructures, including the elec-

---

[15] G. Baker, "Microgrids—A Watershed Moment," *Insight Magazine*, International Conference on System Engineering, June 2020, Vol. 23/ Issue 2.

[16] C. Perrow, *Normal Accidents: Living with High-Risk Technologies*, Princeton University Press, 1999.

[17] G. Baker, "Microgrids—A Watershed Moment," Op. Cit.

tric power systems, water systems, transportation systems, and financial systems. These digital monitoring and control network overlays add a new dimension of EMP risks.

Communication and data network monitoring and control increase the grid's vulnerability to both EMP and cyber debilitation because they introduce new attack vectors exploitable by malefactors. An important case in point is the increased use of Internet-based automation of grid operation as part of smart grid, smart city, and IOT initiatives. To reduce costs, many electric companies, instead of building dedicated monitoring and control data networks, route their data over the Internet. Hackers have used the grid's Internet connectivity to shut down electric power in Ukraine[18] and India.[19] These are important examples of private efficiency creating public vulnerability.[20] To counter this broad movement towards increased vulnerability, we must form public-private partnerships oriented to protecting the public interest. Just as important, we must take steps to provide cost recovery and insurance incentives that encourage private investment in EMP/GMD resilience.

It is important to note that EMP affects the same electronic equipment targeted by cyber-attacks. Conducting Internet paths penetrating infrastructure control systems can also deliver high voltage EMP transients into the same digital devices. And EMP has other paths into equipment as well. EMP is able to bypass cyber security firewalls, air gaps and optical fiber isolation lines by coupling directly to electronic boxes power supply cables. Thus, EMP effects are significantly more ubiquitous than cyber effects since EMP couples to local networks and electronic data and communications systems not linked to the Internet.

Communication and data systems and networks required for grid operation necessarily rise to the top of the DHS priority system identification list. Both normal operation and emergency restoration of the grid in EMP contingencies depend on functional on-site communication systems and the communication/data networks interconnecting grid control centers with generation plants, substations, transmission systems, and distribution systems.[21] The National Security Telecommunications Commission continues to be concerned about the interdependencies between the communications and electric power sectors.

The grid is not alone—the operation and maintenance of all critical infrastructures rely on the larger public switched telephone network (PSTN) which also supports the Internet. These networks also play critical roles during emergen-

---

18 E-ISAC, Analysis of the Cyber Attack on the Ukrainian Power Grid, March 18, 2016

19 https://www.nytimes.com/2021/02/28/us/politics/china-india-hacking-electricity.html

20 L. Branscomb et al, *Seeds of Disaster, Roots of Response: How Private Action Can Reduce Public Vulnerability*, National Institute of Standards - George Mason University, Private Efficiency, Public Vulnerability Project, Cambridge Press, 2006.

21 D. Winks, Protecting U.S. Electric Grid Communications from Electromagnetic Pulse, Foundation for Resilient Societies, April 2020.

cies and in reconstituting societal functions following disasters. Several rules of thumb help in ranking the EMP susceptibility of communications systems. Land line networks are the most susceptible to EMP and GMD because of the large number of nodes and long-interconnecting copper lines—or EMP/E1 susceptible regeneration/repeater stations in the case of fiber-optic networks. Though cell phones themselves are likely to be undamaged by EMP, cell phone communications will fail since cell towers are highly susceptible and are interconnected via the land line system. Telephone central offices are also highly susceptible to EMP (and GMD in the case of long line terminal equipment) effects. Failure of long-haul telecommunication systems will prevent local and long-distance telephone service and Internet connectivity. Satellite phones are also likely to fail since satellites down-link to the PSTN through EMP-susceptible terrestrial receiver stations. Some commercial radio and TV stations may continue to operate if they have survivable backup power. Many HAM stations will continue to function. Some first responder hand-held and land-mobile radio (LMR) radio systems will continue to function if they have survivable backup power. Mobile radio base stations and repeaters may be debilitated. Hand-held and vehicle-mounted satellite UHF radios (e.g., military manpack PRC-117 radio) that connect through high-orbit geosynchronous satellites are likely to continue to operate. EMP testing of specific portable and mobile radio systems and associated base stations and repeaters used by first responders is relatively simple and inexpensive and strongly recommended to ascertain their survivability. In general, radio connectivity is much more likely to remain following EMP exposure. Point-to-point radio systems are the most resilient to EMP environments assuming backup power/battery rechargers are available. Given current vulnerabilities, it is not prudent to rely on network operations center or emergency operations station land-line connectivity.

There is some good news regarding EMP/GMD protection practicality and cost. The public switched telecommunications network (PSTN) is the foundational backbone for U.S. communications. The Telecommunications Act of 1996 opened local PSTN service to competition. The legislation requires incumbent carriers to allow their competitors to have open access to their networks. As a result, carriers are concentrating their assets in collocation facilities known as telcom hotels, collocation sites, or peering points. Internet Service Providers (ISPs) have also gravitated to these facilities to reduce costs. This has curtailed the proliferation of data centers and reduced the requirement for and cost of laying new cable. This means fewer facilities and a lower number of interconnecting cables that require EMP/GMD protection.

Cost Recovery Mechanisms Essential

Achievement of privately-owned infrastructure resilience is unlikely without the establishment of EMP protection cost recovery mechanisms. Under present Federal Energy Regulatory Commission (FERC) rules, BES protection cost recovery is possible only for the transmission portion of the grid. Generation operators may not recover costs for resilience expenses. Legislation is needed to expand cost recovery provisions to include the generation portion of the electric power grid. Some strategies for cost recovery could include identification of "resilience" as an investment justification, modification of tax credits for microgrids and renewables to include resilience, enactment of federal legislation to provide block grants to states for critical infrastructure protection and addressing EMP under the "multi-hazard" rubric to justify protection from the combination of floods, hurricanes, earthquakes, EMP, Solar Storms, and other hazards.

In addition, Tier 1 national security and infrastructure customers—including defense facilities, key data centers, water and wastewater facilities, emergency responders, hospitals, and nuclear power plants—may request firm electric power delivery that requires high reliability and resilient supply and delivery. These customers may rely upon federal or state or municipal appropriations so the "customer pays" principle applies when specific customer priority service is a necessity. Cost savings can be achieved by leveraging existing new builds and replacements to install hardened equipment to minimize the incremental expense of retrofit hardening.

At this point, examples of regulatory agencies specifying or incentivizing EMP/GMD protection of critical infrastructures are scarce. The Energy sector has developed reliability standards through the North American Electric Reliability Corporation (NERC) to protect against GMD including NERC Reliability Standard TPL-007-4 and EOP-010-1. Also, Maine and Virginia have passed electric grid laws that include EMP/GMD disaster mitigation. The federal government must demonstrate a greater interest in regulating or incentivizing adoption through cost recovery, EMP resilience will remain a low priority among critical infrastructure stakeholders.

The Way Forward

EMP has for too long been considered prohibitively difficult and expensive to address. Such is not the case. The major challenge has been the ubiquity of EMP effects. This can be overcome by defining a minimum essential set of systems and network nodes requiring protection and work-around procedures to restore systems that are intentionally allowed to fail. We know how to harden systems. EMP can be viewed and treated as a facility-level electromagnetic interference (EMI) engineering problem. Critical systems must make maximum use of shielded compartments connected with optical fiber. Since hardening costs are proportional to the floor space occupied by electronic boxes and racks, there is a premium on compressing the space occupied by essential electronics. Shielded spaces and cabinets can be fitted with simple, built-in self-monitoring or 'push-button/read meter' shielding effectiveness test devices to ensure protection is surveilled and maintained. Box-level protection is feasible if box EMI field exposure and penetration injection test requirements are adjusted up to 50 kV/m and corresponding coupled current and voltage levels (specifications will be cable dependent and can be handled with look-up tables as in IEC Standard 61000-2-10). In particular, the issuance of an official unclassified EMP protection handbook is long overdue. DHS has been working this issue and is close to a final product for communication and data facilities and networks and associated backup power.

The foundational Report of the President's Commission on Critical Infrastructure Protection of 1997 (PCCIP Report) has not helped the case for national electromagnetic effects resilience, including EMP, GMD and intentional electromagnetic interference (radio-frequency weapons, high power microwave weapons, ultra-wideband weapons, jamming devices, etc.). The report divided infrastructure threats into two categories: 'physical security' and 'cyber security.' This categorization has governed protection program objectives and budgets for over two decades. The 'electromagnetic security' category and associated highly asymmetric effects due to the large areas affected by single events does not fit neatly under the PCCIP's physical security or cyber security definitions. Electromagnetic Security has fallen through the cracks, largely unaddressed in national security planning and system/network design and operation. For instance, EMP did not make the list of DHS' early compilation of the top one-hundred U.S. threats. "Electromagnetic Security" must be included as a separate category in national security strategic planning and budget authorization documents.

One cannot expect instant gratification in the quest for national electromagnetic security. It will take time to delimit the systems that absolutely must survive EMP and GMD. Hardened microgrids are likely the most effective near-term solution for electric power protection. FERC has identified the most essential substations in the bulk electric power grid—attention to these will greatly improve the recoverability, if not the survivability of the transmission system. From a communications standpoint, the regional control centers that tie the generation, transmission, and distribution elements of the electric power grid together are the top priority systems for protection. This is due to their role in controlling the grid during normal operations and during grid restoration including grid isolation, power re-routing, and general situational awareness during grid outages. Control center protection engineering hardware and procedures are available and already demonstrated on two major control centers within the Center Point and Dominion Energy systems. There are approximately 300 major centers across the United States. Federal incentives to protect and to perform testing of these centers and their associated communication and control networks are well advised.

In summary, Presidential Executive Order 13865 has spurred substantial national attention to electromagnetic security vis-à-vis nuclear EMP and solar

GMD. The Executive Order provisions are now legally binding under the 2020 National Defense Authorization Act. The electric power grid, communications, and water sectors are at the forefront of national CI electromagnetic security efforts. It is impractical to harden all critical infrastructure, but careful screening to identify key life/enterprise-supporting and national security systems will enable affordable EMP preparedness. Thanks to DOD's attention to EMP effects and hardening since the 1960s, including the development of standards, protection engineering solutions are known, implemented, and validated for data and communication equipment and centers. Achieving EMP/GMD resilience of the national grid will necessarily involve combined top-down and bottom-up efforts. The top-down approach focuses on protecting generation and transmission systems (BES) under federal government jurisdiction. The bottom-up effort will protect electric distribution system and its CI customers which are under the jurisdiction of State and local governments. Hardened microgrids are a helpful tool as part of the bottom-up effort to protect time-urgent high-risk lifeline and national security infrastructure sites. Protection of the key nation-wide communication networks including the PSTN and Internet is aided by the collocation of network electronic equipment and line terminations in multi-provider network operation centers. Key remaining challenges include (1) priority system identification and down-selection, (2) validating protection methods for high voltage grid systems, (3) filling the present EMP threat-level test data void on large transformers and generation stations, and (4) the establishment of EMP protection incentives and cost recovery mechanisms.

Acronyms

BES	Bulk-power Electric System
CONUS	Contiguous United States
DHS	Department of Homeland Security
DOD	Department of Defense
EMI	Electromagnetic Interference
EMP	Electromagnetic Pulse
FERC	Federal Energy Regulatory Commission
GMD	Geomagnetic Disturbance
GSU	Generator Step-up Transformer
IOT	Internet of Things

ISP	Internet Service Provider
NDAA	National Defense Authorization Act
NSTAC	National Security Telecommunications Advisory Council
PSTN	Public Switched Telephone Network
RTO	Regional Transmission Organization

Capsule Bio

Dr. George Baker is emeritus professor of applied science at James Madison University (JMU), where he also directed the university's Institute for Infrastructure and Information Assurance during 2000-2012. He recently retired from the National Security Council staff, where he coordinated federal interagency implementation of EMP executive order 13865 tasking. From 1999-2000, Baker served as a senior scientist at Northrop-Grumman, advising Defense Threat Reduction Agency (DTRA) nuclear effects R&D programs. He served as Director of DTRA's Springfield Research Facility from 1996-99, a national center for critical system all-hazards vulnerability assessment and protection guidance. Baker's organization developed the JCS Force Protection assessment program. From 1994-1996, he directed the Defense Nuclear Agency's Innovative Concepts Division, managing advanced weapon concept development and protection technology research. From 1987-1994, Baker led the Defense Nuclear Agency's electromagnetic effects programs to protect strategic systems and develop DOD's EMP guidelines and standards. He now applies lessons-learned from DOD experience to critical national infrastructure assurance and community resilience. He has consulted in the areas of critical infrastructure protection, EMP and geomagnetic disturbance (GMD) protection, nuclear and directed energy weapon effects, and risk assessment for customers including DOD, DOE, DHS, the White House, National Guard units, the National Park Service, SAIC, George Mason University, Oregon State University, and Defense Group Inc. During 2001-2008 and 2016-2017 he served as senior advisor to the Congressional EMP Commission. From 2011-2019 he served on the Board of Directors of the Foundation for Resilient Societies, the Board of Advisors for the Congressional Task Force on National and Homeland Security and the JMU Research and Public Service Advisory Board. Degrees include M.S., Physics (University of Virginia) and Ph.D., Engineering Physics (U.S. Air Force Institute of Technology).

The 2021 Texas Blackouts: Causes, Consequences, and Cures

Thomas Popik[1,2] and Richard Humphreys[3]

[1] Chairman & President, Foundation for Resilient Societies
[2] Corresponding Author: thomasp@resilientsocieties.org
[3] Director, Foundation for Resilient Societies

Abstract

In February 2021, rolling blackouts in Texas during Winter Storm Uri demonstrated the vulnerability of the State's electric grid managed by the Electric Reliability Council of Texas (ERCOT). This article examines the technical causes of the ERCOT blackouts, financial and human consequences, and policy changes that could prevent recurrences. ERCOT planned for a winter load peak far below actual electricity demand. Further electricity shortfalls were caused by generation plants with varied energy sources becoming unavailable—natural-gas fired, coal-fired, nuclear, wind, and solar. Prior blackouts during a 2011 period of cold weather had shown the need for better resource planning and plant weatherization, but advance preparation was inadequate. The system of compensating generators in ERCOT was market-based with a $9,000 per megawatt hour cap on wholesale electricity rates—a so-called "Energy-Only market." This regulatory system did not provide adequate incentives for generation plants to be operational during extreme weather, nor did it ensure that natural gas suppliers could deliver fuel to generators. Texas is well-situated for a return to the cost-of-service regulatory model; the State Legislature should consider this policy option.

Keywords: Texas, ERCOT, Electric Grid, Blackout, Uri

Introduction

The State of Texas has its own electric grid, distinct from the Eastern and Western Interconnections that serve most of the continental United States and parts of Canada. Because the Texas electric grid has only a few low-capacity connections with other states, it is not subject to federal regulation of its transmission lines and tariffs. Accordingly, Texas was able to establish America's first electricity market in

1995, two years before Order 888 of the Federal Energy Regulatory Commission (FERC) enabled electricity markets for other U.S. States.

Electric power for most of the land area and population of Texas is supplied by an electricity market managed by the ERCOT. ERCOT is a quasi-governmental nonprofit that sets market rules, conducts daily auctions to determine wholesale electricity prices, and settles accounts between generators and retail distributors. ERCOT also serves as a balancing authority that dispatches generation to balance electricity supply with customer load. The customer load managed by ERCOT is approximately 90% of total electricity consumed in Texas, the remainder being consumed in areas near the state's border served by the Eastern and Western Interconnections.

The ERCOT market is distinctive among U.S. electricity markets in that it is "Energy-Only." An Energy-Only electricity market relies entirely on market forces to ensure both reserve generation capacity and real-time production of electric energy. In contrast, other areas of the U.S. use so-called "capacity markets" in addition to real-time markets or, alternatively, administrative planning processes to assure that sufficient generation capacity exists to avoid shortages during normal and extreme conditions.

Starting on Sunday, February 14, 2021, the Texas region experienced unseasonably cold weather. Temperatures in Austin (approximately the geographic center of the state) plunged to 9 degrees Fahrenheit that evening and remained below freezing until the following Friday. In Texas both fossil fuel-fired plants and wind turbines are generally not designed for extended periods of cold weather. Additionally, because Texas has a moderate climate, homebuilders have found it cost-effective to install resistive heating as standard practice—a heating method that draws large amounts of grid electricity during rare cold spells.

During the week of February 14, fossil fuel-fired generation plants, fuel supply infrastructure, and wind turbines experienced temperature-related malfunctions. In order to maintain internal temperatures, homes and businesses consumed far more electricity than normal in winter. This combination of generation plant freeze-ups and higher electricity demand caused ERCOT to order rolling blackouts from Monday, February 15 until Thursday, February 18. At the peak of the blackouts on February 15, approximately one-third of ERCOT electricity consumers were without electricity. (PowerOutage.US, February 2021)

The severity of the blackouts demonstrated that the electricity sector in Texas had not adequately planned for extreme cold weather like Winter Storm Uri. But an event of this type should have been reasonably anticipated. In February 2011, cold weather hit the Southwestern United States, resulting in freeze-ups and other malfunctions at 210 generating plants in ERCOT. Grid operators ordered a load shed of 4,000 megawatts, resulting in rolling blackouts for 3.2 million electricity customers (FERC, August 2011). Despite that experience, state regulators and utilities did little to weatherize the Texas electric grid.

Generation Planning

ERCOT and its regulator, the Public Utility Commission of Texas (PUCT), do not set requirements for specific generation resources, but instead rely on market forces to determine types of generation and their installed nameplate capacities.[1] Under the Energy-Only market model, regulators allow electricity prices to rise far above normal day-to-day levels as an incentive for utilities to invest in capacity that will remain unused much of the time. This high region of prices is referred to as "Scarcity Pricing."

The Scarcity Pricing Mechanism in ERCOT is defined in Texas Administrative Code §25.505. The price is set at one of two levels depending on "Peaker Net Margin" (PNM). PNM is a mechanism used by the PUCT in an attempt to balance the need to ensure that generators make enough profit to be financially attractive, but also not overly burdensome on consumers. PNM is set to zero at the beginning of the calendar year and then increases throughout the year depending on market prices. Until the threshold PNM value is achieved, the Systemwide Offer Cap is set at the High value (HCAP); once the threshold value is achieved the Systemwide Offer Cap is reset to the Low value (LCAP). In many years, the threshold PNM value is not achieved.

Prior to 2021, the HCAP was administratively raised several times until it reached $9,000 per megawatt-hour. The wholesale price of electricity in ERCOT for 2020 was generally $20-30 per megawatt-hour. ERCOT and the PUCT calibrate the amount of the "price cap" via economic analysis and statistical methods to incent capacity reserve margins of about 10-15%—a process that is inherently indirect and inexact. The regulatory structure in Texas had judged these reserve margins adequate to prevent blackouts except for a small number of hours each ten years (Schneider, 2020).

ERCOT is considered to be a "summer peaking" system. For summer 2020, ERCOT forecasted peak load of 75,200 megawatts while it forecast 57,699 megawatts for winter 2020-2021 (ERCOT, 2020). Much of ERCOT's attention in setting an appropriate price cap has been devoted to ensuring adequate summer generation capacity. It is notable that the price caps set by ERCOT have not been designed to vary by season while the planning process and projected reserve margins are different for winter and summer. There are no explicit capacity planning processes

---

1   According to the Glossary of the U.S. Energy Information Administration, "Generator nameplate capacity (installed)" is defined as "The maximum rated output of a generator, prime mover, or other electric power production equipment under specific conditions designated by the manufacturer. Installed generator nameplate capacity is commonly expressed in megawatts (MW) and is usually indicated on a nameplate physically attached to the generator."

within ERCOT for the so-called shoulder seasons—spring and fall—when electricity demand is normally lower. With the exception of plant outages for planned maintenance, normally conducted in the shoulder seasons, the available capacity in ERCOT is similar in all seasons.

ERCOT uses a two-step planning process for seasonal generation resources. In the first step, nameplate capacity of thermal plants is tabulated, along with derated capacity of intermittent renewable resources and imports. For wind generation, 19% to 43% of nameplate capacity is tabulated, depending on installed region. Although Texas is at a low latitude compared to other parts of the U.S. and therefore receives more intense sunlight (absent cloud cover), solar generation accounts for only 0.4% of tabulated capacity.

Figure 1 shows generation resources planned to be available during the winter of 2020-2021 as part of the first step of ERCOT's Seasonal Assessment of Resource Adequacy (SARA). The vast majority of capacity in ERCOT consists of natural gas-fired plants. Other significant sources of thermal generation include coal-fired and nuclear. There are four nuclear reactor units in ERCOT: two at the South Texas Project and two at Comanche Peak Nuclear Power Plant. Wind turbines are also a significant generation resource in Texas, with good wind conditions in the Coastal, Panhandle, and West Texas regions (West Texas is designated as "Wind-Other" in the ERCOT planning process). Hydroelectric and biomass generation have small capacities in Texas, accounting for 0.5% percent of winter capacity. Because the ERCOT balancing area is unsynchronized with the Eastern and Western Interconnections, imports are constrained to a few High Voltage Direct Current (HVDC) transmission lines and represent less than one percent of winter capacity (ERCOT, 2020).

In the second step of ERCOT's planning process, derating is applied to thermal generation plants so that all resources have deratings. Figure 2 compares final derating factors used in the ERCOT winter planning process. Texas can have frequent cloud cover in winter; accordingly, solar resources are derated to 7% of nameplate capacity. Wind resources in ERCOT are derated by region: 43% for Coastal, 32% for Panhandle, and 19% for what is predominantly West Texas ("Wind-Other"). Hydroelectric generation is a small seasonal resource in ERCOT, heavily derated at 54%. The derating for thermal plants (natural gas-fired, coal-fired, and nuclear) is 81%; their derating factor accounts for maintenance outages ("planned outages") and mechanical malfunctions ("forced outages").

In the ERCOT planning process—and other electric grid planning processes that use single point derating factors—the derating factors represent probabilistic means (or averages) of expected performance. Generation technologies can experience a range of conditions that cause actual electricity production to be well below derated capacity. For example, when the wind is not blowing on the Texas coastline, the effective derating factor will be zero percent, not 43%. Likewise, when the sun sets, the effective derating factor for solar generation is not 7%, it is zero percent. Grid planners in ERCOT and elsewhere are tempted to make optimistic assumptions that diverse generation technologies will not be impacted by the same event at the same time, but these assumptions are often not supported by logic nor experience. The fallacy of ERCOT's optimistic planning assumptions became clear when thermal plants and wind turbines froze up simultaneously in February 2021.

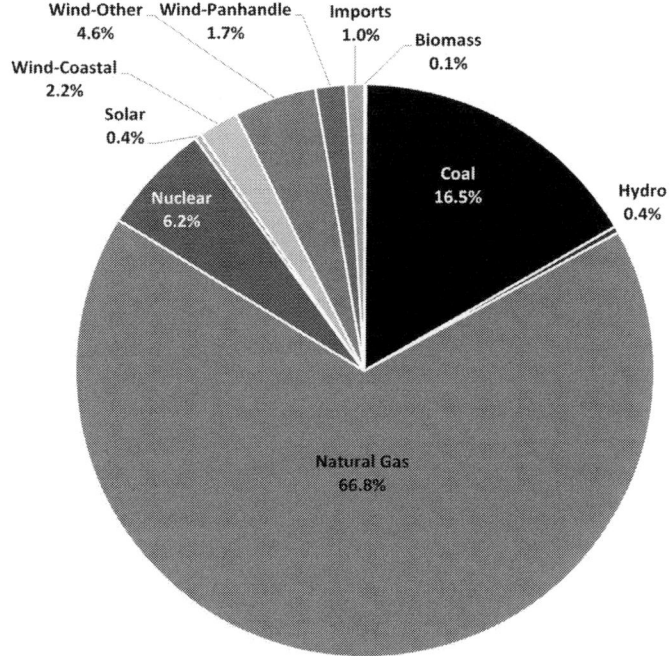

Figure 1. Winter 2020-2021 Seasonal Resources in ERCOT of 83 GW Total

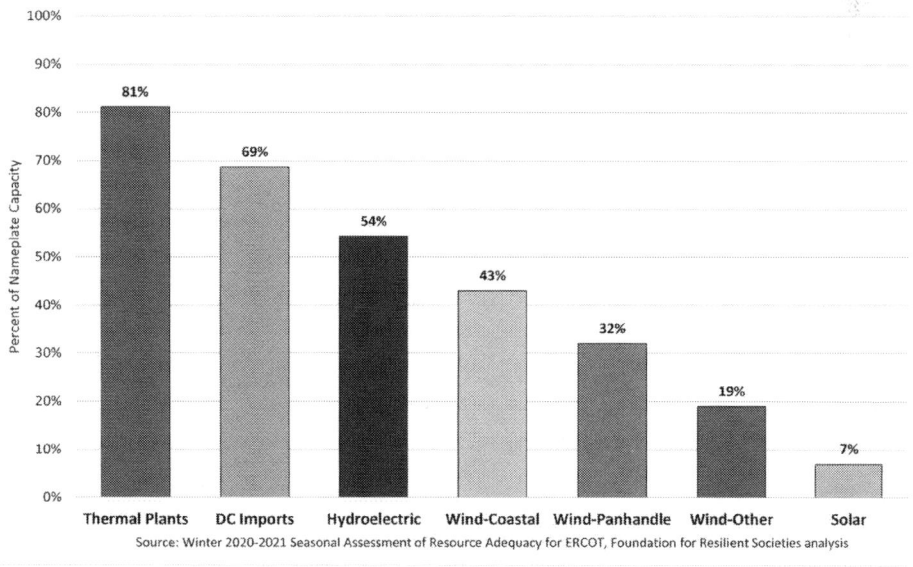

Figure 2. Derating Factors for ERCOT Winter Resource Planning

Sequence of Events

As early as February 8, a full week before rolling blackouts began in ERCOT, grid operators expected extreme conditions. "This statewide weather system is expected to bring Texas the coldest weather we've experienced in decades," said ERCOT President and CEO Bill Magness in a news release. "With temperatures rapidly declining, we are already seeing high electric use and anticipating record-breaking demand in the ERCOT region" (ERCOT, 2021).

The ERCOT regulator, the PUCT, issued its own news release on February 11. "While people often associate the dog days of summer with high electricity consumption, plummeting temperatures predicted for the next few days will place significant demand on the ERCOT grid," said Chairman DeAnn Walker in the release. "The electric system response under stress will, as always, require significant coordination between the Commission, ERCOT, and all entities responsible for providing safe and reliable power" (PUCT, 2021).

In Texas, the natural gas transmission and distribution system is regulated by the Railroad Commission of Texas (RCT). With two-thirds of ERCOT generation being gas-fired, the RCT issued an order on February 12 to reprioritize allocation of gas supplies. Under normal conditions, electric generators with interruptible contracts have fifth (and last) priority after residences and other "human needs" customers, industrial and commercial loads, factories, and operators of gas-fired boilers. The RCT order moved electric generators up to second priority, despite the lower rates (in normal times) paid by generators with interruptible contracts (RUT, 1973) (RUT, 2021).

On February 14, temperatures fell in Texas. As forecast, electricity demand increased as many homes and businesses turned on resistive heating. "We are experiencing record-breaking electric demand due to the extreme cold temperatures that have gripped Texas," said ERCOT CEO Bill Magness in a 9:50 a.m. news release. "At the same time, we are dealing with higher-than-normal generation outages due to frozen wind turbines and limited natural gas supplies available to generating units. We are asking Texans to take some simple, safe steps to lower their energy use during this time" (ERCOT, 2021).

ERCOT reliably operated its system throughout the day of February 14, but conditions degraded soon after midnight. At 12:12 a.m. on February 15, electricity reserves dropped to less than 3,000 megawatts. Three minutes later, reserves dropped below 2,300 megawatts, initiating "Emergency Operations Level 1." At 1:07 a.m. reserves, dropped below 1,750 megawatts, initiating "Emergency Operations Level 2." At 1:20 a.m., ERCOT entered "Emergency Operations Level 3." The situation continued to deteriorate, and ERCOT was soon forced to take action to prevent a cascading collapse of its system. Rolling blackouts began with 10,800 megawatts of load dropped by 2:00 a.m.—about 15% of demand at that time (ERCOT, 2021).

According to the laws of physics, the instantaneous supply of electricity must exactly equal demand at all times in an electric grid. System operators roughly balance supply and demand by "dispatching" generation plants when aggregate customer demand rises or falls. Small imbalances in supply and demand are corrected by governors at generation plants—so called "Automatic Generation Control" (AGC).

During normal operations, the system frequency of electric grids in the United States is 60 cycles per second (60 hertz). Electric grids commonly experience "disturbances"—for example, when generation plants unexpectedly trip off. At the time of a disturbance, the system of generation, transmission, distribution, and load instantaneously adjusts supply and demand without dispatch or active control by temporarily reducing system frequency. As the system frequency falls, demand goes down because electric motors and other frequency dependent loads consume less electricity. AGC systems at thermal plants then supply more fuel to turbines and boilers to increase generation, increasing system frequency. In a similar process at hydroelectric plants, AGC systems increase water flow through turbines. If plants cannot promptly increase their generation, then protective devices in the grid will automatically shed load to regain system balance and return system frequency to 60 hertz—so-called "Under Frequency Load Shedding" (UFLS).

When system frequency drops below 60 hertz for more than a few minutes, this can cause vibrations, fatigue, and permanent failure of turbine blades in thermal generation plants. Accordingly, both ERCOT and the North American Electric Reliability Corporation (NERC)[2] have set UFLS frequency thresholds and time limits to preserve system stability and prevent equipment damage. In the ERCOT system, load is automatically shed when system frequency is below 59.4 hertz for 9 minutes or more (ERCOT, 2021).

The proximate cause of the load drop ordered by ERCOT was a rapid sequence of generation outages—6,078 megawatts in total between 1:20 a.m. and 2:03 a.m. Generation plants initially tripped off because of temperature-related malfunctions (ERCOT, 2021). However, as plants tripped off, the frequency of the ERCOT system rapidly declined, which may have induced other plants to trip off to protect their equipment—even before the 9-minute threshold for UFLS (Texas House of Representatives, 2021).

On February 15 at 1:51 a.m., ERCOT system frequency dropped below 59.4 hertz and stayed below that level for 4 minutes and 37 seconds. Had the frequency remained below this threshold for 9 minutes, UFLS would have been automatically imposed, potentially destabilizing the system and causing a cascading collapse

---

2 The North American Electric Reliability Corporation is the accredited standard-setting body for the high voltage portions of the U.S. and Canadian electric grids. NERC has been selected for this role by its federal regulator, FERC, and has been given authority to both set and enforce reliability standards.

throughout ERCOT. Even without UFLS, damage to generator turbines could have caused long-term plant outages. To maintain reserve margins and prevent additional frequency dips, ERCOT ordered preemptive load sheds at distribution utilities until Thursday, February 18 (ERCOT, 2021).

Figure 3 below shows ERCOT forecast demand versus generation resources available during the February load sheds. The black portion of the chart shows the timing and estimated amount of preemptive load sheds. When load is shed, it is impossible to precisely determine that amount of electricity that consumers would have used if load had not been shed. Therefore, the black part of the chart is the difference between *forecast demand* (based on temperature, time of day, day of week, and past patterns of electricity demand) and actual generation.

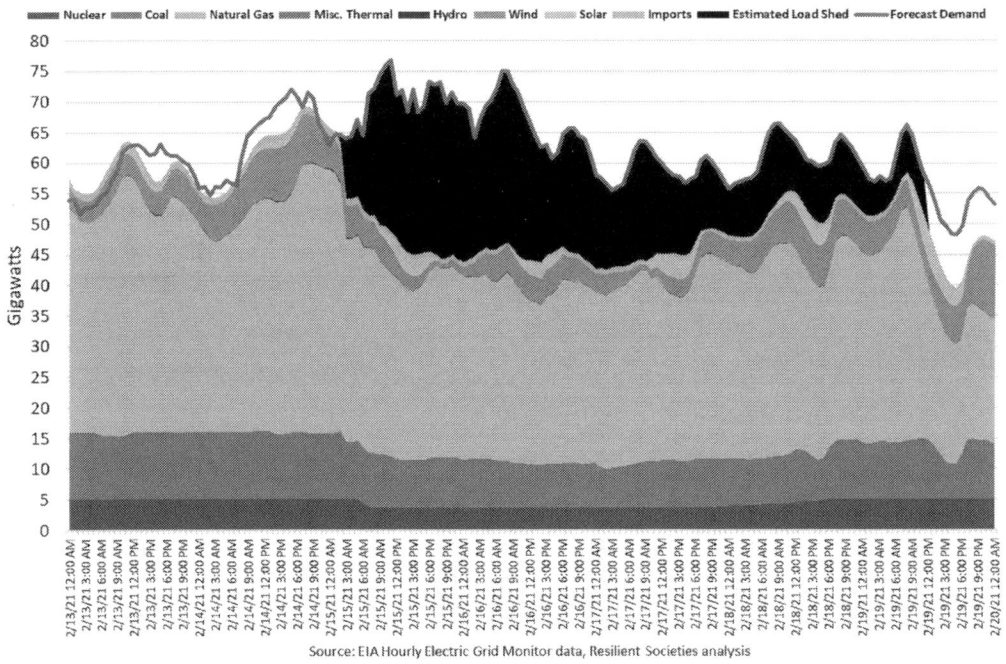

Figure 3. Demand vs. Resources during February 2021 Load Sheds in ERCOT

Figure 3 also shows the types of generation available from February 13 through February 19. Most nuclear reactors, represented in the purple portion of the chart, provided reliable baseload power throughout this period. However, Unit 1 at South Texas Project tripped off due to cold weather on February 15 and took several days to recover. Coal-fired plants, represented by the color gray, initially provided nearly constant baseload power until they began to trip off the morning of February 15. Natural gas-fired plants, represented by light blue, supplied the majority of load. Wind turbines, represented by green, provided significant amounts of non-dispatchable power before the load sheds, but less as they froze up during the week. Solar power, represented by yellow, contributed to load only during daylight hours. Hydroelectric power and imports, represented by the colors dark blue and pink, respectively, contributed negligible amounts to load (EIA, 2021).

While aggressive load sheds avoided a total collapse of the ERCOT system during the early morning of February 15, significant outages continued throughout the day. At 10:11 p.m., 4,395,193 out of 12,448,564 customers were blacked out (PowerOutage.US, 2021). Blackouts were intended to be "rolling"—or rotating among affected customers—but distribution utilities also tried to keep feeders to critical infrastructure such as water purification plants and hospitals continuously energized. As a result, some customers were continuously blacked out for days while others had no interruption of power at all.

One of the most contentious events during this period took place the evening of Monday, February 15. The PUCT met in emergency session due to the concern that real time electricity prices were well below the HCAP level of $9,000/megawatt-hour and that these prevailing prices were too low to incent generation to be available for dispatch. The PUCT approved an Order for PUC Project No. 51617, which consisted of two major provisions: (1) directed ERCOT to manually force the real time price to the HCAP level of $9.000/megawatt-hour as long as load sheds were required; and (2) kept the HCAP in place even though the PNM threshold value was about to be reached, which should have triggered the LCAP (PUCT, 2021). While Provision 1 has received significant press coverage and achieved a national level of notoriety, Provision 2 has received scant attention. In brief, had the PUCT not taken action to avert the triggering of the LCAP, we calculate that an additional $25 billion of cost would have been added to the bills of ERCOT customers due to the spike in natural gas prices.

By the morning of February 17, ERCOT had been able to restore power to a small fraction of the households affected, 1.6 million (ERCOT, 2021). On February 18, ERCOT Senior Director of System Operations Dan Woodfin said, "We're to the point in the load restoration where we are allowing transmission owners to bring back any load they can related to this load shed event." Remaining outages on this day were due to ice storm damage, the need for manual restoration with line crews, and closure of large industrial facilities that had gone offline voluntarily (ERCOT, 2021). As of 7:30 a.m. on February 19, 20,000 megawatts of thermal generation and 14,000 megawatts of wind and solar generation remained on forced outage (ERCOT, 2021). Later that same day, rising temperatures decreased customer demand, allowing all outages to be restored.

ERCOT narrowly avoided an alternative course of events, a disastrous long-term blackout. As CEO Magness testified in March before the U.S. House Energy and Commerce Committee, "Avoiding a complete blackout is critical. Were it to occur, the Texas grid could be down for several days or weeks while the damage to the electrical grid was repaired and the power restored in a phased and highly controlled process … As terrible as the consequences of the controlled outages in

February were, if we had not stopped the blackout, power could have been out for over 90% of Texans for weeks" (Rev.com, 2021).

To recover from a complete blackout, electric utilities use small "blackstart" generators to re-energize larger power plants. Blackstart is difficult because increasing generation must be coordinated with lumpy additions to demand—a process that can cause protective devices in the grid to trip. Adding to this avoided challenge for ERCOT, later research by the *Wall Street Journal* revealed that nine of 13 primary blackstart generators were out of commission at times during the Storm Uri event and six of 15 secondary generators had periodic trouble (Smith, 2021).

Causes

Even while the ERCOT blackouts were still ongoing, robust disagreement about the causes emerged. Four operational causes were proposed early on: higher than expected customer demand due to the low temperatures, thermal plants freezing up, dependence on wind turbines that likewise froze up, and shortages of natural gas for plants relying on this fuel source.

Quantified analysis using EIA data found that electric generation plants of all types failed to perform during the February 2021 deep freeze of Winter Storm Uri. Figure 4 shows actual generation from four major generation types—natural gas, coal, nuclear, and wind—as a percent of specified generation in the ERCOT Seasonal Assessment of Resource Adequacy (SARA) for winter 2020-2021. During the period of rolling blackouts, as represented in the gray portion of the chart, all four generation types performed well below planned capacity.

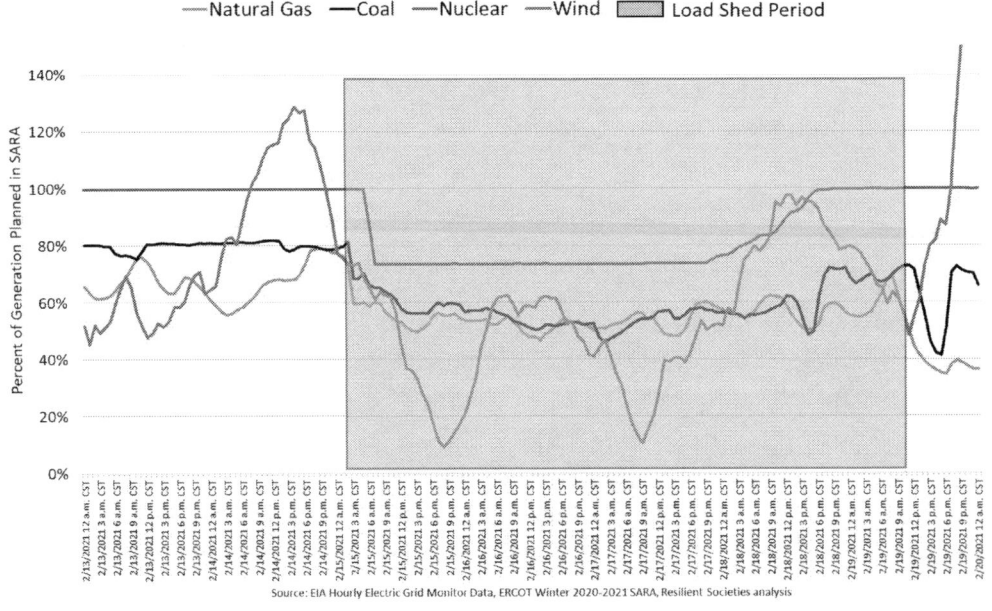

Figure 4. Actual ERCOT Generation in February 2021 as a Percent of Planned Capacity

Moreover, even if ERCOT's generation plants had performed as planned, a blackout still would have occurred because electricity demand was far in excess of the upper bound in the SARA. Figure 5 shows demand at the previous winter peak on January 17, 2018; peak demand for the extreme weather scenario in the winter SARA; planned resources for winter 2020-2021; actual resources on February 15 at 11 a.m.; and estimated peak demand on February 15 at 11 a.m. At planned capacity, ERCOT would have been short nearly 10,000 megawatts at 11 a.m. and short at other times, too, over the course of the blackouts.

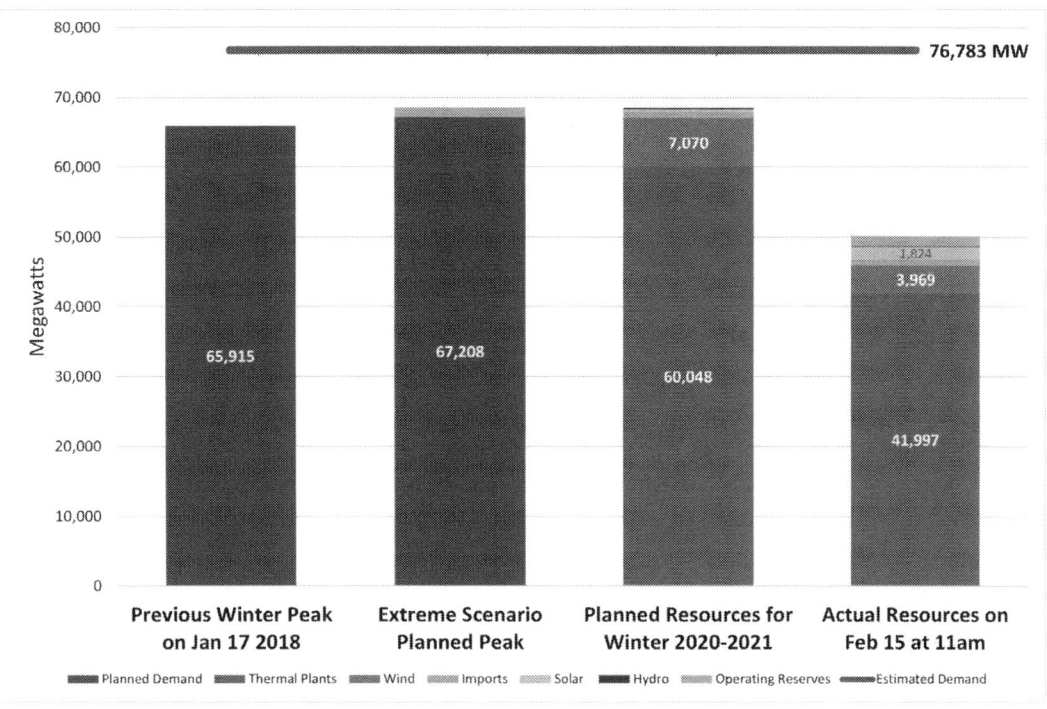

Figure 5. Estimated Peak Demand (76,783 MW) in ERCOT on February 15 at 11 a.m. vs. Resources

Figure 6 shows the megawatt contributions to load sheds on February 15 at 11 a.m. The No. 1 cause was forced outages at thermal plants (18,051 megawatts), followed by demand over the planned scenario (9,575 megawatts). Wind turbine deficits contributed a minor proportion (3,101 megawatts). At this time in the day, solar generation slightly over performed (1,520 megawatts). The contributions of hydroelectric holdbacks and import deficits were negligible (EIA, 2021).

The impact of rolling blackouts on natural gas supplies to generating plants during the February event was a topic of high interest during hearings in the Texas State Legislature. Anecdotally, there were reports of power to oil fields being diverted to hospitals and nursing homes. Because most natural gas production in Texas is "associated gas"—or gas that is obtained as a byproduct of pumping oil from the ground—when power to oil pumps was shut off, gas production stopped as well. Additionally, some pipeline compressors in Texas are powered exclusively by electricity; when electricity to their feeders was shut off, this had the effect of reducing gas pressure and volume of delivered gas to generation plants (Adams-Heard, 2021).

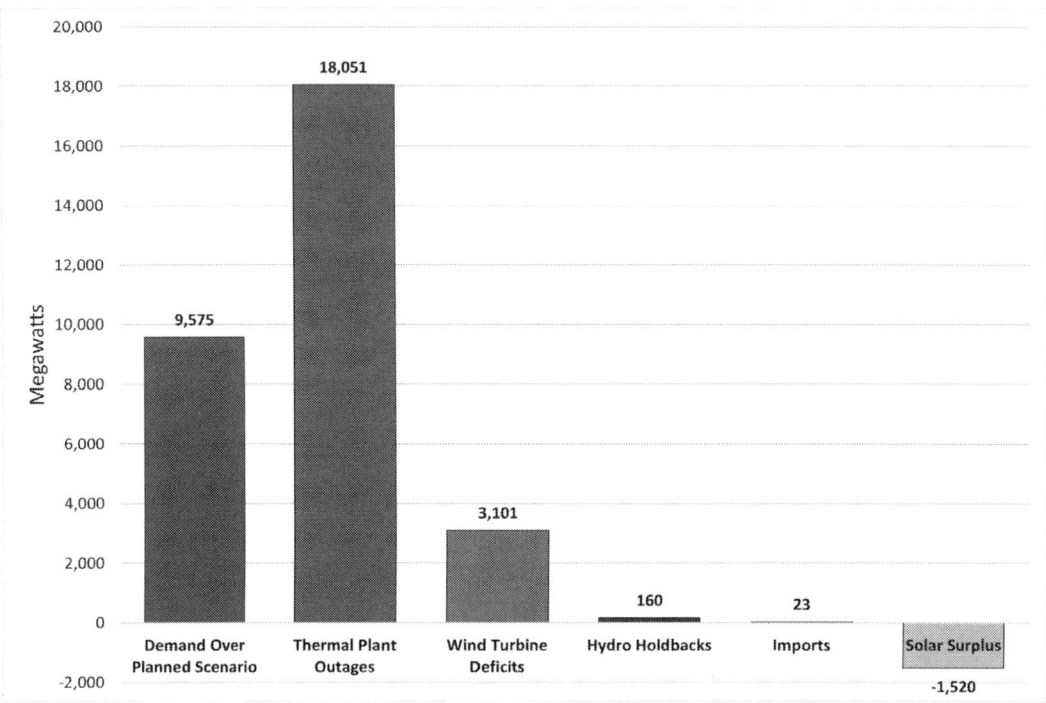

Figure 6. Peak Demand Contributions to Load Sheds in ERCOT on February 15 at 11 a.m.

On April 6, 2021, ERCOT submitted a "Preliminary Report on Causes of Generator Outages and Derates For Operating Days February 14 – 19, 2021 Extreme Cold Weather Event" to the PUCT. Legal restrictions prohibited release of information on individual plant outages, preventing detailed analysis by generation type. However, ERCOT did disclose the megawatts and proportions of generator outages and derates at their peak of 51,173 megawatts at 8:00am on February 16: Existing Outages of 7,487 megawatts (15%); Weather Related of 27,472 megawatts (54%); Fuel Limitations of 6,124 megawatts (12%); Equipment Issues of 6,986 megawatts (14%); Transmission Loss of 1,259 megawatts (2%); Frequency Related of 1,260 megawatts (2%); and Miscellaneous of 585 megawatts (1%) (ERCOT, 2021).

From the winter SARA, we know that natural gas fired generation had nameplate capacity of 52,091 megawatts (ERCOT, 2021). We can reasonably assume no fuel limitations at nuclear and coal-fired plants during the cold weather because they have large quantities of fuel stored on-site. We instead assume all fuel limitations were at gas-fired plants. This allows a calculation of the proportion of gas-fired generation in outage because of fuel limitations: 6,124 megawatts/ 52,091 megawatts = 12%—a significant amount.

Consequences

The consequences of ERCOT's rolling blackouts during Winter Storm Uri have been severe. They include higher costs for electricity ratepayers, bankruptcy-inducing charges to utilities, property damage at homes and businesses, and loss of life.

For the month of February 2020, wholesale electricity prices in the ERCOT real-time market averaged $26 per megawatt-hour. For February 2021, wholesale electricity prices averaged $1,783—an increase of 68 times (Potomac Research, 2021). For 87.5 hours during the week of February 14, wholesale prices were forced to the HCAP price cap of $9,000 per megawatt-hour (Griddy, 2021). Some additional electricity charges will eventually flow through retailers to ratepayers, but significant losses will be incurred by generation and distribution utilities, too.

Exelon Corporation operates three large gas-fired plants within ERCOT—Colorado Bend II, Wolf Hollow II, and Handley. These plants experienced forced outages due to the cold weather and were unable to supply electricity as contracted. Exelon estimates impact to company income of between $560 million and $710 million (Exelon, 2021).

Brazos Electric Cooperative is the largest generation and transmission power cooperative in Texas, serving 1.5 million citizens. Before the events of February 15-19, Brazos was financially strong with "A" to "A+" credit ratings. Brazos refused to pass charges from ERCOT through to their distribution member cooperatives—charges that would have been ultimately paid by individual ratepayers. Brazos instead declared bankruptcy on March 1 (Brazos, 2021).

Griddy Energy was a company with a distinctive business model. Each month Griddy charged its customers a flat rate of $9.99 plus an additional usage charge. The usage charge was calculated by multiplying the real-time wholesale rate of electricity times the kilowatt-hours consumed. The week before the blackouts, Griddy encouraged customers to switch to other electricity retailers but 24,000 customers remained. When the wholesale rate spiked to $9,000 per megawatt-hour ($9 per kilowatt-hour) the week of February 14, additional charges for the average Griddy customer were approximately $1,200 each. Griddy declared bankruptcy on March 15. State Attorney General Ken Paxton and a class action law firm sued to protect Griddy customers from the excess charges. If these lawsuits are successful, unpaid invoices from ERCOT to Griddy will be allocated to other ERCOT retailers (Griddy, 2021; KXII Staff, 2021; Portello-Ronk, 2021; Chediak, 2021).

The total amount of generator, distributor, and retailer losses and excess ratepayer charges during the period of extreme electricity prices cannot be precisely determined from publicly available data, but a range can be estimated. For

ERCOT operating days February 15-21, the total amount of funds obligated to be paid to market participants was $15.2 billion (Ogelman, 2021). However, in Texas a significant amount of electricity is traded in bilateral contracts between generators and distributors—trading that settles outside of the ERCOT market. To calculate a rough upper bound of utility losses and excess charges—including the bilateral trades—we multiplied the electricity consumed in ERCOT during the time of the load sheds (5,048 megawatt-hours) (U.S. Energy Information Administration, 2021) times the HCAP price cap ($9,000 per megawatt-hour). The result was an upper bound figure of $45.4 billion, which compares closely with another published estimate of $47 billion (McWilliams, 2021). A midpoint estimate of utility losses and excess ratepayer charges taken together would be $30 billion.

EIA data shows the vast majority of losses related to the electricity sector were initially taken by generators and retailers, not by consumers. In February 2020, sales of electricity to ultimate consumers totaled $2.578 billion. For February 2021, this figure was $3.951 billion—a moderate difference of $1.373 billion month-to-month compared to total losses on the order of $30 billion. We therefore estimate that losses initially taken by generators and retailers were approximately 95% of total losses related to the electricity sector. Consumer price increases were small; average prices for residential consumers in Texas rose only moderately from $11.96 per megawatt hour in January 2021 to $12.74 per megawatt hour in February 2021 (U.S. Energy Information Administration, 2021). Nonetheless, electricity retailers could try to recover some of their Storm Uri losses through future price increases to consumers, while generators might attempt to bid higher prices in the day-to-day wholesale electricity market.

Who principally gained from high electricity prices? Operators of reliable generation plants made large profits, per the intended design of the Energy Only market system. Suppliers of natural gas also profited from higher prices charged to generators. During the week of February 14, prices at OneOK Gas Transmission soared to $1,250 per million BTU before returning to normal levels of $3 per million BTU. During the same week, spot gas at the Houston Ship Channel hit $400 per million BTU (Gonzales, 2021). As another indicator, revenues for Kinder Morgan, a large natural gas pipeline and storage operator in Texas, surged to $5,211 million in the first quarter of 2021 from $3,106 million in the prior-year quarter; adjusted earnings increased by $907 million. Company executives attributed the better results to one-time gains from Winter Storm Uri (Kinder Morgan, 2021).

Other economic impacts of the Uri blackouts include loss of business and personal income, supply chain interruptions, and property damage when pipes froze. AccuWeather estimated $130 billion of economic damages in Texas (Insurance Journal, 2021). The Perryman Group, an economic consulting firm, estimated damages between $85.8 billion and $128.7 billion (Perryman Group, 2021). Adding $30 billion of utility losses and excess ratepayer charges to other economic losses would result in an estimate for total economic losses between $116 and $159 billion.

In addition to economic losses, numerous lives were lost due to the cold weather and associated blackouts. On April 9, the Texas Department of State Health Services estimated 133 deaths between February 11 and March 5, with the majority due to hypothermia—a preventable cause of death when reliable electricity service is maintained (Texas Department of State Health Services, 2021).

Cures

Multiple cures have been proposed for the conditions that lead to the ERCOT blackouts during Winter Storm Uri. These include reliability standards that would require weatherization, a higher price cap for electricity prices, auction-based incentive payments for generators to maintain capacity ("capacity market"), payments to generators out-of-market to maintain capacity (typically called "Reliability Must Run" contracts), and a return to cost-of-service regulation. Some have suggested that Texas should integrate its grid with the electric grids of other states, a move that would place ERCOT under market and transmission tariff regulation of FERC.

Presently, federal regulation of the Texas grid is confined to the mandatory system of NERC reliability standards; FERC does not regulate the ERCOT market system. In their report on the 2011 Southwest Cold Weather Event, FERC and NERC staff confirmed that NERC and its regional delegate, the Texas Reliability Entity, have authority to set mandatory reliability standards for ERCOT, but did not recommend a standard be set for weatherization. At the time of the February 2021 blackouts, NERC had initiated a project for a weatherization standard, but this effort was years away from completion at the normal pace of standards development. Enforcement of NERC standards has been light-handed, with few monetary fines and administrative exceptions often granted. While FERC has legal authority to require more stringent standards and stronger enforcement, it has been cautious in exercising this authority.

When capacity shortfalls have occurred in ERCOT, the repeatedly imposed "solution" has been to raise the market price cap. To incent more generation capacity, ERCOT increased the HCAP market price cap five times between February 2011 and June 2015, starting at $2,250 per megawatt hour and ending at $9,000 per megawatt hour.

The February 2021 blackouts demonstrated that even $9,000 per megawatt-hour is not enough to incent reliable generation or reduce consumer demand. Why? Because generators can recoup reliability investments only when prices spike very high; these rare events are likely to fall outside the tenure of most utility executives. These same executives are evaluated quarterly on other performance metrics, such as profit and loss. Executive incentives are therefore skewed against long term investments such as weatherization. Moreover, no amount of financial or managerial incentive can cause new generation capacity to be constructed during an energy emergency. In regard to demand reduction incentives, high wholesale electricity prices are unlikely to cause most residential consumers to turn off their heat and risk burst pipes (or hypothermia), especially if the consumers are on rate plans that protect against price spikes. Some industrial users of electricity did voluntarily stop consuming, but this reduced demand was not enough to prevent blackouts for residential consumers.

On March 3, 2021, the PUCT reinstated the ERCOT price cap to the LCAP, which at the time was the higher of either $2,000 per megawatt hour or 50 times the natural gas fuel index price at Katy, Texas. Since then, the PUCT has begun the process (through Project No. 51871) to reduce the natural gas multiplier from 50 to 25 to avoid "absurd results" in the future.

So-called "capacity markets" are an adjunct to the daily electricity markets operated in other RTOs/ISOs such as PJM, NYISO, and ISO-New England. Generator payments for installed capacity are auctioned, typically 1-3 years in advance of the performance period. Capacity payments can be quite large—for example, in New England capacity payments are approximately one-third of the total payments for wholesale power.

A fundamental issue with capacity markets is that the market rules are set by the market participants—including operators of generation plants—consistent with the industry-dominated governance systems of RTO/ISOs. Within the FERC review and approval process, opponents of RTO/ISO market rules have a high legal bar. Financial penalties are a key part of capacity market rules—i.e., the amount of money generators must return to the RTO/ISO if their contracted capacity is not available during a declared energy emergency. Such financial penalties can be a small fraction of overall payments to generators. Therefore, a viable business strategy for generators is to underinvest in reliability improvements and simply pay the penalty if the plant is in forced outage during an energy emergency. But if financial penalties were set higher, this could dissuade participants from entering the capacity market.

When market failures for reliable generation have occurred in RTO/ISO outside of Texas, out-of-market payments—so-called Reliability Must Run (RMR) contracts—have been a costly remedy. In recent years FERC has allowed RMR contracts for Southern California and the Boston area. More recently, Berkshire Hathaway Energy proposed the construction of ten new natural gas fired plants in ERCOT for $8.3 billion. These plants would operate only during energy emergencies. The Berkshire plants would store natural gas on-site, alleviating the problems experienced with fuel supply during the February blackouts. Competing generation companies testified before the Texas State Legislature that this proposal would be unfair because it would undercut previous decisions to invest in generation plants. Moreover, competitors said these emergency generators could cause day-to-day capacity in the Energy Only market to exit—ostensibly because existing generators could not look forward to recouping new investments in reliability during times of high prices.

A *Morning Consult* survey released on February 24 indicated that "56% of U.S. voters say Texas should connect its electric grid with those of other regions, while 24% said the state should continue its independent operation" (Morning Consult, 2021). Presumably, the interests of the vast majority of U.S. voters diverge from Texan interests—but constituents outside of Texas would indirectly have a say in the management of the State's grid if it were to be integrated with the Eastern Interconnection and placed under federal regulation. Sentiment among Texas policymakers has been different. Former Texas Governor Rick Perry was quoted as saying, "Texans would be without electricity for longer than three days to keep the federal government out of their business."

The potential federal regulator, FERC, has responsibilities that go far beyond regulation of electricity markets. FERC is also responsible for hydroelectric dam permits, pipeline approvals and their tariff regulation, liquified natural gas facilities, and grid reliability standards for the nation as a whole. Each year FERC processes thousands of orders, permits and rulemakings. The amount of attention that FERC could give to the problems of Texas would be constrained. Additionally, FERC rulings would necessarily balance the interests of Texas with those of other states.

A rationale for the integration of electric grids is greater resilience; presumably, a system encountering a disturbance or electricity shortage could rely on its neighbor's resources. However, for wide-area events extending beyond the border of a balancing area, reserves in other systems may not be available. Potential wide area events include extremely hot and cold weather, natural gas pipeline interruptions, geomagnetic disturbance (also called "solar storms"), cyberattack, physical attack, electromagnetic attack, and propagating disturbances that result in grid islanding or cascading collapse.

Real-world experience shows that integration of the ERCOT system with neighboring interconnections may have marginal benefit while increasing risk. During the February 2021 events, neighboring electric grids experienced their own power deficits and some imposed rolling backouts. Furthermore, the magnitude of the ERCOT blackouts would have dwarfed reserves likely available in neighboring systems: even California ISO, the largest importer of electricity, imports at most 12 gigawatts while the deficit in ERCOT during February 2021 was over twice that amount. A disturbance in a neighboring electric grid can cause a wide-area cascading collapse—as happened in August 2003, when a transmission disturbance starting in Ohio propagated through Ontario and eight U.S. states. The resulting blackout affected 55 million people.

A potential cure for Texas' market ills would be a return to the "cost-of-service" regulatory system. Roughly one-third of the U.S. still operates under the cost-of-service regulatory model for electricity generation. Under this model, needed generation would be planned by utilities and renumeration would be approved by the PUCT. Most states in an RTO/ISO market system would have difficulty exiting, but Texas would have an easier pathway. Texas has its own electric grid with minimal imports and substantial in-state generation. Importantly, Texas has avoided market regulation by FERC and therefore could return to a cost-of-service model solely by action of its legislature.

By establishing a "deregulated" electricity market, regulators for Texas and other states had hoped to eliminate ratemaking cases and also lower electricity rates for consumers. The subjective nature of ratemaking cases under the cost-of-service model makes it difficult for regulators to enforce efficiencies in plant construction and operation. Under the cost-of-service model, cost overruns for ambitious (or unnecessary) generation projects can be placed upon electricity consumers.

However, recent experience demonstrates that a return to the cost-of-service system could be less expensive for Texas consumers—especially when the extraordinary charges of rare events are factored in. Shortly after the February blackouts, the *Wall Street Journal* published a study titled, "Texas Electric Bills Were $28 Billion Higher Under Deregulation." By comparing rates for consumers in the cost-of-service portions of Texas to the rates in the ERCOT portion, the authors concluded that rates in the cost-of-service portion were 8% lower, on average. The authors also found that consumers in ERCOT paid $28 billion more for their power from 2004 to 2020 than if they had paid rates charged to consumers in the cost-of-service portions of Texas during the same period. Studies by the Texas Coalition for Affordable Power, a government purchasing cooperative, came to similar findings (McGinty, 2021).

We analyzed electricity rate data provided by the EIA. These data show the total electricity rate by state for each year beginning in 1990. The total rate is a combination of the residential, commercial, industry and transportation categories tracked by the EIA (and "other" prior to 2003) (EIA, 2020). Below in Figure 7, we show the result of comparing the average annual electricity rates for Texas, New Mexico, and the U.S. average. New Mexico was selected for comparison for three reasons: (1) New Mexico has retained a cost-of-service electric system; (2) Texas and New Mexico share a long common border; and (3) the Permian basin straddles the common border. The fracking revolution in the Permian basin has been the defining event of the U.S. oil and gas industry in the 21st century and has had a profound influence on the cost of fuel used to generate electricity.

As shown in Figure 7, Texas electricity rates have varied wildly, peaking in 2008 before dropping to a fairly stable level in 2012. By comparison, rates in New

Mexico have risen relatively slowly. Although the rate increase from 1996, when ERCOT began operating the competitive market, to 2019 is less than the U.S. average, it is more than that experienced in New Mexico. And we already know that the 2021 rate for Texas will be significantly higher because of the Storm Uri event. The assertion by one prominent electricity market advocate that "Having straddled the divide between traditional cost-of-service regulation and modern market-based competition, I can assure you the competitive model is the better way to bring price, service and technological innovation benefits to customers" is not consistent with these data (Wood, 2021).

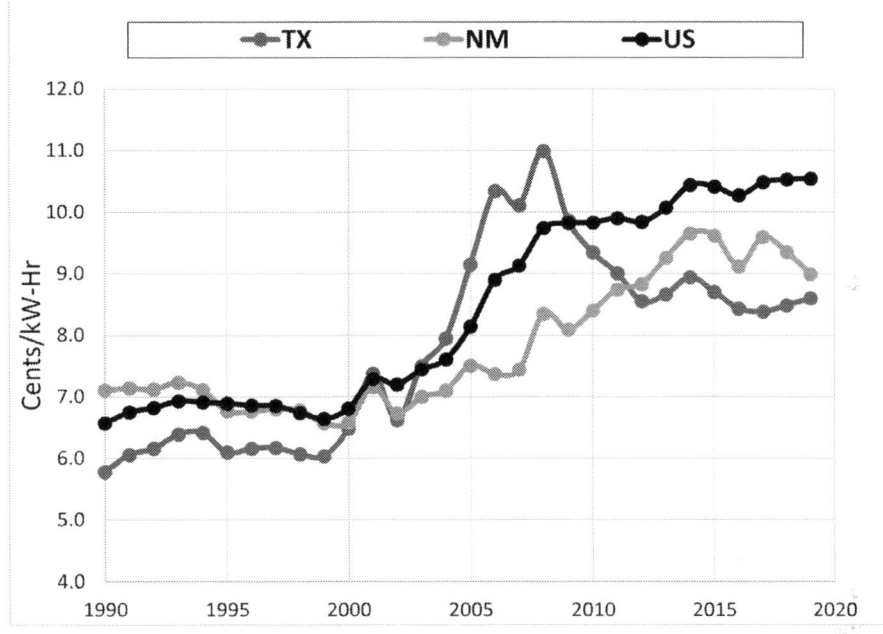

Figure 7. Comparison of Average Electricity Rates in Texas, New Mexico, and the U.S. Average

Other than lower costs to ratepayers, the advantages of the cost-of-service model could be substantial. The types and capacities of generation can be selected for their cost, reliability, and carbon emissions. There is a direct pathway between planned capacity and constructed capacity. Most importantly, if a blackout occurs, the responsible parties can be easily identified and held accountable—and this alone could make blackouts less likely.

Conclusions

For 25 years, Texas has operated the Wild West of electricity markets. During Winter Storm Uri in February 2021, financial losses and human casualties resulted. Repeated increases in the market price cap did not incent sufficient reliable generation but did result in large losses to the electricity sector. Losses also resulted for a small proportion of unfortunate consumers whose rates were tied to wholesale prices, i.e., "Griddy" customers. No financial incentive can increase generation capacity when a blackout is already underway. A total collapse of the ERCOT system was narrowly avoided—not by market forces, but by direct action of grid operators.

Most elaborations of ERCOT's Energy Only electricity market have potential defects. In an Energy Only market, generators have no ready means to recover the cost of reliability improvements and therefore are likely to resist weatherization—whether reliability standards require this or not. Capacity markets provide large payments to market participants without assurance that capacity will be available in an emergency. RMR contracts are expensive and temporary solutions that can also distort day-to-day electricity markets. Integration with neighboring electric grids does not provide sure benefits during wide-area events that also affect neighboring electric grids. In addition to a shared shortage of capacity during extreme weather and other wide-area energy emergencies, integration could also increase susceptibility to cascading collapses.

Because Texas has an independent electric grid that is not regulated by FERC, this State is well-situated for a return to the cost-of-service regulatory model. Under the cost-of-service model, the State could make direct decisions for its generation strategy—including types of generation and their capacities. With direct decisions come accountability. The cost-of-service model could reduce the probability of future blackouts while avoiding the egregious financial losses and human casualties experienced under the current market-based system.

Acknowledgements

The authors gratefully acknowledge the assistance of the late William R. Harris in the research for this article.

Acronyms and Abbreviations

AGC	Automatic Generation Control
BTU	British Thermal Unit
DC	Direct Current
EIA	U.S. Energy Information Administration
ERCOT	Electric Reliability Council of Texas
HVDC	High Voltage Direct Current

FERC	Federal Energy Regulatory Commission
HCAP	High system wide offer cap
ISO	Independent System Operator
LCAP	Low system wide offer cap
NERC	North American Electric Reliability Corporation
PNM	Peaker Net Margin
PUCT	Public Utility Commission of Texas
RMR	Reliability Must Run
RTO	Regional Transmission Organization
RUT	Railroad Commission of Texas
SARA	Seasonal Assessment of Resource Adequacy
UFLS	Under Frequency Load Shedding

Author Capsule Bios

Thomas S. Popik is Chairman and President of the Foundation for Resilient Societies, a nonprofit dedicated to the protection of critical infrastructure from infrequently occurring disasters. He specializes in the regulation of electric grids for reliability under both the cost-of-service and market-based models. He has testified on electric grid reliability before the Federal Energy Regulatory Commission, the Canadian Parliament, and the legislatures of multiple U.S. states and has been quoted in the *Wall Street Journal, Politico, The Economist, Reuters,* and *USA Today.* Mr. Popik holds a Master of Business Administration from Harvard Business School and a Bachelor of Science in Mechanical Engineering from MIT. In his early career, Mr. Popik served as an officer in the U.S. Air Force, with a final rank of Captain.

Richard H. Humphreys studies issues associated with the U.S. electric grid following a 35+ year career in the defense industry. He currently serves on the Board of Directors of the Foundation for Resilient Societies. He spent the bulk of his career with the Boeing Lasers and Electro-Optics group in California and Lockheed Martin's Laser and Sensor Systems group outside of Seattle, Washington. At both Boeing and Lockheed Martin, he served in various management roles, primarily as Program Manager. As Program Manager, he was responsible for leading teams of engineers and scientists in advancing High Energy Laser technology. His teams were successful in advancing fiber laser technology from laboratory proof of concept to fielded weapon systems. He earned B.S. and M.S. degrees from MIT in Chemical Engineering. During his Air Force career, he was stationed at the Air Force Weapons (now Research) Lab, New Mexico and Ft. Meade, Maryland. He continued in the Air Force Reserves, attaining the rank of Major.

References

Adams-Heard, Rachel; Blas, Jarier; and Chediak, Mark. (2021, February). "A Giant Flaw in Texas Blackouts: It Cut Power to Gas Supplies." Retrieved from www.bloomberg.com: https://www.bloomberg.com/news/articles/2021-02-20/a-giant-flaw-in-texas-blackouts-it-cut-power-to-gas-supplies

Blunt, Katherine and Gold, Russell. (2021, February). The Texas Freeze: Why the Power Grid Failed. Retrieved from www.wsj.com: https://www.wsj.com/articles/texas-freeze-power-grid-failure-electricity-market-incentives-11613777856

Blunt, Katherine and Gold, Russell. (2021, February). Amid Blackouts, Texas Scrapped Its Power Market and Raised Prices. It Didn't Work.. Retrieved from www.wsj.com: https://www.wsj.com/articles/texas-power-regulators-decision-to-raise-prices-in-freeze-generates-criticism-11614268158

Brazos Electric Cooperative. (2021, March 1). Brazos Electric Power Cooperative, Inc. Files for Chapter 11 Financial Restructuring. Retrieved from www.brazoselectric.com: http://www.brazoselectric.com/pressrelease.pdf

Chediak, Mark et. al. (2021, February 26). Ercot Still Short $1.3 Billion in Energy Payments: Texas Update. Retrieved from www.bloomberg.com: https://www.bloomberg.com/news/articles/2021-02-26/bankruptcies-loom-from-enormous-obligations-texas-update

Coy, Peter. (2021, February). Ercot's 711-Page Training Manual Tells a Power-Grid Horror Story. Retrieved from www.bloomberg.com: https://www.bloomberg.com/news/articles/2021-02-22/ercot-s-711-page-training-manual-tells-a-power-grid-horror-story

Electric Reliability Council of Texas. (2020, May). Final Seasonal Assessment of Resource Adequacy for the ERCOT Region (SARA) June-September 2020 Retrieved from www.ercot.com: http://www.ercot.com/content/wcm/lists/197378/SARA-FinalSummer2020.xlsx

Electric Reliability Council of Texas. (2020, May). Report on Capacity, Demand and Reserves (CDR) in the ERCOT Region, 2021-2020. Retrieved from www.

ercot.com: http://www.ercot.com/cotent/wcm/lists/197379/CapacityDemandandReserveReport_May2020.xlsx

Electric Reliability Council of Texas. (2020, November). Final Seasonal Assessment of Resource Adequacy for the ERCOT Region (SARA) Winter 2020/2021 Retrieved from www.ercot.com: http://www.ercot.com/content/wcm/lists/197378/SARA-FinalWinter2020-2021.pdf

Electric Reliability Council of Texas. (2021, February 11). Extreme cold weather expected to result in record electric use in ERCOT region. Retrieved from ercot.com: http://www.ercot.com/news/releases/show/224996

Electric Reliability Council of Texas. (2021, February 14). Grid operator requests energy conservation for system reliability. Retrieved from ercot.com: http://www.ercot.com/news/releases/show/225151

Electric Reliability Council of Texas. (2021, February 17). Grid operator continues to restore power. Retrieved from ercot.com: http://www.ercot.com/news/releases/show/225696

Electric Reliability Council of Texas. (2021, February 18). Majority of customers are able to be restored, but electric companies still restoring outages in the field. Retrieved from ercot.com: http://www.ercot.com/news/releases/show/225742

Electric Reliability Council of Texas. (2018, April 4). Inertia: Basic Concepts and Impacts on the ERCOT Grid. Retrieved from ercot.com: http://www.ercot.com/content/wcm/lists/144927/Inertia_Basic_Concepts_Impacts_On_ERCOT_v0.pdf

Electric Reliability Council of Texas. (2021, April 6). Preliminary Report on Causes of Generator Outages and Derates For Operating Days February 14 – 19, 2021 Extreme Cold Weather Event. Retrieved from ercot.com: http://www.ercot.com/content/wcm/lists/226521/51878_ERCOT_Letter_re_Preliminary_Report_on_Outage_Causes.pdf

Exelon Corporation. (2021, February 24). Exelon Reports Fourth Quarter and Full Year 2020 Results And Initiates 2021 Financial Outlook. Retrieved from www.exeloncorp.com: https://www.exeloncorp.com/newsroom/Exelon-Reports-Fourth-Quarter-and-Full-Year-2020-Results

Federal Energy Regulatory Commission and North American Electric Reliability Corporation. (2011, August). Report on Outages and Curtailments During the

Southwest Cold Weather Event of February 1 – 5, 2011. Retrived from www.ferc.gov: https://www.ferc.gov/sites/default/files/2020-04/08-16-11-report.pdf

Gonzales, Leticia. (2021, February 19). Historic Freeze Fuels Monstrous Weekly Natural Gas Price Rally, Leaves Texas Out in the Cold. Retrieved from www.naturalgasintel.com: https://www.naturalgasintel.com/historic-freeze-fuels-monstrous-natural-gas-price-rally-leaves-texas-left-out-in-cold/

Griddy Energy, LLC. (2021, March 15). To Former Customers of Griddy Energy: Notice of Bankruptcy Filing. Retrieved from www.griddy.com: https://www.griddy.com/

Insurance Journal. (2021, March 5). AccuWeather Raises Texas Damage, Loss Estimate from Winter Storm to $130B. Retrieved from www.insurancejournal.com: https://www.insurancejournal.com/news/southcentral/2021/03/05/604122.htm

Jenkins, Lisa. (2021, February 24). Following Mass Power Failures in Texas, Over Half of Voters Say State Needs to Connect Its Grid to Others. Retrieved from https://morningconsult.com: https://morningconsult.com/2021/02/24/texas-power-grid-independence-polling/

Kinder Morgan. (2021, April 21). Kinder Morgan's First Quarter 2021 Earnings Results. Retrieved from ir.kindermorgan.com: https://ir.kindermorgan.com/events-and-presentations/event-details/2021/Kinder-Morgans-First-Quarter-2021-Earnings-Results/default.aspx

KXII Staff. (2021, March 16). AG Paxton Ensures Forgiveness of $29 Million in Electric Bills for 24,000 Texans After Suing Griddy Energy, LLC. Retrieved from www.kxii.com: https://www.kxii.com/2021/03/16/ag-paxton-ensures-forgiveness-of-29-million-in-electric-bills-for-24000-texans-after-suing-griddy-energy-llc/

Magness, Bill. (2021, March 4). Texas Legislative Hearings:Senate Business and Commerce CommitteeHouse Joint Committee on State Affairs and Energy Resources. Retrieved from www.ercot.com: http://www.ercot.org/content/wcm/lists/226521/Texas_Legislature_Hearings_2-25-2021.pdf

Magness, Bill. (2021, February 24). Review of February 2021 Extreme Cold Weather Event –ERCOT Presentation. Retrieved from www.ercot.com: http://www.ercot.com/content/wcm/key_documents_lists/225373/2.2_REVISED_ERCOT_Presentation.pdf

Magness, Bill. (2021, February 25). Texas Legislative Hearings:Senate Business and

Commerce Committee House Joint Committee on State Affairs and Energy Resources. Retrieved from www.ercot.com: http://www.ercot.com/content/wcm/lists/226521/Texas_Legislature_Hearings_2-25-2021.pdf

Malik, Naureen and Chediak, Mark. (2021, February). Texas Power Grid Chair, Directors Quit in Wake of Blackouts. Retrieved from www.bloomberg.com: https://www.bloomberg.com/news/articles/2021-02-23/ercot-chair-vice-chair-and-others-resign-from-board-filing

McGinty, Tom and Patterson, Scott. (2021, February 24). "Texas Electric Bills Were $28 Billion Higher Under Deregulation." Retrieved from www.wsj.com: https://www.wsj.com/articles/texas-electric-bills-were-28-billion-higher-under-deregulation-11614162780

McWilliams, Gary. (2021, March 5). Texas power regulator rejects request to cut $16 billion in charges during freeze. Retrieved from www.reuters.com: https://www.reuters.com/article/us-usa-texas-power-crisis-idUSKBN2AX2MA

Ogelman, Kenan. (2021, March 4). ERCOT Market Update Texas Senate Business and Commerce Committee. Retrieved from www.ercot.com: http://www.ercot.org/content/wcm/lists/226521/Senate_Business___Commerce_Committee_030421.pdf

Perryman Group. (2021, February). Preliminary Estimates of Economic Costs of the February 2021 Texas Winter Storm. Retrieved from www.perrymangroup.com: https://www.perrymangroup.com/media/uploads/brief/perryman-preliminary-estimates-of-economic-costs-of-the-february-2021-texas-winter-storm-02-25-21.pdf

Portillo Ronk Legal Team. (2021, March 16). Information for Creditors of Griddy Energy LLC. Retrieved from www.portilloronk.com: https://www.portilloronk.com/griddy-energy

Potomac Economics, Ltd. (2021, March 10). ERCOT Wholesale Electricity Market Monthly Report. Retrieved from www.potomaceconomics.com: https://www.potomaceconomics.com/wp-content/uploads/2021/03/Nodal_Monthly_Report_2021-02.pdf

PowerOutage.us. (2021, February 15). Major Power Outage Events. Retrieved from https://poweroutage.us: https://poweroutage.us/about/majorevents

Public Utility Commission of Texas, "Second Order Directing ERCOT to Take

Action and Granting Exception to Commission Rules," https://www.puc.texas.gov/51617WinterERCOTOrder.pdf

Railroad Commission of Texas. (1973, January). Order Relating To The Approval By The Commission Of Curtailment Programs For Natural Gas Transported And Sold Within The State Of Texas. Retrieved from rrc.texas.gov: https://rrc.texas.gov/gas-services/curtailment-plan/

Railroad Commission of Texas. (2021, February 12). RAILROAD COMMISSION OF TEXAS EMERGENCY ORDER. Retrieved from rrc.texas.gov: https://rrc.texas.gov/media/cw3ewubr/emergency-order-021221-final-signed.pdf

Rev.com. (2021, March 24). House Hearing on Texas Power Grid Failure Transcript March 24. Retrieved from www.rev.com: https://www.rev.com/blog/transcripts/house-hearing-on-texas-power-grid-failure-transcript-march-24

Texas House of Representatives. (2021, February 25). Joint Hearing: State Affairs and Energy Resources, Part 1. Retrieved from www.house.texas.gov: https://www.house.texas.gov/video-audio/committee-broadcasts/

S&P Global Market Intelligence. (2021, February). Experts mull market, reliability rule changes amid Texas, regional outages. Retrieved from www.spglobal.com: https://www.spglobal.com/marketintelligence/en/news-insights/latest-news-headlines/experts-mull-market-reliability-rule-changes-amid-texas-regional-outages-62688009

Schneider, Jesse and Goggin, Michael. (2020, March 23). ERCOT 2019: Market Performance Assessment. Retrieved from https://gridstrategiesllc.com: https://gridstrategiesllc.com/2019/10/14/ercot-2019-market-performance-assessment/

Smith, Rebecca. (2021, May 27). The Texas Grid Came Close to an Even Bigger Disaster During February Freeze. Retrieved from www.wsj.com: https://www.wsj.com/articles/texas-electrical-grid-bigger-disaster-february-freeze-black-starts-11622124896

Sullivan, Brian. (2021, February 25). Most of Texas Deep Freeze $90 Billion in Losses Avoidable, Modeler Says. Retrieved from www.insurancejournal.com: https://www.insurancejournal.com/news/southcentral/2021/02/25/602807.htm

The Texas Tribune. (2021, February). Texas was "seconds and minutes" away from catastrophic months-long blackouts, officials say. Retrieved from www.texastribune.org: https://www.texastribune.org/2021/02/18/texas-power-outages-ercot/

TimeAndDate.com. (2021, February). Past Weather in Austin, Texas, USA—February 2021. Retrieved from TimeAndDate.com: https://www.timeanddate.com/weather/usa/austin/historic?month=2&year=2021

Texas Department of State Health Services. (2021, April 9). Winter Storm-Related Deaths – April 9, 2021. Retrieved from dshs.texas.gov: https://dshs.texas.gov/news/updates.shtm

U.S. Energy Information Administration. (2021, February). Hourly Electric Grid Monitor. Retrieved from www.eia.gov: https://www.eia.gov/beta/electricity/gridmonitor/dashboard/electric_overview/balancing_authority/ERCO

U.S. Energy Information Administration. (2020, September). Form EIA-860 detailed data with previous form data (EIA-860A/860B). Retrieved from www.eia.gov: https://www.eia.gov/electricity/data/eia860/

U.S. Energy Information Administration. (2021, April). Electric Power Monthly. Retrieved from www.eia.gov: https://www.eia.gov/electricity/monthly/

U.S. Energy Information Administration. (2020, October). Electric Sales, Revenue, and Average Price. Retrieved from www.eia.gov: https://www.eia.gov/electricity/sales_revenue_price

U.S. Senate Committee on Energy and Natural Resources. (2021, March). Full Committee Hearing On The Reliability, Resiliency, And Affordability Of Electric Service. Retreived from www.energy.senate.gov: https://www.energy.senate.gov/hearings/2021/3/full-committee-hearing-on-the-reliability-resiliency-and-affordability-of-electric-service

Wood, Pat. (2021, March 11). Testimony of Pat Wood, III CEO, Hunt Energy Network Before the United States Senate Committee on Energy and Natural Resources March 11, 2021. Retrieved from www.energy.senate.gov: https://www.energy.senate.gov/services/files/371DBE67-1000-41FA-8E76-B467101AABE6

Nuclear Policy in the States: A National Review

Daniel Shea*

*Program Principal, National Conference of State Legislatures, daniel.shea@ncsl.org

Introduction

The nuclear energy industry has regained momentum over the past several years, with state policy serving as a major springboard for that change in fortune. Following a decade characterized by disaster and disappointment for the nuclear industry, policy decisions in the early 2020s have propelled nuclear power forward as a viable resource to support decarbonization efforts while maintaining power system reliability.

Despite only constituting 8% of electric generating capacity in the United States, nuclear power produces nearly 20% of total electricity because nuclear reactors are nearly always operating—outperforming all other resources in this statistic [1] [2]. Perhaps more significantly, given recent trends in public opinion and energy policy, nuclear power accounts for around half of all carbon-free electricity in the U.S.[3] [4] [5]. As lawmakers from across the political spectrum reckon with how the energy transition could affect their communities and constituents, many have increasingly found common ground in the role nuclear energy can play in the process.

While recent federal legislation will have an outsized effect on nuclear power developments over the coming years, state policies have paved the way for many of the clean energy technologies that will transform the U.S. electric grid over the coming decades. State legislatures, in particular, oversee the regulatory environment in which electric utilities operate; these policies affect how utilities plan for the future and the investments they make. While states have widely focused on renewable energy and energy efficiency, a growing number are considering the role nuclear power might play moving forward.

The National Conference of State Legislatures (NCSL) tracks state energy policies across a variety of topic areas[6]. Since 2016, NCSL has seen a near-doubling

---

1   "Electricity generation, capacity, and sales in the United States," U.S. Energy Information Administration, Washington DC, July 2022.
2   "What is Generation Capacity," U.S. Department of Energy, Office of Nuclear Energy, Washington DC, May 2020.
3   A. Tyson, C. Funk, B. Kennedy, "Americans Largely Favor U.S. Taking Steps to Become Carbon Neutral by 2050," Washington DC, March 2022.
4   A. Ray, D. Shea, C. McMichael, A. Igleheart, "2021 Legislative Energy Trends," National Council of State Legislatures, Washington DC, April 2022.
5   J. McDermott, "Majority of US states pursue nuclear power for emissions cuts," Associated Press, Washington DC, January 2022.
6   "Energy State Bill Tracking Database," National Council of State Legislatures, Washington DC, November 2022.

in nuclear energy-related policies considered by state legislatures—up from 74 total bills considered in 2016 to more than 160 bills during the current legislative session. State legislatures have also enacted a greater number of bills over that same timeframe. While five states enacted nine bills in 2016, at least 12 states have enacted 14 bills in 2022.

These policies vary in their approach and scope. In the mid-2010s, the focus among state policymakers mainly involved existing reactor preservation. Many operating nuclear power plants were struggling to compete with natural gas and renewable generation, leading to the premature closure of several nuclear power plants. In response, at least six states enacted policies to prevent the premature closure of existing reactors. While those efforts have remained poignant, in more recent years, a growing number of states enacted policies aimed at developing new nuclear capacity to support of clean energy goals or reliability. This represents a shift from defensive posturing toward a more proactive posture.

These policies have been enacted by both red and blue states—a reflection of the increasingly bipartisan position nuclear power occupies in U.S. political discourse. The passage of recent federal legislation—in particular, the Infrastructure Investment and Jobs Act (IIJA) and the Inflation Reduction Act (IRA)—only appears to have added momentum to initiatives that began at the state level. In the coming years, NCSL anticipates that state legislatures will continue to enact policies in support of nuclear power to leverage funding and financing opportunities in the IIJA and IRA. This article provides a review of these recent state and federal initiatives, along with a brief historical review of nuclear developments in the U.S. over the past two decades.

How We Got Here

The nuclear power industry has experienced a whirlwind over the last 20 years. Following the passage of the 2005 Energy Policy Act, many anticipated a "nuclear renaissance" in the United States. It had been nearly a decade since the last nuclear reactor was brought into service—Watts Bar Unit 1, which began construction in 1973 and wasn't completed until 1996. Since then, new reactor development largely dried up due to high upfront costs and a history of construction delays. But the Energy Policy Act promised to change those dynamics with loan guarantees, cost-overrun support and a production tax credit (PTC) for the first 6,000 megawatts (MW) of new nuclear capacity to come online.

To leverage the federal incentive, Florida, Georgia and South Carolina enacted state policies to further incentivize utilities to pursue new nuclear. Understanding that the upfront costs were still a major hurdle for utilities, state legislators in these states enacted construction work in progress (CWIP) laws for new nuclear projects. CWIP is a financing mechanism that enables utilities to finance capital projects by periodically recovering costs from customers throughout the duration of construction. Normally, utilities can't recover those costs until the project has been brought into service. However, since large nuclear projects can take upwards of a decade to build, CWIP laws aim to make those initial hurdles easier to clear by allowing utilities to recover costs throughout project development, thereby reducing the risk to utility companies and their shareholders, and reducing the overall amount that is needed to finance a project. While state utility regulatory commissions (PUCs) approve costs and oversee progress, consumer advocates have argued these laws shift too much risk to customers.

Between the federal incentives and state CWIP laws, a flurry of activity between 2007 and 2010 suggested that a nuclear renaissance would materialize. In fact, the Nuclear Regulatory Commission (NRC) received applications for construction and operating licenses to build nearly 30 new reactors—a staggering figure since the combined capacity of those units would represent more than a third of the existing fleet.[7]

Disaster and Economic Troubles

However, that momentum came to a sudden halt in March 2011 after the disaster at the Fukushima Daiichi nuclear power plant in Japan. Triggered by an earthquake and tsunami, the event catalyzed opposition to nuclear power over safety concerns. Ultimately, only four of the new reactors broke ground—two at Plant Vogtle in Georgia, and two at V.C. Summer Nuclear Generating Station in South Carolina.

Not only had public sentiment turned against nuclear power, but so had the economics of power generation. In 2005, the average price of electricity in the PJM Interconnection, the largest wholesale electricity market in the U.S., was $63.46 per megawatt-hour (MWh).[8] By 2009, the average price had dropped to $39.04 per MWh. This was no aberration. It was the first hint at the Shale Revolution's impact on the U.S. power market. Hydraulic fracturing unlocked vast natural gas resources, causing the price of natural gas to plummet and—until this past year—largely stabilize.

Over the ensuing decade, natural gas has taken on a larger share of electricity generation, recently accounting for nearly 40% of total electric generation in the U.S.[9] Not only did natural gas almost halve the emissions from coal-fired power, but it complemented another increasingly cheap source of power: renewable ener-

---

7   "Combined License Applications for New Reactors," U.S. Nuclear Regulatory Commission, Bethesda, Maryland, September 2022.
8   "2020 State of the Market Report for PJM," Monitoring Analytics, Eagleville PA, March 2021.
9   "What is U.S. electricity generation by energy source?," U.S. Energy Information Administration, Washington DC, November 2022.

gy[10]. Together, natural gas and renewables set wholesale power prices in organized wholesale electricity markets throughout much of the 2010s. Until this year, those power prices trended lower and lower—generally between $30 and $40 per MWh in the PJM region, but dropping as low as $21.77 per MWh in 2021.

Generally, that's a good thing. Lower wholesale power prices translate into lower power bills for customers. But for nuclear power plants in wholesale markets, those prices led to thinner and thinner operating margins, ultimately causing many nuclear plants in wholesale markets to operate in the red. Since 2013, 13 nuclear reactors with more than 10,000 MW in combined capacity closed prematurely due to these market conditions[11]. That capacity has been replaced largely by new natural gas-fired generation.[12]

States Decide to Act

As nuclear plants began to close, policymakers began considering whether to respond. Nuclear power accounts for only around 8% of total electric generating capacity in the U.S., but generates nearly 20% of total electricity.[13] That is because most nuclear plants operate around-the-clock, with a capacity factor of nearly 93% in 2021[14]. That means that, on average, nuclear plants in the U.S. generated at maximum capacity around 93% of the time last year—nearly twice the capacity factor of resources like coal and natural gas, and triple that of wind and solar. In all, nuclear generates around half of the carbon-free electrons that flow on the U.S. power grid. At a time when electric grid decarbonization became a growing priority, some policymakers felt the need to prevent these large, reliable sources of carbon-free power from closing.

In an effort to preserve carbon-free energy and high-paying jobs, six states have enacted policies since 2016 to provide financial support to struggling nuclear power plants. Four of those states—Connecticut, Illinois, New Jersey and New York—have active policies that provide nuclear power plants with additional revenue. These policies were designed to provide support only to nuclear plants that demonstrate they would likely shut down without state assistance—largely justified based on the avoided carbon dioxide emissions that those power plants represent. Three of those policies were designed in the form of zero emissions credits

---

10 G. McGrath, "Electric power sector CO2 emissions drop as generation mix shifts from coal to natural gas," U.S. Energy Information Administration, Washington DC, July 2021.

11 M. Holt, P. Brown, "U.S. Nuclear Plant Shutdowns, State Interventions, and Policy Concerns," Congressional Research Service, Washington, D.C., June 2021.

12 J. Anderson, K. Hallahan, "Gas-fired power increased with nuclear plant closure; path to climate goals unclear," S&P Global Commodity Insights, New York NY, November 2021.

13 "Electricity generation, capacity, and sales in the United States," U.S. Energy Information Administration, Washington DC, July 2022.

14 "What is Generation Capacity," U.S. Department of Energy, Office of Nuclear Energy, Washington DC, May 2020.

(ZECs), which provide qualifying reactors with a supplemental payment for every MWh of carbon-free electricity sold. A new federal program created by the IIJA, the Civil Nuclear Credit Program, was predicated on these state ZECs programs.

Most recently, the Illinois General Assembly doubled down on supporting the state's nuclear fleet with the passage of the Climate and Equitable Jobs Act in 2021. The new law expanded the state's programs to support five nuclear power plants in the state—up from two nuclear plants that were supported under initial legislation passed in 2016. Last year, the Ohio legislature repealed a similar program designed to support the state's two existing nuclear plants just two years after the law was enacted. The legislature's decision to repeal the program followed federal corruption charges related to individuals involved in the original bill's passage.

The U.S. Congress recently enacted legislation establishing a similar program at the federal level. The new policy is substantially similar to these state ZECs policies. The U.S. Department of Energy is in the process of implementing this new program, which will be discussed in more detail below.

Struggles Persist for New Projects

While some states in the North were acting to preserve their existing reactor fleets, states in the South found themselves managing the new-build projects. The Tennessee Valley Authority became the first U.S. utility to bring a new reactor online in the 21st century. In an interesting twist, it was Watts Bar Unit 2—the sister unit to the last reactor brought online in the 20th century. While construction on Watts Bar Unit 2 began in 1973 alongside Unit 1, the reactor was 60% complete when TVA mothballed the project in 1985[15]. In 2007, TVA decided to complete Unit 2, which became operational in 2016. The project experienced nominal cost-overruns and construction delays—though nowhere near those happening at two projects in Georgia and South Carolina.

Projects in Georgia and South Carolina were building Westinghouse Electric Company's AP1000 reactor—a pressurized water reactor with a designed capacity of 1,110 MW, which represents a significant upgrade from the previous generation of large, light-water reactors. Georgia Power was developing two AP1000s at its Plant Vogtle, while two more AP1000s were being developed at the V.C. Summer plant in South Carolina by Santee Cooper, a state-owned utility, and SCANA Corp., an investor-owned utility.

In March 2017, Westinghouse entered Chapter 11 bankruptcy, throwing both projects into crisis—especially in South Carolina. By August 2017, the V.C. Summer reactors had been abandoned after the developers had already charged customers $2 billion for the project. Neither utility survived unscathed; Domin-

---

15 S. Hoff, M. Gospodarczyk, "First new U.S. nuclear reactor in almost two decades set to begin operating," U.S. Energy Information Administration, Washington DC, June 2016.

ion Energy purchased SCANA Corp., while the South Carolina state legislature required closer state oversight of Santee Cooper. The legislature also repealed its CWIP for nuclear policy, while Florida did the same and Georgia amended its statute to expire following the completion of the Vogtle project.

Ultimately, only the two reactors at Plant Vogtle survived. The plant's first AP1000 is now scheduled to come online in the first quarter of 2023, while the second is expected to follow by the end of 2023. The projects total cost is expected to exceed $30 billion—more than double the original price tag[16].

These events served as a deterrent to large reactor construction. Slowing growth in electricity demand, recent cost-overruns, along with the long timelines to development large reactors—on average, between 10 and 15 years from initial construction to when the reactor is brought online—have led many to question whether there's a role for new nuclear in the clean energy transition[17]. This is perhaps the reason the emphasis in recent years has shifted away from large reactors to prioritize small modular reactors (SMRs), which promise a departure from the previous generation's problems. Whether the industry can deliver on the promise of SMRs will be tested over the coming decade.

State Action to Support New Nuclear

In spite of the beleaguered projects in the South, the nuclear power industry finds itself with wind in its sails once again. While recent federal legislation has added considerably to this progress, state policies led the way. However, the focus has shifted considerably since 2005. The problems associated with large reactor development have not gone unnoticed, and the clear emphasis has been on technologies that tend to be smaller and modular in their design.

If a traditional reactor has a generating capacity around 1,000 MW, small modular reactors tend to be under 300 MW capacity, while microreactors have been designed to generate less than 10 MW. On a basic level, these reactors are scaled to the times. Utilities are no longer experiencing the rapid growth in electricity demand that required huge capacity additions throughout the 20th century; in some regions, demand has flattened or decreased.[18] However, the real advantage according to nuclear advocates is in the modular design and what that means for construction efficiency[19].

---

16 J. Amy, "Georgia nuclear plant's cost now forecast to top $30 billion," Associated Press, Washington DC, May 2022.
17 S. Hoff, M. Gospodarczyk, "First new U.S. nuclear reactor in almost two decades set to begin operating," U.S. Energy Information Administration, Washington DC, June 2016.
18 F. Kahrl, "Why have U.S. electricity sales flattened?," Energy Policy, December 2021.
19 J. Liou, "What are Small Modular Reactors (SMRs)?," International Atomic Energy Agency, New York NY, November 2021.

Building a traditional reactor is an enormous endeavor. At Vogtle, the new-build project required around 9,000 workers at its peak.[20] The reactor components are also built to specification on-site. These factors contributed to cost-overruns and delays. By contrast, SMRs are designed to benefit from factory fabrication and assembly for systems and components, which are then transported and assembled on-site. While still theoretical, centralized, standardized design and fabrication could significantly reduce the problems associated with traditional reactor projects and diminish the upfront barrier due to capital costs.

The reduced size of these reactors holds additional benefits, making these projects easier to site and tie into the existing transmission grid. Their size and capacity is similar to many coal-fired generating units, making siting SMRs at retired or retiring coal power plants of particular interest as the electric sector continues to decarbonize. Not only do these facilities have existing transmission infrastructure and water access that would benefit SMRs, but these projects could support communities and workers affected by the clean energy transition through lost jobs and tax revenue when coal plants shut down.

The U.S. Department of Energy released a recent report on this topic to investigate the potential challenges and benefits of converting retired coal plant sites into SMR sites and concluded that 80% of the nearly 400 retired and operating coal plants identified for the study could be good candidates to host SMRs[21]. In total, these sites could host a combined capacity of 265 gigawatts (GW) in generating capacity—a staggering figure in relation to existing nuclear generating capacity in the U.S., which is around 95 GW. Additionally, the report claims the use of existing transmission and other infrastructure could reduce the cost of capital for "coal-to-nuclear" projects by 15% to 35% compared with greenfield projects.

Increasingly, states are also turning to nuclear power to address reliability concerns as the resource mix shifts toward more variable resources, such as wind and solar[22]. As more variable generation comes online, the grid will require additional "dispatchable" generation to fill in the gaps in generating capacity—resources that can reliably provide power whenever the grid operator calls upon them. Nuclear is one such resource, and one of the few that does so at capacity without generating carbon emissions. In fact, recent research notes that nuclear power plant regulatory standards require these facilities to be designed to safely withstand weather events far beyond those considered for other critical infrastruc-

---

20 "5 Things You Should Know About Plant Vogtle," U.S. Department of Energy, Office of Nuclear Energy, Washington DC, April 2019.

21 J. Hansen, W. Jenson, A. Wrobel, N. Stauff, K. Biegel, T. Kim, R. Belles, F. Omitaomu, "Investigating Benefits and Challenges of Converting Retiring Coal Plants into Nuclear Plants," U.S. Department of Energy, Office of Nuclear Energy, Washington DC, September 2022.

22 "Nuclear Power is the Most Reliable Energy Source and It's Not Even Close," U.S. Department of Energy, Office of Nuclear Energy, Washington DC, March 2021.

ture facilities[23]. As a result, researchers found that nuclear plant operations in the U.S. were rarely affected by extreme weather between 2011 and 2020—causing an average 0.1% loss of capacity factor[24]. While this argument is often a driving force in Republican-controlled states, several Democratic-controlled states have also taken action to support nuclear power for reliability.

California, with the passage of a bill aimed at extending the operating life of the state's last remaining nuclear power plant, is the latest example. Under a 2018 agreement between Pacific Gas & Electric (PG&E), state regulators and environmental groups, PG&E's Diablo Canyon nuclear power plant—a 2,250 MW plant that generates 9% of the state's total electricity—is scheduled to close its two reactors in 2024 and 2025[25]. However, the state's grid has struggled in recent years to cope with several heat waves, leading to rolling blackouts across the state and recent calls to consider extending the life of the plant to support reliability and avoid increasing the use of natural gas-fired generation.

In response to these concerns—and to recently available federal incentives—California lawmakers enacted Senate Bill 846 in September. The law allows Diablo Canyon to operate through 2030, contingent on several requirements. First, PG&E must apply to receive financial support through a new program administered by DOE: the Civil Nuclear Credit Program. Second, PG&E must relicense the two reactors—a costly process addressed by lawmakers through a $1.4 billion forgivable loan from the state. If those two requirements are met, the plant is likely to continue operations through the end of the decade. In late November, DOE announced that Diablo Canyon had been conditionally selected to receive up to $1.1 billion in credits from the Civil Nuclear Credit Program[26]. While the final terms are still subject to negotiation between DOE and PG&E, the news represents another step toward the plant's continued operation.

In the context of advancements in nuclear technologies, coupled with state and utility decarbonization goals and reliability concerns, a growing number of states have started to enact policies to either explore or support new nuclear reactor development or the preservation of existing reactors. As noted, both red and blue states have enacted these policies, demonstrating that nuclear power has increasingly attained consistent bipartisan support in recent years.

Not only has the number of nuclear energy-related bills steadily increased since 2016, but the number of enacted bills has too[27]. In 2016, the National Confer-

---

23 "Nuclear Plant Resilience to Weather-Related Events Between 2011 to 2020," Electric Power Research Institute, Palo Alto CA, September 2022.

24 Ibid.

25 N. Rott, "California lawmakers extend the life of the state's last nuclear power plant," National Public Radio, Washington DC, September 2022.

26 "Biden-Harris Administration Announces Major Investment to Preserve America's Clean Nuclear Energy Infrastructure," U.S. Department of Energy, Washington, D.C., November 2022.

27 "Energy State Bill Tracking Database," National Council of State Legislatures, Washington DC,

ence of State Legislatures tracked 74 bills related to nuclear energy in 17 states. Of those, five states enacted nine bills. In 2022, NCSL is tracking more than 160 bills in 31 states. Of those, at least 12 states have enacted 14 bills in 2022.

And while the ideological and policy reasons for supporting nuclear power may differ, the end result appears to be beneficial to the nuclear power industry. Beyond the preservation of existing reactors, which has already been addressed in this article, these trends can be grouped into the following categories.

Clean Energy Standards

One of the more notable developments in energy policy following the 2016 presidential election was that a large number of Democratic-controlled state legislatures strengthened their support for clean energy. The primary vehicle for state clean energy goals over the past two decades has been through renewable portfolio standards (RPS) that required a certain percent of a regulated utility's retail electricity sales to come from renewable resources[28]. Prior to 2016, most standards were set at relatively modest levels—usually between 10% and 25% of retail sales by a certain date. However, those standards have evolved in two notable ways since 2016.

In the first trend, states increased the requirements—often substantially. Overall, 15 states, two territories and Washington, D.C., have increased their requirements in that timeframe. Of those, 10 states, two territories and Washington, D.C., increased their standards to 100% of retail sales with deadlines ranging from 2030 to 2050, while another three states increased their standards to 50% or greater.

The second trend is that some of those states expanded the types of resources included in their standards. Perhaps unsurprisingly, RPS have traditionally included renewable resources like wind, solar, geothermal and hydropower. Resources like nuclear power or fossil generation outfitted with carbon capture and sequestration (CCS) technologies did not qualify, because the purpose of the RPS model was to support nascent technologies to bring them to cost parity with existing resources. Given that renewables are cheaper to build than most other current energy, it can be said that the RPS model has been successful[29].

However, even with that success, emissions in some markets rose with the closure of nuclear power plants as grid operators relied on natural gas-fired generation to balance variable renewable output[30]. In response to these and other concerns, lawmakers in a number of states shifted the focus slightly from supporting

---

November 2022.

28 C. McMichael, "State Renewable Portfolio Standards and Goals," National Council of State Legislatures, Washington DC, August 2022.

29 D. Baker, "Renewable Power Costs Rise, Just Not as Much as Fossil Fuels," Bloomberg News, New York NY, June 2022.

30 B. Storrow, "3 states with shuttered nuclear plants see emissions rise," Politico, Washington DC, February 2022.

renewable power with the side-benefit of emissions reductions, to prioritizing emissions reductions with the side-benefit of supporting renewable power.

This is where clean energy standards (CES) emerged, with at least eight states deciding to broaden the list of resources supported beyond traditional renewable resources. The focus with CES policies is on emissions reductions, so most of these policies support "carbon-free" or "carbon-neutral" technologies. In states without restrictions on new nuclear, that opens the door for nuclear power and CCS-equipped fossil-fired power plants to qualify under these programs.

It's important to note that renewables in these states still receive the lion's share of the support. CES policies have generally been enacted while strengthening the state's RPS policy. For example, California's CES policy still maintains an RPS requiring 60% renewable power by 2030; New Mexico's requires 80% renewables by 2040. However, the balance—whether 20% or 40%–must come from carbon-free resources, giving nuclear power a potential role to play in meeting state clean energy goals.

Repealing Restrictions on New Nuclear

While states like California and Oregon have enacted CES policies, both states would need to repeal existing restrictions on the development of new nuclear power before additional nuclear capacity could be used to comply with the state CES. Like 10 other states, California and Oregon have restrictions on the construction of new nuclear power facilities.[31]

In many cases, these restrictions are less about nuclear power and more about nuclear waste. Given the impasse in Congress about how to—or whether to—move on from Yucca Mountain as the nation's designated site to house a deep geologic repository for commercial spent nuclear fuel, states have been reluctant to build more nuclear generation without a clear waste disposal solution. A waste solution is at the heart of restrictions on new nuclear in six states. The remaining states either require the state legislature or voters to approve a project before it can commence, while Minnesota is the only state with an outright ban on all new nuclear power facilities.

Of course, these are statutory restrictions and subject to change. Kentucky, Montana, West Virginia and Wisconsin have all repealed similar restrictions since 2016. Similarly, Connecticut enacted a partial repeal—providing for an exemption to its restrictions. While these repeals do nothing more than remove a barrier to development, it is another indication of how states have opened the door once again to nuclear—particularly in states with a historic connection to coal.

---

31   D. Shea, C. McMichael, "States Restrictions on New Nuclear Power Facility Construction," National Council of State Legislatures, Washington DC, August 2022.

Coal-to-Nuclear

Repurposing retired or retiring coal-fired power plants to be used for new nuclear is not a new concept. There are a number of logical similarities between nuclear and coal—the two resources that have long served as the backbone of the electric grid, providing steady, "baseload power." The scale of SMRs theoretically would fit within the parameters of existing coal sites. Existing switchyard, transmission infrastructure and water rights, could be utilized to reduce costs and regulatory hurdles. The existing labor force could be re-trained to operate the nuclear facility—after all, when you boil it down to the basics, both are thermoelectric power plants. These similarities and more have been explored in a variety of research papers, and DOE has recently added to the literature with its own study exploring the potential[32].

It is not surprising that states with historic ties to the coal industry have begun exploring this possibility. Nuclear represents a familiar industry for policymakers in these states, where an emphasis on power reliability and economic contributions—including high-paying jobs—are foundational to the debate over the energy transition.

While Kentucky, Montana and West Virginia have all repealed restrictions on new nuclear development, the two most influential pieces of legislation in this area have been enacted by lawmakers in Indiana and Wyoming.

Wyoming was the first state to pass "coal-to-nuclear" legislation in 2020. House Bill 74 directs state regulators to develop rules and regulations to authorize SMR permitting for owners of existing coal and natural gas power plants that want to replace those facilities with SMRs. The bill requires SMR developers to acquire all of the necessary licenses and permits from the NRC, while providing a streamlined process at the state level—along with the state's explicit support for such projects.

The following year, TerraPower, an advanced reactor company, announced that it had selected a retiring coal-fired power plant in Kemmerer, Wyo., as the site on which to build its first reactor. DOE is investing nearly $2 billion in the project, which has benefitted from the department's Advanced Reactor Demonstration Program[33]. Upon successful completion, PacifiCorp, an investor-owned utility operating across six Western states, plans to acquire and operate the new reactor. In October 2022, PacifiCorp and TerraPower announced plans to explore the potential of deploying up to five additional TerraPower reactors, paired with energy storage systems, in the utility's service territory by 2035.

---

32 J. Hansen, W. Jenson, A. Wrobel, N. Stauff, K. Biegel, T. Kim, R. Belles, F. Omitaomu, "Investigating Benefits and Challenges of Converting Retiring Coal Plants into Nuclear Plants," U.S. Department of Energy, Office of Nuclear Energy, Washington DC, September 2022.

33 "Next-Gen Nuclear Plant and Jobs Are Coming to Wyoming," U.S. Department of Energy, Office of Nuclear Energy, Washington DC, November 2021.

In 2022, the Wyoming legislature enacted Senate Bill 131, which made several technical changes to the original law, including broadening its definition of qualifying reactors to accommodate TerraPower's specific design. The legislation also added spent fuel management requirements and established certain tax exemptions if the nuclear facility sources at least 80% of its fuel from domestic supplies.

Indiana enacted its own coal-to-nuclear legislation in 2022. Senate Bill 271 similarly directs state regulators to develop rules and regulations that accommodate the construction and operation of SMRs at retiring coal and natural gas facilities. However, the bill also addressed some of the financial uncertainty around nuclear development by authorizing utilities to receive CWIP financing for these projects. Other states are also exploring the potential role for new nuclear, including Montana, which approved a study to explore the feasibility of replacing coal units with SMRs.

Support for New Nuclear

For all the interest in coal-to-nuclear, this is but one distinct trend in broader support for advanced nuclear among states. Like Montana, a number of states are exploring this by commissioning studies to consider the role new nuclear could play in the energy transition. Michigan, Nebraska, New Hampshire and Virginia have all funded studies to this effect, while a handful of additional states have considered doing so.

And while studies can often be a precursor for more substantive legislation, they're not a prerequisite. Alaska, Connecticut, Nebraska and Virginia enacted legislation over the past two years that would support new nuclear development, while Missouri has also shown signs of interest.

In 2022, Alaska enacted Senate Bill 177, which aims to streamline the permitting of microreactors—defined by the statute as reactors with a generating capacity of 50 MW or less. The bill empowers municipal governments to approve microreactor projects and requires the state to develop regulations overseeing microreactor permitting.

Connecticut enacted two relevant bills in 2022. The first, House Bill 5202, would allow the state's lone nuclear power plant, Millstone, to expand and construct another reactor on-site. However, the bill does not allow that reactor to be a large, traditional reactor. While the plant operator currently has no plans to pursue an SMR, the legislation allows for that in the future. The second bill, House Bill 5200, aims to position the state as a leader in hydrogen production and generation. The role of nuclear power in hydrogen production is currently being explored through DOE pilot programs, and this legislation includes nuclear as a potential resource to consider in developing carbon-free hydrogen as a clean energy fuel.

Nebraska Legislative Bill 84, enacted in 2021, extended existing incentives for renewable energy under its ImagiNE Nebraska Act to apply to advanced reactor companies. Meanwhile, Virginia House Bill 894, enacted in 2022, directs state agencies to convene stakeholders and identify strategies and policies to promote SMR development in the state while minimizing the impact on prime farmland and encouraging investment in industrial sites.

Finally, the Missouri House passed House Bill 1684 in early 2022, which would have provided an exception to the state's ban on CWIP financing for advanced nuclear and renewable facilities of 200 MW capacity or greater. It is the second year in a row that the House passed the measure but it failed to move in the Senate. If enacted, the bill would certainly shift the conversation around new nuclear development in the state.

However, the dynamics have shifted since the Missouri Senate decided not to take up House Bill 1684 earlier this year, following Congress' passage of the Inflation Reduction Act (IRA) in August 2022. The new federal package has several provisions that could support new reactor development regardless of additional state policies. However, it seems likely that states will consider policies moving forward that leverage the federal incentives to further incentivize a broad swathe of clean technologies—nuclear among them—that are supported by the IRA and the IIJA, which Congress enacted in November 2021.

The Impact of Recent Federal Action

While state legislative action has played an important role in preserving existing reactors and laying the groundwork for new nuclear development, recent federal action is likely to have a dramatic effect across the energy sector in its scope and breadth. Congress has acted on nuclear issues in recent years—most notably in an effort to streamline the NRC's regulations and licensing procedures to accommodate advanced reactor designs. However, the IIJA and IRA are expected to have a profound effect on the energy sector, and the nuclear energy industry is widely expected to benefit through several key provisions from those laws.

The IIJA invested $73 billion in decarbonizing and improving the reliability of the energy sector. The nuclear power industry, in particular, will benefit from several provisions. Primary among those is through the Civil Nuclear Credit Program (CNCP), discussed earlier in relation to the Diablo Canyon nuclear power plant in California. The law allocated $6 billion for the CNCP program, which is modeled off state ZECs programs to provide financial support to struggling nuclear power plants through payments for every MWh of electricity generated. Nuclear power plant owners have been calling for a program like the CNCP for some time, given that many reactors operating in states without ZECs or other programs have also been at risk of premature closure. The CNCP, which is administered by the DOE, now has the potential to support existing reactors nationwide into the

2030s, with priority allocated to reactors that source their fuel domestically. DOE has recently concluded the first award cycle, conditionally awarding Diablo Canyon with up to $1.1 billion in credits. The department issued draft guidance on the second award cycle.

Additionally, the IIJA supports the DOE's Advanced Reactor Demonstration Program (ARDP), which aims to speed up the commercialization of advanced nuclear technologies. The ARDP received an additional $2.5 billion through 2025 to support demonstrations. These awards have been instrumental in developing the TerraPower demonstration project in Wyoming, along with a second project being developed in eastern Washington by X-energy, an advanced reactor company.

Several other provisions require DOE to develop a report on how nuclear energy can contribute to meeting the nation's resilience and carbon-reduction goals, and requires the development of a standard for qualifying "clean hydrogen" from a variety of sources, including nuclear power.

While the IIJA was considered beneficial to nuclear, the IRA has only increased the industry's enthusiasm for what the future may hold for advanced nuclear in the U.S. The IRA includes a number of tax credits that could be used by nuclear power facilities—particularly for developers of new nuclear facilities—including:

- Investment tax credit for owners of new carbon-free generation, worth 30% of the amount paid to build a facility;

- A new clean electricity production tax credit for any carbon-free generator that begins construction in 2025 or later, worth at least $25 per MWh of electricity generated;

- Coal-to-nuclear bonus tax credit, offering a 10% addition for new facilities sited in coal and other fossil fuel communities that are affected by the clean energy transition;

- Clean hydrogen production tax credit based on the carbon-intensity of the hydrogen production;

- Nuclear power production tax credit for existing reactors of up to $15 per MWh from 2024 through 2032 to prevent premature closure.

The IRA also addresses growing concerns over the U.S. nuclear sector's reliance on foreign-sourced fuel. The commercial fleet of nuclear reactors in the U.S. imports most of its uranium from countries like Kazakhstan, Canada, Australia and Russia[34]. In fact, the U.S. only produces 5% of the uranium used by the cur-

---

34 "Nuclear Explained: Where our uranium comes from," U.S. Energy Information Administration, Washington DC, July 2022.

rent reactor fleet. And that's just the raw uranium. Russia is the leading producer of enriched uranium—the form required to be used as fuel[35]. Nearly 40% of the world's supply of enriched uranium came from Russia in 2020, and the recent war in Ukraine has only exacerbated these concerns.

This is even more pronounced when it comes to the production of high-assay low-enriched uranium (HALEU) fuel, which is required for most advanced nuclear technologies[36]. To support domestic production of HALEU fuel, the IRA provided $700 million to DOE to support the development of HALEU facilities in the U.S.

The allure of the nuclear power industry—from an economic, workforce, decarbonization and grid reliability perspective—has been enhanced by the passage of these federal packages. It seems inevitable that states will spend the next several years positioning themselves to benefit from the suite of incentives provided under these new laws.

Conclusion

As the U.S. moves forward with the clean energy transition, the role of nuclear power remains to be seen. While many states are exploring its potential, the nuclear energy industry and advanced reactor companies leading the way in new technology development will ultimately need to deliver on the promise in order for nuclear to gain broad acceptance as a technology solution.

State legislative policy has been increasingly supportive of the potential for nuclear power. NCSL's bill-tracking database reveals the increased interest in this topic area, and a growing number of states have enacted legislation to support new and existing reactors. These policies have been enacted by states across the political divide, reflecting the increasingly bipartisan nature of nuclear power.

Recent federal legislation is likely to accelerate these trends. In the coming years, NCSL anticipates that state legislatures will continue to enact policies in support of nuclear power to leverage funding and financing opportunities in the IIJA and IRA.

Author Capsule Bio

Daniel Shea is a program principal in the energy program at the National Conference of State Legislatures, where he covers nuclear power, utility regulation and electric grid policy.

---

35 K. Foltynova, "Russia's Stranglehold On The World's Nuclear Power Cycle," RadioFreeEurope, Washington, DC, September 2022.

36 "What is High-Assay Low-Enriched Uranium (HALEU)?," U.S. Department of Energy, Office of Nuclear Energy, Washington DC, April 2020.

Incentivizing Good Governance Beyond Regulatory Minimums: The Civil Nuclear Sector

Debra K. Decker,[1,2] Kathryn Rauhut[3]

[1] Senior Advisor, Stimson Center
[2] Corresponding Author, ddecker@stimson.org
[3] Non-Resident Fellow, Stimson Center

[see Author Capsule Bios below]

Abstract

The consequences from a blended cyber-physical terrorist attack on a nuclear power plant are potentially catastrophic. Sabotage of the plant or theft and subsequent use of radiological materials can potentially lead to blackouts, deaths, and injuries and even a release of radiological materials. This threat continues to evolve in sophistication and complexity and is outpacing the ability and resources of governments to anticipate risks and to protect their critical infrastructure and the public from harm. Policymakers are working to keep up with the rapid onset of these threats to reinforce the resilience of critical infrastructure. Cyber vulnerabilities including insider threats are also evolving, with cyberattacks on nuclear facilities the tip of the iceberg as more sophisticated advanced persistent threats develop. This paper suggests governments look beyond regulations and policy directives to harness the power and energy of the market to incentivize operators to voluntarily adopt security measures beyond regulatory requirements.

Good organizational governance is important and necessary to secure critical infrastructure including nuclear facilities and increasingly can be rewarded by the market. The definition of what is good organizational governance matters to investors, lenders, insurers, regulators, and the public. Is the organization going to be able to function effectively as an enterprise and provide a return to investors, pay back its loans, protect its workers and community, including the environment? In the nuclear field, the stakes can be high—with stakeholders depending on a stable baseload electric supply without safety or security incidents, especially of a radiological nature.

This article documents findings from a multi-year project to identify incentives for nuclear security beyond regulatory minimums, with a focus on nuclear power plants. We assessed the importance of standards and developed a "Good Governance Template" to support owners/managers in obtaining benefits and reducing potential liabilities. We found that market incentives are developing in areas such as insurance, credit, and other rating systems to support the development of good governance, including incentives for companies to demonstrate due care in the management of risks, especially cyber risks. Building a business case for nuclear security based on these incentives is an important step forward in securing our nuclear future, especially in terms of cyber risks.

Keywords: Governance, nuclear security, nuclear safety, nuclear power, regulation, standards, guidance, incentives, liability, cyber, insurance, credit ratings, ESG ratings, sustainability, due care

Introduction

The nuclear sector, like other critical infrastructures, will continue to be a target—for terrorists, domestic activists, and foreign state actors penetrating domestic critical infrastructures. Given these threats with new avenues like cyber for attack and the potentially high consequences of any incident, ensuring nuclear safety and security remains a critical issue. By definition, critical infrastructure performs essential functions for a community. The designation of what constitutes critical infrastructures may differ somewhat between countries and across regions, but the approaches to managing risks and the oversight mechanisms to ensure safe and secure performance are similar. Regulatory authorities establish minimum baseline requirements. Policy directives supplementing these are put forth from a central authority such as through an Executive Order or a European Union Council Directive. Oversight of compliance and implementation is complex, especially in sectors that present high risks. With all this, however, the policy goals are the same—to have the critical infrastructure organization internalize some of the external costs from potential malperformance.

Although regulations and directives may be essential to ensuring some minimum levels of protection, performance, and resilience of critical infrastructures, compliance may not be achieved and is by no means sufficient. Some countries' regulatory authorities may not have the capacity or capability to provide adequate oversight to ensure compliance or to insist on performance improvements. Even in countries that have well-developed oversight authorities, regulations and other requirements typically do not keep up with the emerging challenges in today's fast-paced societies. Overly prescriptive regulations can be not only costly and burdensome but also counterproductive by impeding optimization of organizational safety and security. Technological innovations, increased digitization and adoption of novel processes may present efficiencies but can also pose new risks beyond what regulators and policymakers conceived. Recognizing this, some oversight authorities like the US Nuclear Regulatory Commission (NRC) are moving towards performance-based systems.[1]

Thus, to ensure safe and secure performance of our most critical assets and systems, owners as well as managers and operators must be incentivized to invest in good governance in a dynamically changing world. Safety and security must not be costly burdens seen to constrain but optimized to also benefit business and ensure balanced investment in managing across risks.

This project on incentivizing good performance in the civilian nuclear industry sector started with the Obama Administration's goal of strengthening nuclear security internationally, including in the United States, as interest in nuclear energy increases—not just for power but also for other industrial and research purposes. The four international Nuclear Security Summits under U.S. President Obama from 2010 to 2016 helped to raise awareness of nuclear risks, with some nuclear materials and facilities vulnerable to extremist and terrorist threats and insiders always a concern. The civil nuclear industry is slowly growing worldwide although plants are closing domestically. The drivers for nuclear's global growth include increasing energy demand as the world population grows and the need for carbon-free energy as well as desalination. New advanced reactors are also part of the energy mix that are expected to be less expensive, safer and more secure. These may well jumpstart future new nuclear growth.

The goal of our research was to find whether security could be embedded in the interests of nuclear licensees, as safety is embedded: Is there a way to ensure civil nuclear security beyond regulatory minimums? Security is part of overall safety. Security violations can become safety violations in the view of nuclear regulators. In many languages, safety and security are in fact the same word. Safety incentives should logically work to incentivize security. We attempted to identify the right business case that could cause licensees to properly adjust their performance to a new fast-changing environment that regulations and directives could not quickly anticipate and regulate. We sought the "holy grail": a market-based incentive or incentives that could apply benefits to reward good governance not only to the nuclear power industry but also to the broader nuclear sector, such as nuclear fuel facilities, transport, and research/test reactors. If incentives could work in the nuclear sector, they could be applied across the spectrum of other critical infrastructure sectors as well.

---

1   See, for example, guidance from the U.S. NRC at: https://www.nrc.gov/reading-rm/doc-collections/nuregs/brochures/br0303/index.html

In interviewing nuclear industry stakeholders, we found that cybersecurity was one of the major operator concerns. The Obama Administration had itself recognized that cybersecurity of critical infrastructure is a major source of risk, so it worked with stakeholders to develop a Cybersecurity Framework and explored incentives to foster adoption (U.S. Department of the Homeland Security Integrated Task Force, 2013). Many of those incentives required legislation and political will, which were slow to arise. Only recently have government mandates and incentives matured, with the Cyberspace Solarium Commission recommendations and related legislation (Cyberspace Solarium Commission n.d.). The Solarium Commission and earlier reports recognized that market forces can work to mitigate risks.

We sought to identify and help magnify those forces that could apply to better managing not just cyber risks but also other sources of risk. We found new market incentives evolving as States' regulatory systems are unable to keep pace with risks from technological changes in and outside facilities, including blended physical-cybersecurity threats and new types of possible incidents such as those involving drones or deep fakes.

Methods and Results

This paper is the summation of five years of research, interviews and roundtables which considered various incentives that could motivate operators to voluntarily adopt security measures beyond regulatory minimums. We went through a systematic series of questions and developed and tested hypotheses around different market levers. We started first by considering who, in addition to regulators, were looking at nuclear performance and how those evaluations might be used in the market. We then considered how voluntary consensus standards could be used to bring external benefits to operators and recognized that standards compliance was not enough in itself. Good governance as well as stewardship of nuclear materials is required. Low probability, high consequence events like terrorism demand difficult tradeoffs and resources may not always be readily available. Strong security does not necessarily mean more security but can often mean a rightsizing of existing resources (Forging Strong Security Norms, Kempfer, Rauhut, Umayam, 2018). With stakeholders, our team developed and discussed a "Good Governance Template" that could guide senior leadership in their decision-making processes to ensure and demonstrate good security without revealing sensitive information. The template is a set of principles with related questions (e.g., on resilience and contingency planning) which help owners/operators illustrate and track "reasonableness" by providing a transparent statement of criteria evaluated by those managing risks. The template is a written set of risk mitigation protocols that illustrate regular risk assessments and corresponding personnel training and document best practices, thus garnering benefits for good governance from regulators, insurers, financiers/investors, judges, and attorneys.

The largest benefit we identified from an initial roundtable of stakeholders was reduction in potential liability for an incident as well as the significant potential loss of reputation from that incident. Subsequently, we found that credit ratings, which measure many factors including general governance, influence funding costs and are thus a concern of owners/managers. Also helping to drive good governance, including over security, is the development of cyber ratings and ESG—environmental, social, and corporate governance—ratings. These are independent factors influencing some investors, financiers and insurers but also are becoming factors for credit raters. The Governance Template, a simple tool, if properly applied, could help owners and managers improve their ratings.

Who, in addition to regulators, is addressing nuclear security?

The International Atomic Energy Agency (IAEA), the UN-affiliated agency established to promote the "safe, secure and peaceful use of nuclear technologies," defines nuclear security accordingly: "Like nuclear safety, nuclear security aims to protect people, property, society and the environment from harmful effects of ionizing radiation" (International Atomic Energy Agency n.d.).

The IAEA develops guidance documents for nuclear security—but these are guidance only, slow to be published and the world changes quickly. The IAEA has many types of review missions. Countries have taken advantage of its Integrated Nuclear Security Support Plan (INSSP) peer-reviews that over the past five years include a cyber security component for both operations and infrastructure derived from IAEA published guidance. On a facility basis, the IAEA conducts International Physical Protection Advisory Service (IPASS) missions and has started including cybersecurity in these. However, ensuring performance improvements requires follow-up missions and the funding, staffing and resources do not always exist for such follow up missions. These are confidential missions with only some states revealing their performance assessment. This lack of transparency may make the reviews more attractive to some operators but limit their utility for market rewards and benchmarking by other states.

Nuclear facilities/materials should be secure from sabotage or theft and safe from all hazards, including accidents and other incidents. The World Association of Nuclear Operators (WANO), whose U.S. office sits with the Institute for Nuclear Power Operations (INPO), does full peer reviews of nuclear operators every four years with interim reviews every two years, but these consider safety and reliability and exclude security. WANO is also working with other organizations such as the IAEA and the Japan Nuclear Safety Institute to see what other reviews can be judged as equivalent to WANO peer reviews. Although WANO might not directly review security, cyber security and supply chain security are of high concern within the nuclear industry; their inclusion in future reviews appears inevitable.

The World Institute for Nuclear Security (WINS) has supported the development of professional training and certifications for nuclear security officers. Some country regulators have minimum requirements for nuclear security officers. Such professional certifications can help evidence good security training but not necessarily performance. Others support nuclear security, such as with exercises, but not necessarily the development of good, embedded standards. And almost all these efforts are not made public so cannot get rewarded.

Some press investigations have consolidated public information of US nuclear power plant ratings, including the Nuclear Regulatory Commission scoring as part of its reactor oversight process—but these are time-consuming, occasional efforts (Proctor 2018).

Could Voluntary Consensus Standards Help Reduce Risks?

To develop a business case for nuclear security, we hypothesized with industry stakeholders how they could come together to decide on what good practices are necessary as well as sufficient to merit rewards. At industry's request, we presented a paper making the case for voluntary consensus standards at the joint Industry-Civil Society Nuclear Summit in 2016 (Nuclear Energy: Securing the Future – A Case for Voluntary Consensus Standards, Decker and Rauhut 2016).

The paper points out the plethora of standards development bodies around the world beyond the International Standards Organization (ISO) and includes statements from industry calling for some standards particularly for managing cyber risks. This was a new development as U.S. private sector participants working with the U.S. Department of Homeland Security (DHS) and the National Institute of Standards and Technology (NIST) on cyber security had wanted to ensure that NIST developed a cybersecurity framework not a standard.

We were thus encouraged to explore the standards development world. If you were compliant with some performance standards, could you get benefits from insurers, financers, regulators, the public? We looked at what standards had been developed already in the nuclear area and whether standards really work to ensure better quality practices in those who follow them, including within the nuclear industry.

Some guidance for security that could lend itself to standards development comes from many treaties, conventions and UN Security Council resolutions that call for nuclear safety and security, in particular the Amendment to the Convention on the Physical Protection of Nuclear Material and related IAEA guidance. This prompted our study of where standards can best be applied (The Quest for Nuclear Security Standards, Decker and Rauhut 2016).

ISO, American Society of Mechanical Engineers (ASME) and its N-Stamp, ASTM, ASIS, and others have developed voluntary consensus standards for products and quality performance. Management standards in safety/risk management, such as ISO quality management (ISO 9000 series) and its risk management guidance (ISO 31000), are generally not used in the nuclear industry. However, the industry has strong standards over product quality.

There has been a move to develop specific standards in the nuclear industry for quality management, such as for nuclear supply chain management, but these are not yet widely adopted. On security, the IAEA just issued in 2021 guidance on computer security that suggests "competent authorities" may look to some ISO/IEC [International Electrotechnical Commission] 27000 series information security management standards (IAEA 2021).

In discussions with these official standards organizations as well as some private providers of rating services in other fields, we found that organizations who went through the process to be shown compliant by ISO or other standards did so as a contractual requirement of performance or as a market differentiator. The U.S. Department of Defense asked ASIS, an official American National Standards Institute developer which is known for its security standards certifications, to develop standards for private security forces with certified training and then required those certifications for securing related Defense Department contracts.

That the nuclear industry has not widely adopted third-party quality management standards is clearly due to lack of perceived benefits from external certifications/accreditations. That said, the industry generally operates to its own high standards, which get even more stringent after each major incident. On safety, INPO has done many trainings and certifications; but regulators such as the U.S. Nuclear Regulatory Commission require these (Institute of Nuclear Power Operations n.d.). WINS has certified more than 400 professionals in nuclear security, often with financial support. Without regulatory requirements or external funding, it is unclear to what extent such initiatives would persist.

Unfortunately, standards can become a check-the-box routine without significant national and organizational commitment to the good governance that can drive good safety and security cultures. In Korea in 2012, the testing of nuclear power plant parts was discovered to have been falsified, costing billions of dollars and sending many to jail (Park 2013). The Fukushima nuclear power disaster, although precipitated by a tsunami, was more attributable to poor management and "regulatory capture," with the regulators more controlled by the nuclear industry than regulating it (Kaufmann and Penciakova 2011).

This became clearer as we pursued discussions with the Organisation for Economic Co-operation and Development's Nuclear Energy Agency (NEA) in our quest to find the conditions from which benefits could accrue for good security. How can you demonstrate good security? The NEA has heavily emphasized the importance of human and organizational elements in nuclear safety culture. In discussions with the NEA, we agreed that good governance was the key to good security just as it is to safety. Standards may be good but are not sufficient—governance drives culture which drives adherence to the spirit of any adopted standards (Decker 2016).

Doubling Down on Security Culture:
Good Governance is Good Business

Culture is important to good performance. Some recent examples of accidents where safety culture was identified as a contributing cause include BP's Texas City refinery explosion in 2005 (Chemical Safety Board), the Washington Metropolitan Area Transit Authority Metrorail collision in 2009 (National Transportation Safety Board), the Deepwater Horizon oil spill in 2010 (United States Coast Guard), and the Upper Big Branch mine explosion in 2010 (Mine Safety and Health Administration).

A lot of work has been done on safety culture and some work has been done on security culture, but leaders and how they govern drive culture. Good leadership and good safety and security culture are closely related. In the nuclear area, a U.S. Nuclear Regulatory Commission study of INPO's safety culture evaluations and plant performance showed the correlation between culture and fewer unplanned scrams, forced outages and better overall operating performance (Morrow and Barnes 2012).

Creating a governance framework for good nuclear security could prove cost-effective for operators, that is, it could derive licensee benefits from using it, we hypothesized. This would not be an in-depth standard or IAEA guidance, but a framework for management—for reflection, review, documentation and perhaps also a tool for communicating with stakeholders that demonstrates managements' due diligence, that management has seriously reflected on and pursued good security measures.

Industry was already thinking along these lines and had presented an initial security governance framework at the 2016 Nuclear Industry Summit in their report "The Role of the Nuclear Industry Globally." We took that initial draft of a governance framework and further developed it in discussions with operators, insurers, regulators, lawyers, and others who could help provide insight on possible incentives for good governance. We looked to other industry sectors, such as aviation and maritime and especially the chemical industry—and built out the framework in more detail. We supplemented it with IAEA guidance, WINS guidance, and incorporated WANO/INPO leadership principles (Duncan 2019).

The result was a Good Governance Framework that could be used by operators and was tested with stakeholders (Stimson Center n.d.). The team discussed the tool with various stakeholders and across various cybersecurity hypothetical scenarios. Although the Framework uses the term "Security" throughout, changing this to "Safety and Security" was deemed to provide even broader benefits.

We also investigated evaluations of governance and how those were evolving beyond just the maritime, chemical and aviation sectors and looked to the assessment of insurers and other evaluators of good governance. We found that rating systems help assess an organization's governance and reassure stakeholders of effective oversight and management as well as secure returns. Good governance can also help protect owners/managers from some potential liability. More investors, lenders and the public are looking to environmental, social, and governance factors in their assessment of organizations, and ratings have been developed in that area. Insurers and credit rating agencies are also becoming more sophisticated as more data become available, especially in the area of cyber risks.

Discussion

The journey to finding overall good governance as the basis for potential market rewards was a long one. This was an iterative process, with the framework being tested and refined across many stakeholder groups, with a focus on those conveying benefits.

Regulatory Benefits

Could you gain some regulatory benefits from owners, managers and operators doing a self-assessment of security using a Good Governance Framework? Although we were exploring benefits to be derived from the external market, we found that regulators are always a primary concern of licensees.

What did regulators say about supporting the nuclear security governance framework we were developing:

- Yes! It's another tool in the regulatory toolkit.

- If we know that an operator has not been doing well but is working on bettering their governance model, we can give them the benefit of the doubt in some of our oversight evaluations.

This stakeholder approval was a by-product of the effort, but an important one.

Insurance Benefits

As part of risk management, organizations take out insurance. Many countries require operators to be insured to demonstrate that the country is compliant with international treaties (World Nuclear Association 2021). Commercial insurers generally exclude nuclear risks, thus specialized nuclear insurers exist that provide coverage for nuclear operators. They share risks among themselves by establishing pools of insurance within and across countries (Nuclear Risk Insurers n.d.). Thus, we hypothesized that insurance had to be a lever for good governance internationally.

Insurers evaluate risks for underwriters and help operators in pre- and post-incident performance. They recommend ways to reduce the likelihood of a loss and its consequences. They also can assist in reducing the consequences of an incident by providing advisory services and assistance post incident.

The two major categories of insurance are property insurance, which includes business continuity, and liability insurance, which covers third parties' losses. Other specialized insurances exist, including for cyber coverage. Cyber is one of the key areas that worry nuclear insurers. With plants becoming more digitized, potential attack vectors increase—with increased risks to software and hardware, to information technology and operational technology. The electric sector is a prime target for advanced persistent threat actors who act through trusted parties, including managed service providers. Supply chain and cyber-related risks including ransomware attacks worry the sector.

Policies in the past had been silent on cyber coverage, so these were deemed by default to be covered risks. However, now they are generally excluded and must be specifically written back into a policy or obtained through a separate cyber risk policy that details coverage.

The specialized nuclear insurers survey nuclear power plants to assess plant performance and the insurance risk presented. As only 441 power plants currently operate in the world, with 56 under construction (primarily in China), specialized assessors—typically engineers and nuclear professionals—are hired by insurers to survey these plants (WNA 2021 and Reitsma 1998). While security and security culture are not standalone parts of the structured assessments, engineering consultants and pool representatives informed us that it is incorporated into their overall assessment. In the United States, which has the largest number of nuclear power plants, American Nuclear Insurers (ANI), a joint underwriting association, and Nuclear Electric Insurance Limited (NEIL), a mutual insurance company, respectively cover primarily liability and property insurance. Each operator takes on the risk of the others. Risk assessments and to some extent pricings for coverage are informed by confidential ratings that INPO issues. We also found that evidence of good governance, such as the model we developed, could help inform insurance underwriting.

However, insurance costs are a very small part of a nuclear power plant's cost. Capital costs (for the facility itself) and salaries are the largest expenses with fuel costs much lower than gas or coal plants (WNA 2021). Treaty terms cap liability limits for radiological events, while governments typically absorb much of the liability costs of the operators which keeps insurance rates low. Also, note that insurance did not factor into some large nuclear events like Chernobyl and Fukushima.[2] We found possible better insurance terms from better nuclear security, but these were not a driver of many operating decisions.

Also, insurers do not base their prices solely on risk, so demonstrating good governance and reducing risks would not necessarily lead to better insurance terms. Insurers also price based on portfolio performance, their loss experience and market competition.

The only lever insurance can provide to promoting good governance is the question of an entity's ability to obtain insurance at all. In only a few cases internationally have insurers requested changes in an enterprise's operating procedures before confirming underwriting. Insurers' engineers, while undertaking surveys, will influence operators to improve resilience to cyber incursions. They provide recommendations and promote best practices observed internationally, such as from the IAEA, NEA, WINS, and national regulatory bodies.

This may change. Small modular reactors (SMRs) and advanced modular reactors (AMRs) are likely to become a significant part of the future nuclear power industry. With different cyber risk exposures than legacy nuclear systems, these new plants will present insurers with new challenges. An advantage of digital systems utilized for SMRs and AMRs is that they will be designed and manufactured to work in the digital age, with associated security concerns addressed from the initial design. They are also much more digitally complex than older legacy systems that have backfitted digital systems and hardwired safety systems. SMRs and AMRs with remote monitoring systems will have to be assessed to be reliable and resilient. Assessment of their safety and security will be tied not only to their having safety and security "by design" but also to their having a "commoditized" approach to their manufacture and performance. This will make supply chain even more important. New types of insurance might be needed with more attention to governance quality standards as cyber and supply chain risks become better understood.

The nuclear pools have followed the market trend, i.e., to specifically exclude cyber in property insurance policies, and operators have shown a lack of interest to separately insure it. They self-insure or do not insure. The pools concluded that operators were comfortable managing the cyber risk themselves within their safety and security frameworks.

The pools do not exclude cyber from nuclear third-party liability cover for radiological events, but as mentioned earlier these are generally capped. However,

---

2   See: https://www.oecd-nea.org/law/table-liability-coverage-limits.pdf. Note that Chernobyl and Fukushima were not privately insured (https://www.oecd-nea.org/ndd/workshops/nuclearcomp/presentations/documents/1.SebastiaanReitsma-OECD-NEALiabilityWorkshop-December2013.pdf). Japan was not party to a convention until after the Fukushima incident, and the Soviet Union's responsibilities for the Chernobyl incident were limited under the then-existing convention details (https://www.oecd-nea.org/law/chernobyl/LAMM.pdf).

potential liability from events not involving radiological releases must be considered as cyber risks increase. Lloyd's, the specialist insurance/reinsurance market, has called for better clarity in policies and noted the major and potentially catastrophic impact of a cyberattack on an electric grid (The Council of Insurance Agents and Brokers 2019 and Lloyd 2015).

The importance of good governance and stewardship of nuclear assets including management of cybersecurity and supply chains cannot be understated. New technologies, including deep fakes, can escalate the impact of cyber incidents. Owners/managers must assess risks as part of good governance; and transferring some risks to insurers should be better studied and well considered. The insurance industry's assessment of cyber risk is quickly increasing with insurance becoming more costly as underwriters handle more cyber incidents and want to manage their exposures.

Reduced Liability and Increased Reputational Benefits

Two effective inducements for incentivizing security governance were operator concerns for reputation and liability from events without radiation releases. The international liability regime covers incidents that release or threaten to release radiation; a blackout or other disruption to the power supply at a nuclear power plant would not be covered (Nuclear Energy Agency 2019). In the aftermath of a terrorist incident at a nuclear facility, an operator could be held liable for negligence, that is the failure to act reasonably and adequately to protect the public and environment from harm. To demonstrate this, we held several roundtables in London with judges, attorneys, regulators, insurers, and operators. We developed hypothetical cybersecurity scenarios in which there was a blackout at a nuclear power plant with catastrophic consequences. One roundtable featured a mock trial in which former judges heard evidence about the hypothetical incident and ruled on whether the operator of the hypothetical plant in question would be held liable for civil and criminal charges for failure to prevent or mitigate a cyber terrorist-related event[3] (Stimson 2017 and Stimson 2018). In order to do so, the group tested iterations of the Good Governance Template and whether or not use of the template could have prevented or mitigated the effects of an incident.

The purpose of these roundtables was to explore liability mechanisms to identify economic incentives to make business decisions above and beyond compliance with regulatory minimums. Reasonable precautions must be taken to have systems and processes in place to address incidents with due diligence to ensure that processes are working consistently, reasonably and in accordance with industry norms. These factors are required to evidence an operator's duty of care. In

---

3   See some summaries at https://www.stimson.org/wp-content/files/file-attachments/LiftingTheLid-R4-WEB.pdf and, an earlier event, at https://www.stimson.org/2017/demonstrating-due-care-cyber-liability-considerations-nuclear-facilities/.

addition, operators must operate with continuous improvement and look to best practices in managing their facility.

The importance of developing and implementing a good model of governance and transparently reporting on that model proved to provide public assurance and support owners' and managers' self-attestations of operating with due care (World Institute for Nuclear Security 2018). It was found that significant civil and criminal liability can be reduced if operators have taken reasonable measures to protect the public and environment.

These personal impacts from demonstrating good governance proved to be compelling. Some benefits from good governance go even further. Entities can apply in the United States for certain protections from litigation if they comply with principles under the Homeland Security Act of 2002 known as the SAFETY Act. Enacted after 9/11, it was intended to motivate production of anti-terrorism products and services. The Act provides a unique way for organizations to limit liability in the event of a cyber or physical act of terrorism. It provides significant protection for products and services that meet specific anti-terrorism performance metrics. Security companies that have received SAFETY Act protection include ABM Security Services and Wackenhut Security. The National Football League, Major League Baseball and National Basketball Association have also had their security and best practices certified, and finally, the Southern Company obtained Safety Act coverage for its cyber/risk mitigation program for its electricity generation, transmission and distribution, gas services, business corporate services, and other activities.[4]

Finance and Investor Benefits

We next explored the issue of financing and whether demonstration of good governance of security and safety could attain better financing terms? Nuclear facilities are very expensive to build and require many investors and lenders (although this will likely change with SMRs and AMRs). Public companies, private companies, utilities that have nuclear generation, government-owned entities can all get rated, rating agencies explained. Because an entity is publicly owned does not mean that it is not subject to a rating review.

- *Export finance banks*: We researched export financing and spoke with several export banks. We found countries are looking to support their exports and build strategic relationships and are not that concerned about getting paid back over the many decades the financing would likely be outstanding, or so it seemed.

- *New builds*: Security risk is also not a concern for others financing new builds— project overruns are. Initial funding arrangements were all based on strategic

---

[4] See currently approved SAFETY Act technologies at: https://www.safetyact.gov/lit/at/aa.

country decisions, project-specific financing and country-related overall risk profiles—not the potential risks inherent in the eventually operational plants.

- *Operational Plants:* For going concerns—enterprises that were already operating—security can be a factor. Organizations are sensitive to changes in their risk profiles because they get evaluated by credit rating agencies like Standard & Poor's, Moody's and others around the world. Stock analysts and investor advisors all have a lot to say. What does good governance of security mean to them? If an entity's ratings go down, the cost of borrowing goes up including on new debt issues. The value of the company itself can go down with lower stock ratings for poor governance. This impacts both public and private equity investors' valuations of the company.

We found that good credit ratings can translate to better financing terms for organizations and the ability to tap into a larger investor group. Some investors such as pension funds can only invest in certain grades of investments. *The Economist* notes, "A downgrade can cause a company's funding costs to rocket, or a run on a bank. It can also force a corporate or sovereign borrower out of an index, draining the pool of investors willing or permitted to lend to it" (*The Economist* 2020).

Until now, most companies in the nuclear sector have had their credit ratings affected more by the general outlook for nuclear or the country risk of where they are located than by their individual performance, according to our interviews. This is changing somewhat as more data-driven risk evaluations are occurring in the rating agencies and as more investors consider sustainability and ESG goals in their portfolio holdings.

Credit, ESG and Cyber Ratings Driving Change

Credit rating agencies assess the ability of a country or entity to repay a debt. "Sovereign ratings" are given to a country to assess its political stability, foreign reserves, and other information. Ratings are also assigned to public and private companies and their various debt instruments. The rating agencies also give "ratings outlooks" that give their analysts' opinions regarding the direction of the rating for a future period given an entity's performance and anticipated market conditions.

The United States Securities and Exchange Commission recognizes nine credit rating agencies. (U.S. Security and Exchange Commission n.d.) The biggest are Moody's, Standard & Poor's (S&P) and Fitch. These three globally dominate, but other rating authorities in Europe, Switzerland, China, Russia and elsewhere recognize others also. Of particular interest—given where nuclear facilities are located—may be the European credit authorities' lists and rules, the Russian credit rating organization ACRA that partners with China, and Chinese rating agencies like China Chengxin Credit Rating Group that has a subsidiary joint venture with Moody's.

Credit rating agencies are not without controversy. The 2008 financial crisis highlighted the inability of the agencies to rate accurately, with misleading ratings on many financial instruments. Conflict of interest questions relate to how ratings agencies are paid; in the U.S., the organization being rated pays.

Given perceived overreliance on such agencies, the European Union and other members of the G20 took steps to ensure "that banks, market participants and institutional investors make their own credit assessments and not rely solely or mechanically on CRA [credit rating agency] ratings" (European Commission 2013). The EU cited the lack of transparency in agencies' sovereign ratings among other issues.

Given these and other concerns, under international regulatory requirements, banks have to risk-weight their assets (Chen 2020). Banks use complex rating systems beyond the rating agencies to make judgments on credit quality. Published operating information of a company is just one factor used in these assessments. But some lenders are beginning to look at textual information including public sentiment in assessing credit risks. And public sentiment is affected by entity and media reporting as well as credit ratings. This is significant with companies now clearly needing to manage their public reputations as part of good governance and good ratings.

Cyber risks in the electric utility area and nuclear sector in particular are indeed already concerns of analysts, as this sector is well known to be a target of terrorists, other States and hacktivists; and cybersecurity is increasingly affecting ratings. In 2017, the U.S. credit bureau Equifax suffered a major cyberbreach that released the personal information of nearly 150 million people (Fruhlinger 2020). [Note that credit bureaus rate individuals while credit rating agencies rate entities, so this was a release of individual's data.] The CEO resigned and asserted that the failure of one person in IT had left the company exposed to the exploit (Bernard and Cowley 2017). The company faced fines and class-action lawsuits that led Moody's to downgrade the company's ratings; this was one of the first time that Moody's had taken a negative rating action due to a cyber incident (Moody's 2019, 5). This affected the value of the company and its share price declined. However, as so many companies have experienced cyber incidents, the stock market appears to be suffering from breach fatigue and Equifax' share price has since rebounded (Osborne 2021). Early in 2021, it was found that Eletrobras, the largest power utility company in Latin America, was hit with a ransomware attack including as a target Eletronuclear, its subsidiary involved in the construction and operations of nuclear power plants (Cyber Reports 2021). Moody's, for one, deemed this a credit negative.

Analysts say that key to maintaining value after a cyber incident is to react quickly, responsibly and transparently to the incident. To attempt to quantify a company's cyber risk exposure—both IT and OT—and measure its resilience, in

2021 Moody's invested in BitSight and VisibleRisk to bring big data and more analyses to its cyber risk assessments (Moody's n.d. and VisibleRisk n.d.).

Investors look beyond credit ratings to other ratings and assessments of organizations. These investors can be individual ones looking not just for performance based on risk and returns but also for ethical matches for their portfolios. Shareholder activism has forced increased management interest in good governance (Broadridge n.d.). Investor and lender interest has led to Environmental, Social and Governance evaluations—or ESG, an outgrowth of earlier efforts at corporate social responsibility. The increase in interest in companies with good ESG profiles comes from individual investors as well as pension funds and other controllers of large sources of wealth, known as asset managers. This is not just about investors gaining more of a conscience, but also about analysts recognizing that such companies attract talent and have lower turnover thus potentially higher profits and better long-term sustainability, or at least that is the thinking (Thygensen 2019). And good governance is important. McKinsey notes, "Frequent governance reviews are … simply good corporate hygiene" (Birshan et al. 2020).

Approaches to ESG and sustainability reporting are proliferating, but their governance evaluations do not yet directly address oversight of safety/security for protection of workers and the environment (*The Economist* 2020). We see this changing, especially as we see ESG and credit ratings being developed into more finely tuned and integrated models—although some ESG may look at nuclear negatively (nuclear waste disposal) or positively (low carbon), which Canada's Bruce Power is capitalizing on with its green financing framework (Bloomberg News 2021). The ratings agencies' governance assessment differs from the internal good governance measures that we used in our model. Their models have higher-level measures that may include, for example, board structure, independence, diversity, and compensation but do include risk oversight (ISS n.d.). Some agreement on acceptable/important ESG indictors may well be forged as countries issue their own ESG rules, with the EU just publishing new disclosure rules on sustainability (think climate effects) for fund managers that the U.S. looks set to emulate (Eaglesham and Hirtenstein 2021 and Gnanarajah and Shorter 2021).

Moody's has been working on an effort to integrate ESG concerns into its overall ratings. Some cyber issues fall into ESG evaluations and could directly affect credit ratings, e.g., data privacy issues in the health care or financial services sectors. But other ESG effects on an entity's credit worthiness are more subtle. In discussions with Moody's, it was noted that operational aspects and risk transfer aspects of organizations' cyber risk profile are not fully captured in ESG ratings. For the Governance rating, 30-40 questions are considered with 80-90 sub-questions. Questions concern, for example, board structure, policies and procedures; board independence; compliance and reporting. Management credibility and track record are important, e.g., the organization performs as management plans and says it will. Controversies in the news are tracked and included in evaluations. Moody's, as an SEC-approved credit agency has access to operations, information and internal reports that go beyond companies' public reporting. The INPO rating system for nuclear performance is shared with Moody's and other approved credit rating agencies (as well as insurers and INPO members, as earlier mentioned). Moody's executives noted that good governance of security affects environmental and social evaluations, and that ESG ratings should not be stove-piped. Indeed, the company is right now trying to integrate all evaluations.

Morningstar is an investment research organization that provides evaluations of relative risk and returns with a star-rating system. Its Morningstar ratings and its analyst recommendations are highly influential among fund managers. The firm has expanded its services into credit ratings and ESG ratings. Morningstar's Sustainalytics, an ESG rating organization, explained the ratings basis for its ESG system including such factors as overall industry exposure to ESG risks. Importantly, the firm monitors 70,000 news sources bi-weekly to rate the news' risk and impact on organizations and how that news might affect shareholders and stakeholders. In terms of evaluating governance, the firm considers business ethics and a company's handling of adverse events.[5]

The move toward greater evaluations of governance and reputation in assessing ESG ratings, and the move toward integration of evaluations (within ESG ratings, with credit ratings and from news sources), demonstrate that good governance of security should help in the future drive for better ratings and their benefits. Some aspects of security governance are already starting to affect ratings, at least in the cyber area. A rating can be affected but not so substantially—yet! The financial materiality of cybersecurity is only now being identified.

Other Efforts

Some press investigations have consolidated public information of U.S. nuclear power plant ratings (Cascadia Times 2013), including the Nuclear Regulatory Commission scoring as part of its reactor oversight process—but these are time-consuming efforts (Proctor 2018). Note, we did not look at National Nuclear Security Administration (NNSA) Performance Evaluations—although that would be an interesting exercise given the many past issues of government nuclear facilities.[6]

---

5   For other information on Sustainalytics, see: https://www.sustainalytics.com/about-us.

6   For some recent performance evaluations of government-owned but contractor-managed nuclear facilities, see: https://www.energy.gov/nnsa/articles/nnsa-releases-performance-reports-labs-plants-and-sites. Some issues on management of these facilities can be found in press reports as well in analyses of the Project On Government Oversight and the Exchange Monitor. Some good early work on incentives for nuclear security in government facilities with nuclear warheads and weapons-usable materials (before the advent of WINS in 2008), can be found at: https://scholar.harvard.edu/files/matthew_bunn/files/incentives_for_nuclear_security.pdf.

An INPO tactic that drives security and managers' quest for good ratings is management's consideration of quest for a good rating and thus a good reputation amongst peers. Peer pressure is perceived to be important. In 2019, the "Federal Energy Regulatory Commission (FERC) and North American Electric Reliability Corporation (NERC) issued a joint white paper proposing to 'name and shame' electric utilities violating NERC Critical Infrastructure Protection (CIP) Reliability Standards" (Jeweler et al. 2019). The organizations were receiving many Freedom of Information Act requests for these, and the thinking was that public exposure of noncompliance notices could lead to better compliance. However, fearing that this could also lead to even worse security breaches, the proposal was abandoned in 2020. In any event, reputation concerns can lead owners/managers to have better security governance, and enhanced reputation can then feed into credit, ESG, insurer benefits and better performance.

Conclusion

We have explored how market incentives could be used as a force multiplier to incentivize nuclear security beyond regulatory minimums and found that evidence of due care is a necessary prerequisite for achieving benefits. Recognizing that complete security can never be achieved, facilities could be inspired to good security and safety governance beyond regulatory minimums through a Good Governance Template that inspires reflection, requires systematic reviews and transparent risk assessments, and demonstrates due care.

We found that judgments of rating agencies, insurers, courts, and financiers can motivate good security performance of a nuclear facility operator by affecting public reputation and by modifying potential liability of the facility's owners/operators in the event of an incident. Evidencing good performance also potentially affects the availability of financing/investment as well as financing terms and conditions. Insurance availability, especially for cyber coverage, will become a more important incentive for good governance as owners/operators have expanded exposure to more complex technologies and an enlarged threat surface.

Each potential lever of influence has certain limitations, but when taken as a whole—as a reflection on a company's reputation—are very important. The overall reputation of a company is an important consideration in the judgments these parties make, and positive judgments bring benefits to the entities. Overall reputational considerations—not one individual market benefit—appear to drive owner/managers in a more holistic way. Peer judgments are important to an operator's own self-assessment, which should not be undervalued. Further, reputation influences regulators as well as the public and employees.

In sum, we found that the whole of incentives is bigger than the sum of its parts—that multiple and collective incentives promote the best security state of practice and obtain the most benefits. Continual improvement, doing the right thing, right-sizing security, supporting a questioning attitude, seeking and adopting best practices—these are all mantras in the nuclear industry that the industry itself should continue to foster in licensees. Licensees will then benefit from better stewardship and governance of their facilities in the virtuous circle of knowledge and continuous learning.

Acknowledgements and Funding

The authors thank the John D. and Catherine T. MacArthur Foundation, the Carnegie Corporation of New York, the Stanley Foundation as well as the governments of Canada, Finland, and the United States for their financial support.

We would also like to give special thanks to the law firm of Pillsbury Winthrop Shaw Pittman and many of its staff for all their *pro bono* support and especially to Elina Teplinsky a partner at Pillsbury who has supported this work from its beginning. We also want to recognize the World Institute for Nuclear Security for collaborating with us—in particular, Roger Howsley, its former Executive Director, who was a visionary and gave this project his unwavering support. There were so many others who advised on this project, including Symantec and Lofty Perch on cyber issues, Moody's Corporation and Sustainalytics on ratings' incentives, Edlow International on transport risks and Nuclear Risk Insurers, the Nuclear Energy Institute and the Canadian Nuclear Association—to name just a few. We also want to recognize two remarkable leaders who are no longer with us: Frank Saunders, formerly with Bruce Power, and Greg Kaser, formerly with the World Nuclear Association. Thank you all. We deeply appreciate your contribution to helping us seek ways to make the world safer and more secure. We also would like to thank Stimson Research Intern Jerry Zhang for helping to edit this paper.

Acronyms and Abbreviations

AMR	Advanced modular reactor
ANI	American Nuclear Insurers
DHS	U.S. Department of Homeland Security
ESG	Environmental, Social, and Governance
FERC	Federal Energy Regulatory Commission
IAEA	The International Atomic Energy Agency
INPO	Institute for Nuclear Power Operations

INSSP	Integrated Nuclear Security Support Plan
IPASS	International Physical Protection Advisory Service
ISO	International Standards Organization
NEA	Nuclear Energy Agency
NEIL	Nuclear Electric Insurance Limited
NERC	North American Electric Reliability Corporation
NIST	National Institute of Standards and Technology
NRC	Nuclear Regulatory Commission
SMR	Small modular reactor
WANO	World Association of Nuclear Operators
WINS	World Institute for Nuclear Security

Author Capsule Bios

Debra K. Decker is a Senior Advisor at the Stimson Center, where she works on cyber and nuclear security issues. She has advised on strategy and risk management with private and public sector organizations, including the U.S. Federal Bureau of Investigation and the U.S Departments of Defense and Homeland Security. In the public sector, she has specialized in threats stemming from weapons of mass destruction and in the vulnerabilities of critical infrastructure. She was involved in the development of the National Institute of Standards and Technology first Cybersecurity Framework and the 2013 ASIS Technical Advisory Committee for developing a national risk assessment standard. Earlier in her career, she was a Research Associate at Harvard's Belfer Center for Science and International Affairs.

Kathryn Rauhut is Non-Resident Fellow at the Stimson Center. An attorney specializing in international security, she works primarily in the field of cyber and nuclear security accountability and liability issues. She is a member of the California Bar Association, the American Bar Association, and the International Nuclear Lawyer's Association. She has completed a decade of international work in Europe while living in Vienna, Austria. Prior to her work with Stimson, she was Strategic Advisor to the World Institute for Nuclear Security and the Internet Security Alliance. Before that, she was Deputy General Counsel of Lawrence Livermore National Laboratory in California, where she had earlier served as a prosecutor. Ms. Rauhut, along with Ms. Decker, have been advisors to the International Atomic Energy Agency on supply chain risk issues.

References

Bernard, Tara, and Stacey Cowley. 2017. "Equifax Breach Caused by Lone Employee's Error, Former C.E.O. Says." *The New York Times*. October 3, 2017. https://www.nytimes.com/2017/10/03/business/equifax-congress-data-breach.html.

Birshan, Michael, Madelein Goerg, Anna Moore, and Ellora-Julie Parekh. 2020. "Investors Remind Business Leaders: Governance Matters." McKinsey & Company. October 2, 2020. https://www.mckinsey.com/business-functions/strategy-and-corporate-finance/our-insights/investors-remind-business-leaders-governance-matters.

Bloomberg News. 2021. "Nuclear Energy Generator Splits ESG Buyers with Green Bond." November 18, 2021. https://www.bloomberg.com/news/articles/2021-11-18/nuclear-energy-generator-splits-esg-buyers-with-green-bond-sale.

Broadridge. "ESG Webinar: How to Engage Shareholders Through Technology." Accessed December 9, 2021. https://www.broadridge.com/webinar/esg-webinar?id=ICSCIO19jl5d4afe9903727e96f88518d91d37ee51&so=se&po=&di=&ct=&ot=wb&mt=ja&yr=20&rg=gl&on=01&ep=pd&gclid=EAIaIQobChMI66WXlozi6gIVSr7ACh0PuArMEAAYASABEgKuevD_BwE.

Cascadia Times. 2013. "The Most Dangerous Nuclear Power Plants in America." December 18, 2013. https://www.times.org/nuclear-power-back/2018/3/8/the-most-dangerous-nuclear-power-plants-in-america.

Chen, James. 2020. "Basel II." Investopedia. October 31, 2020. https://www.investopedia.com/terms/b/baselii.as.

Cyber Reports. 2021. "Eletrobras, Copel energy companies hit by ransomware attacks." February 7, 2021. https://cyber-reports.com/2021/02/07/eletrobras-copel-energy-companies-hit-by-ransomware-attacks/.

Cyberspace Solarium Commission. "Cyberspace Solarium Commission." Accessed December 9, 2021. https://www.solarium.gov/home.

Decker, Debra. "Before the Next Chernobyl." CNN Opinion. April 26, 2016. https://www.cnn.com/2016/04/26/opinions/chernobyl-nuclear-safety-opinion-decker/index.html.

Decker, Debra, and Kathryn Rauhut. 2016. *Nuclear Energy: Securing the Future – A Case for Voluntary Consensus Standards*. Washington, D.C.: Stimson Center. https://

www.stimson.org/2016/nuclear-energy-securing-future-case-voluntary-consensus-standards/.

Decker, Debra, and Kathryn Rauhut. 2016. *The Quest for Nuclear Security Standards*. Muscatine, IA: The Stanley Foundation. https://stanleycenter.org/publications/pab/Decker-RauhutPAB216.pdf.

Duncan, Brian. 2019. *WANO Principles: Nuclear Leadership Effectiveness Attributes*. PL2019-01. London, United Kingdom: The World Association of Nuclear Operators. https://www.wano.info/getmedia/f6e15600-4526-42f6-b77d-066deba2561d/PL-2019-01-Nuclear-Leadership-Effectiveness-Attributes-(A4).pdf.aspx.

Eaglesham, Jean, and Anna Hirtenstein. 2021. "ESG Disclosure Rule from Europe Challenge U.S. Fund Manager." *The Wall Street Journal*. March 22, 2021. https://www.wsj.com/articles/esg-disclosure-rules-from-europe-challenge-u-s-fund-managers-11616405401.

European Commission. 2013. "New Rules on Credit Rating Agencies (CRAs) – Frequently Asked Questions." January 16, 2013. https://ec.europa.eu/commission/presscorner/detail/de/MEMO_13_13.

Fruhlinger, Josh. 2020. "Equifax Data Breach FAQ: What Happened, Who was Affected, What was the Impact?" CSO. February 12, 2020. https://www.csoonline.com/article/3444488/equifax-data-breach-faq-what-happened-who-was-affected-what-was-the-impact.html.

Gnanarajah, Raj and Gary Shorter. 2021. *Introduction to Financial Services: Environmental, Social, and Governance (ESG) Issues*. CRS Report No. IF11716. Washington, D.C.: Congressional Research Service. https://crsreports.congress.gov/product/pdf/IF/IF11716.

International Atomic Energy Agency, "Nuclear Security Series." Accessed December 9, 2021. https://www.iaea.org/resources/nuclear-security-series#:~:text=The%20IAEA%20establishes%20and%20maintains%20the%20guidance%20series,the%20environment%20from%20harmful%20effects%20of%20ionizing%20radiation.

International Atomic Energy Agency. "Overview of Management, Governance, and Organizational Structure." Accessed December 9, 2021. https://www.iaea.org/about.

International Atomic Energy Agency. 2021. *Computer Security for Nuclear Security*. Vienna, Austria: International Atomic Energy Agency. https://www-pub.iaea.org/MTCD/Publications/PDF/PUB1918_web.pdf.

Institute of Nuclear Power Operations. "About Us." Accessed December 9, 2021. http://www.inpo.info/AboutUs.htm#:~:text=Our%20National%20Academy%20for%20Nuclear%20Training%20provides%20training,and%20take%20the%20various%20online%20courses%20INPO%20offers.

ISS. "Governance Qualityscore." Accessed December 9, 2021. https://www.issgovernance.com/esg/ratings/governance-qualityscore/.

Jeweler, Matthew, Brendan Hogan, Richard Mroz, Robert Ross, and Cassie Lentchner. 2019. "Name-and-Shame Proposal of Electric Regulators Highlights Need for Cyber Insurance." November 5, 2019. https://www.pillsburylaw.com/en/news-and-insights/name-and-shame-proposal-of-electric-regulators-highlights-need-for-cyber-insurance.html.

Kaufmann, Daniel, and Veronika Penciakova. 2011. *Preventing Nuclear Meltdown: Assessing Regulatory Failure in Japan and the United States.* Washington, D.C.: The Brookings Institute. https://www.brookings.edu/opinions/preventing-nuclear-meltdown-assessing-regulatory-failure-in-japan-and-the-united-states/#:~:text=To%20a%20significant%20extent%2C%20it%20appears%20that%20regulatory,that%20the%20NRC%20is%20not%20effectively%20enforcing%20regulations.

Lloyd's. "Business Blackout." Accessed December 9, 2021. https://www.lloyds.com/news-and-insights/risk-reports/library/business-blackout/.

Moody's. "Moody's and Cyber." Accessed December 9, 2021. https://about.moodys.io/cyber.

Moody's. 2019. "Credit implications of cyber risk will hinge on business disruptions, reputational effects." Accessed December 17, 2021. researchdocumentcontentpage.aspx (moodys.com)

Morrow, Stephanie, and Valerie Barnes. 2012. *Independent Evaluation of INPO's Nuclear Safety Culture Survey and Construct Validation Study.* Rockville, MD: Nuclear Regulatory Commission. https://www.nrc.gov/docs/ML1217/ML12172A093.pdf.

Nuclear Risk Insurers. "Nuclear Pools." Accessed December 9, 2021. https://www.nuclear-risk.com/nuclear-pools/#.

Park, Ju-min. 2013. "South Korea Charges 100 with Corruption over Nuclear Scandal." Reuters. October 10, 2013. https://www.reuters.com/article/us-korea-nuclear-idUSBRE99905O20131010.

Proctor, Darrell. 2018. "Three U.S. Nuclear Plants Get Poor Marks from NRC." Power. May 30, 2018. https://www.powermag.com/three-us-nuclear-plants-get-poor-marks-from-nrc/.

Reitsma, Sebastiaan. 1998. "Nuclear Insurance Pools: World-Wide Practice and Prospective." Vienna, Austria: International Atomic Energy Agency. https://inis.iaea.org/collection/NCLCollectionStore/_Public/31/051/31051428.pdf.

Stimson Center. 2017. "Demonstrating Due Care: Cyber Liability Considerations for Nuclear Facilities." April 24, 2017. https://www.stimson.org/2017/demonstrating-due-care-cyber-liability-considerations-nuclear-facilities/.

Stimson Center. 2018. *Lifting the Lid on Nuclear Liability*. Washington, D.C.: Stimson Center. https://www.stimson.org/wp-content/files/file-attachments/LiftingTheLid-R4-WEB.pdf.

Stimson Center. "Nuclear Security Governance Template." Accessed December 9, 2021. https://www.stimson.org/2021/nuclear-security-governance-template/.

The Council of Insurance Agents and Brokers. 2019. "Lloyd's Moves to Address Silent Cyber Risk." July 11, 2019. https://www.ciab.com/resources/lloyds-moves-to-address-silent-cyber-risk/.

The Economist. 2020. "Markers Marked: Credit-rating Agencies are Back under the Spotlight." May 9, 2020. https://www.economist.com/finance-and-economics/2020/05/07/credit-rating-agencies-are-back-under-the-spotlight.

The Economist. 2020. "In the Soup: The Proliferation of Sustainability Accounting Standards Comes with Costs." October 3, 2020. https://www.economist.com/business/2020/10/03/the-proliferation-of-sustainability-accounting-standards-comes-with-costs.

Thygesen, Tine. 2019. "Everyone Is Talking About ESG: What Is It and Why Should It Matter To You?" *Forbes*. November 9, 2019. https://www.forbes.com/sites/tinethygesen/2019/11/08/everyone-is-talking-about-esgwhat-is-it-and-why-should-it-matter-to-you/?sh=2cf5219c32e9.

U.S. Department of Homeland Security Integrated Task Force. 2013. *Executive Order 13636: Improving Critical Infrastructure Cybersecurity, Incentives Study Analytic Report*. Washington, D.C.: Department of Homeland Security. https://www.cisa.gov/sites/default/files/publications/dhs-eo13636-analytic-report-cybersecurity-incentives-study.pdf.

U.S. Securities and Exchange Commission. "Current NRSROs." Accessed December 9, 2021. https://www.sec.gov/ocr/ocr-current-nrsros.html.

VisibleRisk. "Cyber Risk Qualification." Accessed December 9, 2021. https://visiblerisk.com.

World Institute for Nuclear Security. 2018. *Corporate Governance Arrangements for Nuclear Security.* Vienna, Austria: World Institute for Nuclear Security. https://www.wins.org/document/corporate-governance-arrangements-for-nuclear-security/.

World Nuclear Association. "Economics of Nuclear Power." Accessed December 9, 2021. https://world-nuclear.org/information-library/economic-aspects/economics-of-nuclear-power.aspx.

World Nuclear Association. "Liability for Nuclear Damage." Accessed December 9, 2021. https://www.world-nuclear.org/focus/fukushima-daiichi-accident/liability-for-nuclear-damage.aspx.

World Nuclear Association. "World Nuclear Power Reactors & Uranium Requirements." Accessed December 9, 2021. https://world-nuclear.org/information-library/facts-and-figures/world-nuclear-power-reactors-and-uranium-requireme.aspx.

Evolution and Trends of Industrial Control System Cyber Incidents since 2017

Robert Grubbs,[1,2] Jeremiah Stoddard,[3] Sarah Freeman,[4] Ron Fisher[5]

[1] Senior Cyber Intelligence Analyst, Idaho National Laboratory
[2] Corresponding Author, Robert.Grubbs@INL.gov
[3] Critical Infrastructure Security Analyst, Idaho national Laboratory
[4] Industrial Control Systems Cyber Security Analyst, Idaho National Laboratory
[5] Director of Infrastructure Assurance and Analysis, Idaho National Laboratory

[see Author Capsule Bios below]

Abstract

The industrial control systems (ICSs) that manage our critical infrastructure are increasingly converging with corporate networks and the Internet as technology and businesses prioritize digital connectivity. These connections make them more vulnerable and available to malicious cyber actors who traditionally targeted the companies' more public-facing information technology (IT) networks. This paper will review select publicly reported cyber incidents to highlight the continued and growing threat to ICS devices and operational technology (OT) environments. It will summarize the incident and when available, will provide information on the cyber actors, the vulnerabilities they exploited, and any publications the U.S. Government (USG) provided in response. Data belonging to the Department of Homeland Security (DHS) will be used to highlight quantitative trends concerning ICS incidents. This paper builds on "History of Industrial Control System Cyber Incidents" (Hemsley & Fisher 2018), a paper that highlighted select noteworthy threats and incidents to ICS systems up to 2017. This paper will similarly review select incidents occurring after the last previously reviewed incident, Triton/HatMan, December 2017, and will note ICS incident trends including IT/OT convergence and advances in cyber-threat actors' capabilities in observed in the examined incidents.

Keywords: Industrial Control System, Information Technology, Operational Technology, Compromise

Introduction

Control systems manage and regulate devices or other systems, ranging from simple household appliances such as a refrigerator or air-conditioning unit in a single-family home, to large-scale systems governing public transportation or factory machinery. Industrial control systems (ICSs) are a collection of control systems and their instrumentations used to govern or automate industrial processes and exist in operation technology (OT) environments. ICSs are frequently managed via a Supervisory Control and Data Acquisition (SCADA) system that provides a graphical user interface (GUI) for the operator to perform their duties, including observing the system, receiving and acting upon alarms, or adjusting processes governed by the SCADA. These industrial processes are essential to the critical infrastructure sectors, including but not limited to water and wastewater systems (WWS), energy, fuel, and transportation, which are the backbone of modern conveniences. Whereas the primary benefit of using control systems in consumer devices is convenience, at the corporate and national critical infrastructure level ICS and SCADA systems provide significant cost efficiencies and thus permeate the operation and control of those infrastructures. Table 1 provides an example of how ICS and SCADA are widely utilized in critical infrastructures.

Table 1. Examples of Control Systems in Critical Infrastructures.

Critical Infrastructure	Control Systems/ICS Example(s)
Energy Sector	SCADA and Distributed Control Systems (DCS) used to operate and manage hundreds of thousands of miles of transmission and distribution of power grids and oil and natural gas pipelines; and the complexity of operating and maintaining petroleum refineries.
Water/Wastewater Sector	SCADA used to operate and monitor water treatment, water testing, water quality, and water flows to storage through end use.
Transportation Sector	Control systems are embedded in all modes of transportation (e.g., trucking, automotive, rail, air, water) to efficiently transport goods and people. As movement towards autonomous vehicles continue, this will increase significantly the control systems in automobiles and other transportation equipment.
Public Health	Control systems increasing utilization in medical devices including dialysis equipment, pacemakers, and health monitoring equipment.

Even though the services ICSs provide touch our lives every day, from a cyber-perspective, ICS/SCADA and OT generally receive less attention than the information technology (IT) environments that govern our modern Internet-dependent businesses and lifestyles. As businesses and the technologies that run them become more Internet-connected, many devices and systems that have not traditionally been Internet-connected are coming online, increasing the cyber-footprint for many companies not accustomed to minding cybersecurity best practices.

This paper will examine incidents that either compromised ICSs or disrupted ICS/SCADA operations due to a compromised IT environment, and when available, will note the attack vector and threat type. Some of the attack vectors include ransomware, insider threat, supply chain and brute force attacks, and these incidents were carried out by both cyber-criminal groups and advanced persistent threat (APT) (i.e., nation-state) cyber actors. The incidents covered in this paper do not review every single recorded ICS compromise during the examined timeframe, but rather a selected list. Some of the compromises directly targeted ICS devices, whereas in other incidents, ICS devices were indirectly targeted and affected.

The incidents selected for review are notable for a variety of reasons including, but not limited to: having occurred since 2017 to avoid anything in the Hemsley & Fisher paper, the attack vector used in order to demonstrate the diversity of ways a network or environment can be targeted, the notoriety and amount of media coverage of the event, leading to an expectation it would be covered (e.g., Colonial Pipeline, JBS meat plant, Oldsmar), the amount of publicly available information allowing for comprehensive and verifiable incident review and independent research, or to specifically highlight one facet of the incident, such as how the victim handled the incident publicly (e.g., Volue ASA). Lastly, a few incidents listed were chosen because the company did not make the initial compromise public and only later agreed to be anonymously covered in Cybersecurity and Infrastructure Security Agency (CISA) reporting, highlighting that there are many more incidents than those available on the public Internet.

According to metrics provided by CISA, for the first three quarters of the fiscal year 2021 (FY-21) only 12.6% of victim notifications performed by CISA were to the Energy, Food & Agriculture, Nuclear, Transportation or WWS sectors. Not all of these victim notifications involved an OT compromise, but these sectors are highly reliant upon OT processes. Though IT environments are more frequently targeted by cyber actors, the low percentage of notifications is an indicator many cybersecurity events in OT environments may go unreported and remain unknown to their customers until well after the incident is over.

Timeline of ICS Incidents

This paper timeline starts in 2018, picking up from the previous ICS paper (Hemsley & Fisher 2018) to provide a continuous glimpse of ICS incidents over time. These papers combined provide insights into the increasing level of vulnerabilities and threats to ICS and highlight the growing number of attack vectors available to threat actors.

Table 2 below lists the incidents covered in this paper temporally.

Table 2. ICS Incidents Covered in this Paper.

YEAR	ATTACK TYPE	VICTIM(S)	SUMMARY
2018	Third-party / supply chain	Energy Services Group	Attack on billing software company disrupts a natural gas company
2019	Insider Threat	Unidentified Power Plant	Employee installed ransomware via infected peripheral device
2019	Remote Exploit	sPower	Remote exploit caused Denial-of-Service (DoS) and device restarts
2019	Insider threat	Post Rock Water District, Ellsworth County (KS)	Ex-employee attempted to alter water disinfectant levels using still-valid user credentials
2019	Brute Force	Energy Companies Across Europe and U.S.	APT actors use Kubernetes cluster in brute force attacks
2020	Remote Exploit	Camrosa Water District (CA)	Cyber actors encrypt files, exfiltrate personal information
2020	Word Press vulnerability / watering hole	Florida Water Infrastructure Construction Company	Cyber actors turn legitimate water sector site into a watering hole attack page
2021	Unauthorized Remote Access	San Francisco Bay-area Water Treatment Plant (CA)	Cyber actors use TeamViewer to delete programs used to treat water
2021	Ransomware in the IT environment	Eletrobras & Copel Electric Power Utilities	Ransomware affects operations at two plants; cyber actors exfiltrate sensitive business and network data
2021	Unauthorized Remote Access	Oldsmar (FL) Water Treatment Plant (WTP)	Cyber actors use remote access in attempt to change water chemistry
2021	Unknown ransomware in the OT environment	Nevada-based WWS	Ransomware affects the ICS/SCADA environment
2021	Supply chain	Metropolitan Water District of Southern California (MWD)	China-based APT cyber actors compromise MWD device using Pulse Secure exploit

2021	Ransomware in the IT environment	City of Tulsa (OK)	Ransomware affects city services and customer-facing website
2021	Ryuk ransomware in the IT environment	Volue ASA (Norway)	Ransomware disrupts operations; company lauded for transparency and accountability in public response
2021	Ransomware in the IT environment	Colonial Pipeline	Ransomware disrupts operations on US' largest pipeline
2021	ZuCaNo ransomware in OT environment	Maine-based WWS	Treatment center needed to be run manually until operations returned to normal
2021	Ghost variant ransomware in the OT environment	California-based WWS	Ransomware sat on several SCADA servers for a month until detected

Chronological List of ICS Incidents

Energy Services Group LLC

In March 2018, unidentified cyber actors compromised a software platform developed by Energy Services Group LLC that is used for billing and customer transactions (Lyngaas 2018) The attack on the billing software impacted the Texas-based Energy Transfer Partners LP, a natural gas and propane pipeline company, with more than 71,000 miles of pipelines across 38 states and Canada (Energy Transfer 2018). The attack specifically targeted an Electronic Data Interchange (EDI) for the Eastern Panhandle pipeline serviced by Energy Services Group LLC and caused the system to be taken offline. Taking the system offline did not disrupt the flow of natural gas in the pipeline (Ciscomag 2020).

This incident demonstrates the reliance OT systems have on IT infrastructure for many critical infrastructure operations. Even though OT systems may still function correctly, if the owner/operator cannot properly determine usage or billing rates, they may choose to take a service offline. This incident also highlights the supply chain and third-party concerns inherent to OT environments as more of their control systems are regulated by IT systems. While the ICS owner/operator may be secure, their IT partners that manage their data can be compromised which can still lead to service interruptions.

Unidentified Power Plant

Sometime in early 2019 cyber actors convinced a trusted visitor of an unidentified power plant outside of the United States to plug a universal serial bus (USB) mouse into a computer system. The affected computer was a human machine interface (HMI) providing the operator views of the power plant. Once the infected mouse was plugged in, the cyber actors were able to remotely deploy ransomware. The cyber actors did not do any damage to any of the ICSs, despite having access. The power plant paid the ransom but did not get their files back and had to rebuild their network, impacting operations at the plant for three months. The trusted visitor was eventually arrested and charged with knowingly plugging in the infected mouse into an ICS computer in exchange for money (Tomlinson 2020).

This incident highlights how ransomware groups may try to bypass traditional remote, network-based efforts by looking to co-opt insiders. Whether the insider is acting intentionally, as in this case, or is an unsuspecting accomplice, the insider threat posed by trusted visitors or employees of ICS companies remains high and is an appealing choice to cyber-criminals if they have a specific target victim in mind.

sPower

In March 2019, unidentified cyber actors attempted to exploit an Internet-facing firewall, resulting in device restarts, DoS, and periodic loss of view against the Salt Lake City-based solar and wind energy developer sPower for approximately 12 hours. While the power company lost visibility into its network, no actual power outages were reported (Tomlinson 2019). A DoS attack occurs when cyber actors and/or botnets flood the targeted network with enough traffic that it cannot process requests or it crashes, preventing the network from being accessible for legitimate use (CISA 2009). The DoS attack likely targeted a Cisco Adaptive Security Appliance (CASA), an Internet-facing device that functions as a firewall and virtual private network (VPN) that has been associated with numerous vulnerabilities (Behr 2019). The CASA devices have previously been successfully targeted via CVE-2018-0296 and CVE-2018-0101[1] by malicious cyber actors who seek to cause a denial-of-service condition by causing the affected devices to reload unexpectedly (Cimpanu 2018).

---

1 CVE-2018-0296: According to Mitre.org, CVE-2019-0296 is a vulnerability in the web interface of the Cisco Adaptive Security Appliance (ASA) could allow an unauthenticated, remote attacker to cause an affected device to reload unexpectedly, resulting in a denial of service (DoS) condition. It is also possible on certain software releases that the ASA will not reload, but an attacker could view sensitive system information without authentication by using directory traversal techniques. The vulnerability is due to lack of proper input validation of the HTTP URL.

CVE-2018-0101: According to Mitre.org, CVE-2018-1010 is a vulnerability in the Secure Sockets Layer (SSL) VPN functionality of the Cisco Adaptive Security Appliance (ASA) Software could allow an unauthenticated, remote attacker to cause a reload of the affected system or to remotely execute code. The vulnerability is due to an attempt to double free a region of memory when the webvpn feature is enabled on the Cisco ASA device. An attacker could exploit this vulnerability by sending multiple, crafted XML packets to a webvpn-configured interface on the affected system. An exploit could allow the attacker to execute arbitrary code and obtain full control of the system or cause a reload of the affected device.

This attack, directed against transmission-level assets, is the first of its kind; although this event did not result in disruptions in electricity delivery, it was the largest attack against the U.S. electric sector by affected megawatt (MW) (nearly 20 MW). This incident demonstrated the fragility of IT infrastructure within the OT environment. Manufacturers of OT systems often go to great lengths to ensure the reliability and availability of their technologies, often implementing robust resiliency testing. IT asset resiliency however, for assets deployed within the OT environment, is often overlooked. The disruption of IT can still impact OT functions.

Post Rock Water District, Ellsworth (KS)

In March 2019 a former employee of the Post Rock Water District in Ellsworth County, Kansas allegedly logged into their computer system in an effort to alter the disinfectant levels. The former employee worked for the WWS utility from 2018 until January 2019, and remotely logging in after hours to monitor the facilities computer system was part of his normal work duties. It is likely that the ex-employee successfully logged in after his termination date, using credentials which were not properly revoked at the time of his resignation (O'Donnell & Welch 2021; Morgan 2021). The unauthorized intrusion caused an unplanned shutdown of the plant's processes, affecting the facility's cleaning and disinfecting procedures. It is alleged in the indictment that the former employee logged in with the intention of harming the drinking water treated by the Ellsworth County Rural Water District (ksn.com 2021).

This incident demonstrates the insider threat attack vector that IT and OT companies face, and it was compounded by poor operational security (OPSEC) practices. The mandatory and timely deletion of credentials for exiting employees, and periodic audits comparing valid user credentials to current employees can help diminish this attack vector.

Unidentified Energy Companies in Europe and the U.S.

Beginning in mid-2019 and continuing through early 2021, APT actors targeted unidentified energy companies in Europe and in the United States in a global brute force campaign. The APT actors—Russian General Staff Main Intelligence Directorate (GRU) 85th Main Special Service Center (GTsSS), military unit 26165—have been attributed in open-sources by the private sector as APT 28, Fancy Bear, Pawn Storm, Sofacy Group, Sednit, STRONTIUM, Tsar Team, and other names (defense.gov 2021; mitre.org 2021).

The APT actors employed a Kubernetes[2] cluster to conduct brute force at-

---

2   A Kubernetes cluster is a set of nodes that run containerized applications. Kubernetes clusters allow containers to run across multiple machines and environments: virtual, physical, cloud-based, and on-premises. Kubernetes containers are not restricted to a specific operating system (OS), unlike virtual machines.

tacks against various targets globally. A significant number of the targeted entities used Microsoft Office 365 cloud services. The actors also targeted other service providers and on-premises email servers using a variety of different protocols. The Kubernetes-enabled brute force attack provided initial access to the victim's networks, allowing access to protected data such as email, and identifying valid account credentials. Using identified account credentials in conjunction with exploiting publicly known vulnerabilities, such as exploiting Microsoft Exchange servers using CVE-2020-0688 and CVE-2020-17144,[3] for remote code execution and further access to target networks is a known tactic, technique and procedure (TTP) for these actors (defense.gov 2021). Once inside the network the actors performed privilege escalation, spread laterally, and installed reGeorg web shells to widen their footprint and secure footholds across the network, allowing the actors remote access beyond the initial intrusion (Hope 2021).

The adoption of sophisticated technology, in this case the Kubernetes cluster, by APT cyber actors helps increase the efficiency of their attack operations. Using a commercially available product has numerous benefits; it saves the actors time and money in developing custom tools; it diversifies and increases the attack vector spectrum, forcing network defenders to account for attacks coming from unexpected or non-traditional technologies, protocols, ports, etc.; and it potentially allows attackers to "hide in plain sight," carrying out their malicious activity under the guise of a product already trusted by network defenders. Kubernetes also enables effective and efficient management of attack servers (e.g., when an actor chooses to introduce new attack tools).

Although Kubernetes is becoming increasingly popular, it is not as well-known as cloud-based solutions for resource management. The adoption of this technology for attack operations alludes to a sophisticated actor interested in computer network operations (CNO) evolution.

Camrosa Water District (CA)

In August 2020, the Camrosa Water District (CA) discovered a cyber-attack resulting in certain devices on its network becoming encrypted. Further investigation, with assistance from a third-party cybersecurity firm, revealed unauthorized access by cyber actors dating back a full year, from August 2019. During that timeframe the cyber actors had access to Camrosa Water District file servers storing personally identifiable information (PII) that included the names and Social Se-

---

[3] CVE-2020-0688: According to Mitre.org CVE-2020-0688 is a remote code execution vulnerability that exists in Microsoft Exchange software when the software fails to properly handle objects in memory, aka "Microsoft Exchange Memory Corruption Vulnerability."

CVE-2020-17144: According to Mitre.org, CVE-2020-17144 is a Microsoft Exchange Remote Code Execution Vulnerability This CVE ID is unique from CVE-2020-17117, CVE-2020-17132, CVE-2020-17141, CVE-2020-17142.

curity numbers for current and former employees, as well as current and former customers. The current and former customers billing information, including their checking or savings account information, used to pay via an automated clearing house (ACH), may have also been visible to the actors (Stafford 2020).

Camrosa and their third-party cybersecurity partner did not ultimately find any indication the actors viewed or exfiltrated any personal information, but they did offer a free one-year subscription to an identity protection service to everyone potentially impacted (Stafford 2020).

That Camrosa decided to offer the complimentary identity protection service shows how a critical infrastructure asset owner can be impacted financially without its utility services being disrupted or suffering a ransomware attack. The PII of employees and customers that OT-focused businesses house is just as valuable to cyber-criminals as the PII owned by IT companies, and cyber actors may choose to target OT companies, believing them to be easier to exploit than IT companies.

Florida Water Infrastructure Construction Company

In December 2020 unidentified cyber actors, possibly associated with the DarkTeam Store and/or the Tofsee botnet malware, compromised a Florida water infrastructure construction company's website, injecting it with malicious code, to create a watering hole attack page. The malicious code seemed to target water utilities, particularly those in Florida, according to Dragos (Backman 2021). That may simply be due to more Florida-based water utilities needing to visit the Florida-based water infrastructure construction company than water utilities in other states.

The cyber actors possibly exploited a WordPress vulnerability in a plug-in used by the WordPress-based site, and inserted malicious code into a website footer, on 20 December 2020. Over the next 58 days, over 1000 computers visited the compromised but otherwise legitimate website. The 1000 plus visitors included municipal water utilities, state and local agencies, various water sector private companies, and legitimate Internet bot and website crawler traffic (Backman 2021).

Notably, a computer on an Oldsmar, FL city-owned network visited the watering hole site on 5 February 2021. This is the same day the Oldsmar water treatment plant (WTP) reported an incident. The Oldsmar city computer visiting the watering hole occurred at 0949ET, after the initial unauthorized login to the Oldsmar WTP, but before a second unauthorized login wherein the cyber actor attempted to alter the water supply. [See below - Oldsmar WTP]

Malicious code reverse-engineered from the watering hole site ultimately pointed to only one other website that had the same unique combination of sophisticated code, a Dark Web site that supplies stolen or illegitimate gift cards and account credentials called DarkTeam Store. However, closer inspection of Dark-

Team Store's website revealed at least part of the site is not a market, but instead a check-in, or command and control (C2), site used for a variant of botnet malware called Tofsee (Backman 2021). It is unclear as of this publication date if DarkTeam Store is associated with the Tofsee botnet, or if its site was compromised by Tofsee and used as botnet infrastructure.

ICS-focused security vendor Dragos noted in a follow-up to their original reporting on the Oldsmar WTP incident that the cyber actor who compromised the site "likely deployed the watering hole on the water infrastructure construction company site to collect legitimate browser data for the purpose of improving the botnet malware's ability to impersonate legitimate web browser activity." In other words, the compromise of the Florida water infrastructure construction company's website was intended to improve a botnet, and not lead to the compromise of the Oldsmar WTP.

Dragos directly contacted Idaho National Laboratory (INL) personnel supporting CISA to initially report its findings, as noted on its blog (Backman 2021). INL and CISA worked to notify several dozen additional water sector entities that visited the watering hole attack page who were identified by Dragos and shared with CISA.

An Unidentified San Francisco Bay-Area WTP

Sometime in January 2021 an unknown cyber actor gained illegitimate access to a San Francisco Bay-area WTP and attempted to stop or alter the treatment of the plant's drinking water. The cyber actor used legitimate credentials from a former plant employee, allowing access to the former employee's TeamViewer account. The TeamViewer account enabled remote access to the plant's computers, where the cyber actor deleted programs used to treat drinking water. The plant discovered the deleted programs the following day and reinstalled them and changed system passwords. There were no subsequent reports of people being sickened by the plant's drinking water (Teague 2021).

The WWS has notable security weaknesses, specifically as it relates to remote management tools and architectures. The lack of centralization for the water sector does provide some measure of security; however, it also means there is no uniform or easily identifiable solution for security. According to the National Rural Water Association, "It's really difficult to apply some kind of uniform cyber-hygiene assessment, given the disparate size and capacity and technical capacity of all the water utilities." The sector cites remote management as a tool that saves time and money, but WWS facilities typically do not have the most comprehensive security standards and cybersecurity personnel in place to ensure they are implemented and maintained correctly from a security perspective (Collier 2021).

Eletrobras and Copel Electric Power Utilities (Brazil)

In late January 2021, two different state-owned electric utilities in Brazil were victims of ransomware attacks. The utilities announced the attacks in early February (Ilascu 2021). Eletrobras is the largest power utility company in South America, generating roughly 40% of Brazil's electrical supply (Thomas 2021). Copel is the largest power utility company in the state of Paraná (estimated population of 11.5 million) (City Population, 2021). Eletrobras also owns Eletronuclear, a subsidiary that operates two nuclear power plants (Ilascu 2021).

The ransomware attacks at both utilities disrupted operations and forced the companies to temporarily suspend some operations. Copel confirmed that it immediately followed security protocols including instructing personnel to stop using its computer systems when it learned of the attack (Ilascu 2021). The Eletrobras network attacked by ransomware was not connected to any Eletrobras OT networks for the nuclear power plants; however, Eletronuclear did suspend the use of some administrative software used by the nuclear power plants (Reuters 2021).

Copel did not publicly disclose the attack, but it was listed in a publicly available filing to the Securities and Exchange Commission (SEC) (Seals 2021). The Darkside ransomware cyber-criminal group claimed responsibility for the Copel attack, claiming to have stolen more than 1,000GB of data. The stolen data included: sensitive infrastructure access information including plaintext passwords; personal details about management and customers; network maps; backup schemes and schedules; as well as Active Directory (AD) data, including user groups and password hashes for all domain users (Ilascu 2021). Eletrobras has not publicly provided any details on the identity of the cyber actors behind the attack, nor has it stated if the cyber actors exfiltrated any data in the attack. However, given the near simultaneous nature of the attacks, it is reasonable to suspect Darkside as being the cyber actors behind the Eletrobras as well (Thomas 2021).

Oldsmar WTP

In February 2021 an unidentified cyber actor (Cyber Actor 1) used unauthorized remote access to view the control systems and attempted to make changes to the water chemistry at the Oldsmar WTP. The cyber actor initially remotely logged into the system around 0800ET. This login was dismissed by a plant employee, who assumed it was normal remote access by an authorized user. Roughly five and half hours later, about 1330ET, Cyber Actor 1 again remotely accessed the plant's control system. This time Cyber Actor 1 again took control of the cursor and began clicking through the plant's controls on the HMI. A plant supervisor working remotely immediately noticed the attempt and reverted the concentration back to the normal amount (Greenberg 2021; Evans 2021; Rasmussen 2021).

Though ultimately unsuccessful, Cyber Actor 1 attempted to alter the water chemistry by increasing the amount of sodium hydroxide, or lye, from 100 parts per million (PPM), to 11,000 PPM. Lye is commonly used in water treatment to control the acidity of the water, but too much can be corrosive to the plant and pipes, and dangerous to humans. Even if the WTP personnel had not noticed the changes, the chemically altered water would not have reached the population the plant serves for another 24 to 36 hours, and automated pH testing safeguards would have caught the change and triggered an alarm, giving the plant plenty of time to stop the water before it reached its customers (Greenberg 2021; Evans 2021; Rasmussen 2021).

Cyber Actor 1 accessed the Oldsmar WTP's network by exploiting an outdated Windows 7 operating system (OS) and poor password security, according to the FBI (Pulse Secure 2021). Though reporting repeatedly indicates Cyber Actor 1 used the TeamViewer tool software—typically used for remote access IT troubleshooting and to share screens—to gain access to the plants control system, this cannot be confirmed according to analysis done by CISA (CISA 2021).

The attack on the WTP described above was almost certainly done independently of the activity described below, despite the coincidence and amount of initial reporting that link the two incidents, according to Dragos in an update to their original report that linked the two incidents (Cyber Defense Magazine 2021).

The WTP attack occurred the same day an Oldsmar city computer visited a website that had been compromised by a cyber actor (Cyber Actor 2) and injected with malicious code. The website hosting the malicious code—now a watering hole attack site—belonged to a Florida water utility contractor site [See above-Florida Water Infrastructure Construction Company], a type of site commonly visited within normal duties for the city. Notably, the 0800ET unauthorized login was prior to the 0949ET visit by an Oldsmar city computer visit to the compromised website, indicating the unauthorized logins were separate cyber actors with separate access vectors (Pulse Secure 2021). The Oldsmar cyber incidents are visually displayed in Figure 1.

Though remote visibility tools are not intended as a security feature, in this instance the shared screen capability may have helped the plant staff discover the unauthorized access, as the employee who first noticed the intrusion became aware when the cursor on his screen began moving strangely around the screen, out of his control. The plant employee noticed it again hours later when Cyber Actor 1 began clicking through the controls.

While remote access and remote management tools are convenient and possibly helped in noticing the intrusion and attempted disruption in this case, they also afford actors the opportunity to disrupt OT operations. Visual tools such as TeamViewer may offer cyber actors who are not familiar with ICS/SCADA programming the ability to disrupt operations more easily than they could relying upon nominal ICS/SCADA skills to deploy their malware or conduct other malicious cyber-operations. This incident highlights the cybersecurity risks associated with remote management of OT devices.

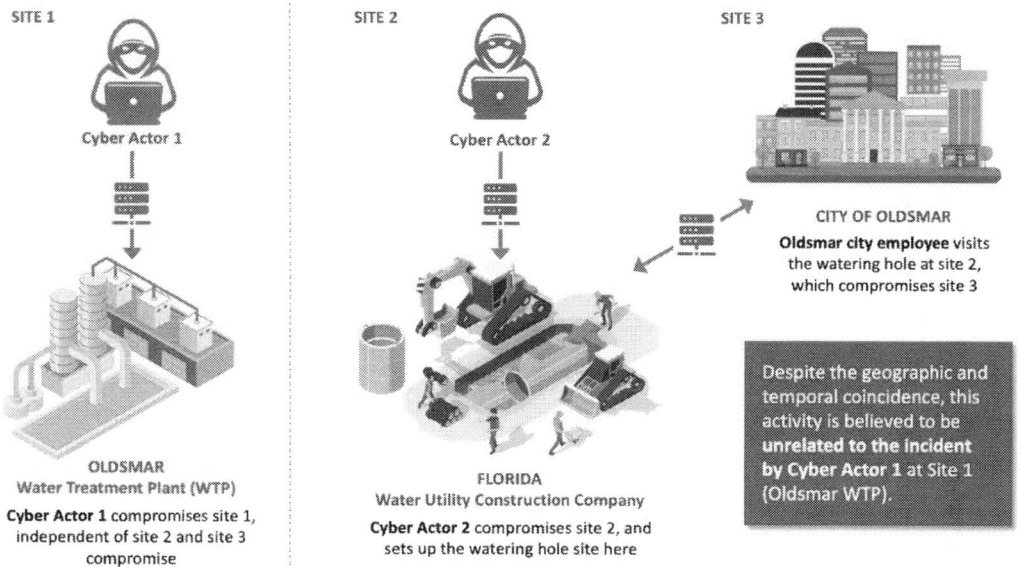

Figure 1. Oldsmar Cyber Incidents.

Nevada-based WWS Facility

In March 2021 unidentified cyber actors used an unknown ransomware variant against a Nevada WWS facility. The ransomware affected the victim's SCADA system and backup systems. The SDADA system provided visibility and monitoring but was not a full ICS (CISA 2021).

Metropolitan Water District of Southern California (MWD)

Sometime prior to April 2021, China-based APT cyber actors compromised Pulse Secure (since acquired by Ivanti, also known as Ivanti Pulse Secure), a software maker whose Pulse Connect Secure secure sockets layer (SSL) VPN software is used in organizations worldwide. The software allows for secure remote access from any Internet-connected device, including mobile, into corporate resources. The cyber actors identified and exploited previously known Pulse Secure vulnerabilities from 2019 and 2020, as well a new zero-day tracked as CVE-2021-22893 (Cyber Defense 2021). The CVE includes an authentication bypass vulnerability that can allow an unauthenticated user to perform remote arbitrary file execution on the Pulse Connect Secure gateway and has a critical common vulnerability scoring system (CVSS) score, according to the company (Pulse Secure 2021).

The MWD of Southern California was among the most critical and notable victims of the Pulse Secure breach. The MWDSC is the largest wholesale provider of drinking water in the country and its water treatment plants are among the largest in the country (Metropolitan Water District of Southern California 2018). The MWD discovered a compromised Pulse Secure appliance after viewing the alert about APT malicious activity and vulnerability was released by CISA. The WMD immediately took the compromised device offline and believes that none of its systems or processes were affected. The company also did not observe any data exfiltration (Suderman 2021).

The Pulse Secure compromise demonstrates the susceptibility of ICS companies and OT environments to the problems that impact IT environments. The continued targeting of market-leader technology enabling wide-scale exploitation (as also seen in the 2020 SolarWinds and 2021 Microsoft Exchange compromises) (Solar Winds 2021; Osborne 2021) by APT cyber actors can give those actors user credentials and accesses to the company's network that can be leveraged into access into the OT environment and ICSs, without actually compromising the ICS devices themselves. The convergence of the IT and OT environments that can allow a corporate IT compromise to lead to OT impact is a trend that will continue to increase as the lines between those once-separated environments blur.

City of Tulsa Municipal Networks

In late April 2021 cyber actors, likely associated with the cyber-criminal group Conti, installed ransomware on city networks, disrupting the availability of city websites and causing delays to city services. The city became aware of the ransomware in early May when the cyber actors contacted the city via a message on a compromised city server, stated they had compromised the server, provided instructions for paying the ransomware on the dark web along with visual proof of the compromise (Whaley 2021; Canfield 2021; Phillips 2021).

The city claimed to be well prepared for a cyber-incident, with detection systems in place that automatically alerted the IT teams, who immediately started shutting systems down. However, the cyber actors used a well-known TTP and sprung the ransomware during a weekend, when there are fewer people in the office to notice. The timing of the ransomware deployment, when the IT office was minimally staffed, allowed the attack to disrupt services despite the city being prepared, including the ability to obtain police reports, pay utility bills, or have new utilities connected. Residents reported being without water for days after requesting new service. They eventually resorted to manually turning their water services on in their homes themselves (Whaley 2021; Phillips 2021).

The city's chief information officer (CIO) detailed the damage to the media four months after the initial attack, estimating that roughly 40% of the city's 471 servers were damaged or encrypted, as well as 20% of the city's more than 5,000 desktop and laptop computers. The CIO expected a full recovery by October, five months after the attack was discovered. City officials also announced that more than 18,000 exfiltrated files had been made public by the cyber actors but noted nearly all of them were publicly available online police reports and did not contain residents' Social Security numbers or financial information (Canfield 2021). The files may have contained other PII such as name, date of birth, address, and driver's license numbers (Dellinger 2021).

This incident neatly demonstrates how ICS services, such as connections for new utility customers, can be impacted by disruptions to the IT environment even when the OT environment remains unaffected. Nearly all public-serving utility companies have public-facing portals and websites for their customers to request services and pay bills, and when the back end to those portals and sites are compromised, the utility services are also likely to also be impacted.

Volue ASA[4]

On 5 May 2021, Norwegian company Volue ASA "Volue" announced on its corporate website it was the victim of a Ryuk ransomware attack. Volue is a green-energy company providing technology for energy production, trading, distribution, and consumption. The attack limited some front-end customer platforms and encrypted company data. The company stated that all of its data was backed up in cloud storage, and the backup data was not impacted by the ransomware. Forensic analysis showed the Ryuk ransomware only targeted Volue infrastructure and networks and did not seek to spread to or encrypt third-party networks or customer information (Volue 2021; Kovacs 2021).

Upon discovering the ransomware attack, the company immediately deployed its cybersecurity task force and shut down operations and affected applications. The company advised customers to immediately shut off their service, and to change passwords associated with their Volue account. Volue alerted the Norwegian Computer Emergency Response Team (KraftCERT) and shared indicators of compromise (IOCs) with them and allowed KraftCERT to alert other companies that may be at risk, as well as Norwegian law enforcement. Volue also brought in a third-party cybersecurity firm to assist with the recovery (Kovacs 2021; Gjerstad 2021). The company set up a website that provided updates about the incident and the recovery process. The website provided daily updates and webcasts on the recovery efforts, available in both English and Norwegian, and had point of contact (POC) information available for the chief executive officer (CEO) and the chief financial officer (CFO) (Volue 2021). Later, a separate webpage detailed Volue's cybersecurity roadmap, encompassing what it had done to recover from the attack, and what it planned to do in the future to avoid similar attacks (Gjerstad 2021).

---

4   ASA: The Norwegian term "Aksjeselskap" is used for a stock-based company. It is usually abbreviated AS. Public companies are called Allmennaksjeselskap (ASA), while companies without limited liability are called Ansvarlig selskap (ANS). https://snl.no/allmennaksjeselskap; https://snl.no/aksjeselskap

Volue's commitment to transparency, ownership and resolution was applauded across the cybersecurity community. Cybersecurity firms, publications and bloggers welcomed how Volue so quickly addressed the attack publicly, kept everyone aware of its actions through clear and concise written and video updates, and provided POC info for key personnel, and not an anonymous hotline or junior employee. The Volue response has been lauded as the model for handling cyber-attacks when they occur (Varghese 2021; Abrams 2021; Mills 2021; James 2021).

Colonial Pipeline

In May 2021 cyber-criminals successfully deployed ransomware onto IT networks belonging to the Colonial Pipeline company. The Colonial Pipeline is the largest refined products pipeline in the U.S., a 5,500-mile pipeline moving more than 100 million gallons of gasoline, diesel fuel and natural gas every day, providing roughly 45% of the fuel consumed on the East Coast, and reaching more than 50 million Americans. The ransomware forced Colonial Pipeline to shut down pipeline operations for several days, leading to fuel shortages causing spikes in gasoline prices, panic buying by consumers and outages at many service stations, mostly across the Southeast. Airline operations were also impacted by the fuel shortages. The attack has been attributed to Darkside, a cyber-criminal group likely operating out of Russia. It is considered the largest publicly disclosed cyber-attack against U.S. critical infrastructure in history (Colonial Pipeline 2021; Greenberg 2021; Kerner 2021).

On 6 May 2021 cyber-criminals logged into a Colonial Pipeline VPN using legitimate credentials belonging to a Colonial Pipeline employee. While the credentials were legitimate, the VPN account was inactive and not meant to be in use, though it still provided access to the network. The employee likely used the same credentials across multiple websites, and the cyber-criminals discovered the password from a separate data breach. It is unknown how the cyber-criminals obtained the VPN username. The VPN did not support multi-factor authentication (MFA) (Culafi 2021; Novinson 2021).

Once the cyber-criminals had accessed the VPN, they exfiltrated roughly 100GB of data, deployed their ransomware and left a ransom note on the IT network, demanding 75 Bitcoin (approximately $5 million at the time) in exchange for the files, while threatening to release the information to the public (Wilkie 2021; Robertson and Turton 2021). The cyber-criminals' ransomware locked up numerous corporate systems, including ones used for billing. Colonial Pipeline discovered the ransom note at approximately 0500ET on 7 May 2021. By 0555ET the company began suspending pipeline operations, with the entire pipeline shut down by 0610ET.

The decision to suspend operations was driven by the need to contain the attack and ensure the ransomware did not spread to the OT environment, according to testimony given by the CEO to a Senate committee (Wilkie 2021). Privately, the company also decided to shut down operations due to the billing system being compromised, amidst fears it would not be able to determine how to bill customers, according to people briefed on the matter (Bertrand et al. 2021). The company also had concerns about whether its network backups were also corrupted and would be safe to use (Culafi 2021).

On 7 May 2021 Colonial Pipeline paid a $4.4 million ransom in Bitcoin through a negotiator. The CEO cited the need to have "every tool available . . . to get the pipeline back up and running." The CEO said the decision to pay the ransom was not publicly disclosed at that time due to OPSEC concerns and to avoid providing publicity for the cyber-criminals. The company was initially reported to have been unwilling to pay the ransom. It is unclear if that was incorrect reporting or deliberate misinformation by the company (Wilkie 2021; Walsh 2021).

By 8 May 2021 Colonial Pipeline had begun restoring some services to the pipeline. Colonial Pipeline had contacted the USG, local law enforcement and a third-party cybersecurity firm to assist with the effort. While the main lines remained non-operational, Colonial Pipeline turned on smaller lateral lines connecting terminals and delivery points. By 12 May 2021 Colonial Pipeline initiated the restart of all pipeline operations, though it would take several days for the supply chain to return to normal. Service stations across the Southeast were still without gasoline until at least 18 May 2021. The restoration effort was done in accordance with federal regulations and with support of the USG (Colonial Pipeline 2021; Eaton 2021).

The fallout of the attack continued for Colonial Pipeline even after restoring operations, as the company announced in mid-August that PII for nearly 6,000 people, mostly current and former employees and their families, was included in the initial 100GB data exfiltration. The PII included name, date of birth, Social Security numbers, military and driver's license numbers, and health insurance information (Fung 2021). Colonial Pipeline reached out to the personnel impacted in the PII breach, making them aware of credit monitoring services (Colonial Pipeline 2021).

The Colonial Pipeline incident very publicly, and to a global audience, demonstrated the crippling damage a cyber-attack can cause to a critical infrastructure asset owner and the impact that can have on the public, even when the OT environment is not compromised. Colonial Pipelines' decision to shut down the pipeline affected millions of Americans in their everyday life, from both a convenience and a financial point-of-view. The attack itself reinforces the need for MFA as well as regular network audits, as the VPN was not in use but still provided connectivity. From a best practice's stance, it also highlights the danger of re-using passwords across multiple platforms or websites, and not changing passwords that may have been exposed via separate data breaches.

Maine-based WWS Facility

In July 2021, unidentified cyber actors using remote access targeted and successfully installed ZuCaNo ransomware onto a SCADA computer at a Maine-based WWS facility. The ransomware disrupted the system, resulting in the treatment center needing to be run manually, with more frequent operator rounds. The system was eventually restored using local control (CISA 2021).

ZuCaNo ransomware is a variant of the well-documented Xorist ransomware family, and mitigation and removal techniques are readily available online (Remove Malware 2021). These tutorials and software solutions tend to be catered to IT environments. However, a successful deployment on an OT system may be much harder to manage and require more technical expertise unique to the OT environment, making the mitigation and malware removal more difficult, time-consuming, and expensive for the operator.

California-based WWS Treatment Center

In August 2021 unidentified cyber actors successfully deployed a Ghost variant ransomware onto a California-based WWS treatment center. The ransomware had been in the system for about a month and was not discovered until three SCADA servers displayed a ransomware message (CISA 2021).

Shifts in Cyber-Attacks Requires Shifts in Cyber Policy

Most notable cyber-incidents prior to 2017 have been attributed to a nation-state or specific APT actor and have been handled diplomatically in a reactive manner via sanctions, or individual charges. The legal framework for those diplomatic responses is the Executive Order (E.O.) 13694, enacted April 1, 2015 that "authorized the imposition of sanctions on individuals and entities determined to be responsible for or complicit in malicious cyber-enabled activities that result in enumerated harms that are reasonably likely to result in, or have materially contributed to, a significant threat to the national security, foreign policy, or economic health or financial stability of the United States." E.O. 13694 was updated with E.O. 13757 that allows for the Department of Treasury's Office of Foreign Assets Control (OFAC) to designate sanctions upon individuals and entities whose conduct meets the criteria set forth in E.O. 13694.

The USG uses that framework to punish nation-state cyber activity, such as in April 2021 when the U.S. Department of Treasury announced broad sanctions across numerous Russian-government affiliated companies following the late-2020 SolarWinds hack, an incident attributed to the Russian Foreign Intelligence Service (SVR) associated APT29/Cozy Bear threat actors. In October 2020 the US Department of Justice charged six members of the Russian state-sponsored Sandworm team (Greenberg 2020). The U.S. Department of Justice has also charged several Iranian and Russian citizens for their involvement with cyber activity related to the Trickbot trojan, and intentions to interfere in the 2020 U.S. Presidential election (Justice 2017), (Justice 2021).

That framework functionally works at the nation-state policy level; however, because it is reactive, the hack has already occurred. In addition, those legal actions are frequently inadequate, with charges being mostly symbolic (assuming Iran and Russia are not likely to extradite their own government and military members), or so long after the incident occurred it is out of the public's mind and the ire is lost. The charges against the Sandworm team came in 2020 but were levied for actions connected to the Ukrainian Christmas blackout of 2015, a Kyiv blackout attack in 2016, the global NotPetya outbreak of 2017 and the Olympic Destroyer malware associated with the 2018 Winter Olympics (Greenberg 2020).

Given that diplomatic and legal responses are negligible and frequently years after the cyber incident, the policy to address malicious cyber activity needs to change too. While the reactive diplomatic response should stay in effect, a proactive U.S.-facing policy framework is necessary to protect U.S. critical infrastructure.

The federal government and U.S. states are moving in that direction. Other E.D.'s including 13800 and 14028 have sought to strengthen the cybersecurity of federal networks, critical infrastructure and the US (CISA n.d.), (CISA n.d.). The National Defense Authorization Act for Fiscal Year 2022 (NDAA) ultimately did not contain a much-debated provision that would have required critical infrastructure owners and operators to report covered cybersecurity incidents to CISA; however, it did contain numerous cybersecurity provisions, including the authorization of the CyberSentry program, focused on the cybersecurity of ICS (Greig 2021).

The NDAA also introduced the Joint Cyber Defense Collaborative (JCDC), in which CISA and its partners—including federal, state, local, tribal, and territorial (SLTT) governments and the public and private sectors—work together to drive down the risk of cyber-attacks. The JDCD is "designed to strengthen the nation's cyber defenses through planning, preparation, and information sharing." It includes cyber operational planning, public and private sector information fusion and analysis, and cybersecurity guidance dissemination to its stakeholders (CISA n.d.). The JCDC will improve upon existing analysis and dissemination vectors, such as the Information Sharing and Analysis Centers (ISACs) and state fusion centers, to ensure more critical infrastructure owners and operators receive the cybersecurity information they need.

The USG has also shifted policy to actively caution U.S. entities that failing to protect their customers information may have legal or financial implications. The December 2021 Log4J vulnerability prompted the Federal Trade Commission (FTC) to demand US companies to update their systems, or potentially face an FTC lawsuit. The FTC referred to their $700 million settlement with Equifax stemming from the 2017 data breach, and specifically highlighted Equifax's failure to patch a known vulnerability in their Log4J warning (FTC 2022). CISA has also issued an Emergency Directive (ED) for Log4J (CISA 2021). ED's serve as mandates to civilian federal agencies, which are legally required to comply.

The shift toward getting U.S. entities to proactively prevent an incident, rather than reactively and punitively punishing foreign nation-state's cyber actors, is a notable change and the preferred action in how the USG should look to apply policy in the cyber space going forward. Increased information sharing between the public and private sector, improved platforms for information dissemination by the USG, and USG programs designed to assist specific sectors such as CyberSentry are good examples of the USG's role in assisting and educating industry on cybersecurity risk to allow industry to create or update cyber-defense plans, incident response plans, and risk models.

Lessons Learned

Many of the incidents covered in this paper highlighted ICS/SCADA operations disrupted by malicious cyber actors who did not actually compromise the OT environment. Several of these incidents' disruptions were caused by ransomware compromising an IT system or network that led to a disruption of the OT environment, or an intentional shutdown of the OT services by the afflicted company. Businesses trying to reduce costs or increase convenience by utilizing technology such as remote management and visibility tools, or billing services connected to both IT and OT environments, has created a hybrid IT/OT environment wherein cyber actors do not need to compromise the OT environment to disrupt ICS/SCADA operations. This shift in business operation tactics has led to cyber actors targeting ICS/SCADA companies and under-funded and under-staffed sectors such as WWS that may not have the resources or staff necessary to defend their networks.

Perhaps more critically, this IT/OT merge has also lowered the bar necessary to attack OT environments. Previous well-documented ICS/SCADA disruptions such as Stuxnet, Black Energy or CRASHOVERRIDE were sophisticated pieces of malware specifically targeting ICS/SCADA devices and custom written by well-funded and trained APT cyber actors. The ability to use readily available and cheaply acquired ransomware or malware designed for IT environments to attack an OT environment is a shift in the attack paradigm, opening the opportunity to more cyber actors.

Unlike most IT environments such as a business office where most employees are not working over the weekend and critical updates can be done during that time, many OT environments cannot be turned off for scheduled updates and patching due to the 24/7 nature of the plants and factories running them. This creates an environment rife with outdated and legacy operating systems and software versions full of vulnerabilities. This lack of patching and updates creates a target rich environment for cyber actors looking for vulnerabilities and outdated OSs and software. The 24/7 nature of OT environments and the critical infrastructure that depends upon them has led malicious cyber actors to target these OT environments, assuming the services they provide—water, gas, electricity, etc. —are too important to be down for an extended period of time. ICS/SCADA companies also house valuable PII information that can be leveraged for ransom or sold, just like IT environments. Cyber actors are starting to recognize these factors and targeting ICS/SCADA companies in the same way they have traditionally targeted IT environments.

With actors targeting OT environments with some of the same TTP's used in IT environment attacks, a review of IT best practices can show how they manifest in an OT environment. Table 3 below shows the same list of incidents, with columns added for the likelihood the attack could have been prevented if the victim had been using common IT best practices, with the possible solution for prevention listed if available. The preventability of each incident was scored as "unlikely," "possible," or "likely" per known best practices applicable to the incident. An incident is labeled as "unknown" if a lack of information available makes a judgment impossible.

Table 3. ICS Incidents Covered in this Paper and Potential Mitigation Strategies.

YEAR	VICTIM	THREAT TYPE	PREVENTABLE	POSSIBLE SOLUTION(S) AND COMMENTS
2018	Energy Services Group	Third party / supply chain	Unknown	
2019	Unidentified Power Plant	Insider Threat	Possible	Enhanced insider threat training. IT policy on allowing foreign USB devices into the facility, and allowing them to run on the HMIs.
2019	sPower	Remote Exploit	Unlikely	A review of the firewall hardware and the hardening policies applied.
2019	Post Rock Water District, Ellsworth County (KS)	Insider threat	Likely	Regular audits of current users/employees.

2019	Energy Companies Across Europe and US	Brute Force	Unlikely	Kubernetes as an attack tool was a very new TTP at that time.
2020	Camrosa Water District	Remote Exploit	Unknown	
2020	Florida Water Infrastructure Construction Company	Word Press vulnerability / watering hole	Likely	WordPress is widely known to be commonly targeted, with nearly 3700 CVE entries and nearly 22,000 total vulnerabilities (Mitre, n.d.) (Abela 2021).
2021	San Francisco Bay-area Water Treatment Plant	Unauthorized Remote Access	Likely	Human Resources (HR) and IT should be lockstep in policy that user credentials are revoked / removed the same day an employee exits the company.
2021	Eletrobras & Copel Electric Power Utilities	Ransomware in the IT environment	Unknown	
2021	Oldsmar (FL) Water Treatment Plant	Watering hole attack	Possible	The muddled reporting makes the attack vector unclear. If it was outdated Windows 7 OS and poor password security, as FBI reports, then it likely could have been preventing with Windows 7 OS updates and better password security. See CISA Alert AA21-042a for additional recommendations.
2021	Nevada-based WWS	Unknown ransomware in the OT environment	Unknown	

2021	Metropolitan Water District of Southern California (MWD)	Supply chain	Possible	The actors exploited two known Pulse Secure CVEs, but also used a zero-day. Impossible to judge actors' success with just the zero-day. See CISA Alert AA21-110A for additional information on Ivanti Pulse Connect Secure products.
2021	City of Tulsa (OK)	Ransomware in the IT environment	Unknown	If the actors used Conti ransomware, CISA Alert AA21-265A could have been applied.
2021	Volue ASA (Norway)	Ryuk ransomware in the IT environment	Unknown	
2021	Colonial Pipeline	Ransomware in the IT environment	Likely	The password used was likely discovered in a data breach and used across multiple sites. Better password policy may have prevented that from being successful. The VPN accessed with the credentials did not support MFA. Requiring MFA for the VPN would likely have prevented access. See CISA Alert AA21-131A for additional information.
2021	Maine-based WWS	ZuCaNo ransomware in OT environment	Unknown	See CISA Alert AA21-287A for mitigation recommendations.
2021	California-based WWS	Ghost variant ransomware in the OT environment	Unknown	See Alert AA21-287A for mitigation recommendations.

It is impossible without access to the full forensic reports and proprietary information related to each incident to know if the possible solutions would have prevented the incident. It is also possible the cyber actors have unused exploits or attack vectors available that were unnecessary once they had gained access, that would have worked despite the possible solution. Likewise, perhaps the IT staff of the victim made the intrusion worse with poor incident response techniques or plans, or the decision to take systems offline made by a CEO was too hasty, unnecessarily causing the disruption. However, with the information available, the majority of the incidents are deemed "likely" or "possible" to have been prevented had common best practices for IT environments been in place.

While patching and updating ICS systems can be difficult in the 24/7 environments in which they are often found, it is vital to keep the associated and connected IT environments up to date. Common ICS security recommendations such as ensuring segmentation between IT and OT networks, limiting external connectivity of OT systems and enabling MFA where it is necessary, and establishing user roles and privileges based on work responsibilities, should also be followed. CISA and the Department of Energy maintain comprehensive recommended practices lists and tools for self-evaluating cybersecurity (CISA n.d.) (Defense.gov 2020), (Department of Energy, n.d.). Having an ICS-specific incident response plan is also critical, as unlike an IT network compromise, there are potential threats to life and property that can occur in an OT environment as a result of a cyber compromise (CISA October 2019). No network is invulnerable, but many of the reviewed incidents may have been prevented with better IT and OT cybersecurity policies in place.

Conclusion

ICS incidents continue to be a concern to critical infrastructures. This paper highlighted the increasing trend of how the interconnectivity of devices and services connecting the IT and OT environments and the increasing sophistication of cyber actors, both nation-state (APT) and cyber-criminal, have put many businesses and services that may not consider themselves traditional targets of malicious cyber actors at risk of a cyber-attack. Cyber actors have learned they do not need to compromise the OT environment to disrupt OT services; the convergence of IT and OT has blurred that line. Similarly, cyber actors lacking ICS/SCADA-specific knowledge have realized that an IT intrusion can be just as effective as an OT disruption, lowering the sophistication necessary to target OT environments. This trend has increased the vulnerability to OT systems since both IT and OT exploits can be used to impact OT systems.

Regardless of whether they originate from an IT or OT environment, disruptions of services erode public trust and cause costly outages that ICS/SCADA companies cannot afford. Some ICS/SCADA companies are starting to realize it is not a matter of if, but when, they will be compromised, and are accordingly. Investing in cybersecurity, having an OT-specific incident response plan for a compromise, and being transparent and up-front about compromises to the public is the way forward.

Acronyms and Abbreviations

APT	Advanced Persistent Threat
C2	Command and Control
CEO	Chief Executive Officer
CFO	Chief Financial Officer
CIO	Chief Information Officer
CISA	Cybersecurity and Infrastructure Security Agency
CNO	Computer Network Operations
CVE	Common Vulnerabilities and Exposures
CVSS	Critical Common Vulnerability Scoring System
DCS	Distributed Control System
DHS	Department of Homeland Security
DoS	Denial of Service
ED	Emergency Directive
E.O.	Executive Order
FTC	Federal Trade Commission
GRU	Russian General Staff Main Intelligence Directorate
GTsSS	85th Main Special Service Center
GUI	Graphical User Interface
HMI	Human Machine Interface
HR	Human Resources
ICS	Industrial Control System
INL	Idaho National Laboratory
IOC	Indicator of Compromise
ISAC	Information Sharing and Analysis Center
IT	Information Technology
MFA	Multi-factor Authentication
MW	Megawatt

MWD	Metropolitan Water District of Southern California
NDAA	National Defense Authorization Act
OPSEC	Operational Security
OS	Operating System
OT	Operational Technology
PII	Personally Identifiable Information
POC	Point of Contact
PPM	Parts Per Million
SCADA	Supervisory Control and Data Acquisition
SLTT	State, Local, Tribal and Territorial
SSL	Secure Sockets Layer
TTP	Tactic, Technique and Procedure
USB	Universal Serial Bus
USG	United States Government
VPN	Virtual Private Network
WTP	Water Treatment Plant
WWS	Water and Wastewater Systems

Robert Grubbs is a Senior Cyber Intelligence Analyst for the Infrastructure Assurance and Analysis division of Idaho National Laboratory (INL). In his current role he provides on-site operational support and intelligence analysis. He has supported the U.S. government for more than 20 years as a federal employee and as a contractor, beginning with four years of college internships with the Department of State. Since graduation he has supported work across the intelligence community (IC) and financial sector in network engineering, network and telecommunications analysis, and cyber intelligence and counterintelligence roles. He has a degree in English with a focus in Technical Writing and Editing from Virginia Polytechnical Institute and State University (Virginia Tech) and is a SANS-certified Certified Forensics Examiner (GCFE).

Jeremiah Stoddard is a Critical Infrastructure Security Analyst for the Infrastructure Assurance and Analysis division of Idaho National Laboratory. In his current role he provides support for efforts on software bill of materials (SBOM) as well as vulnerability disclosure. Mr. Stoddard attended Idaho State University and received a bachelor's degree in History and a Master of Business Administration with an emphasis in cybersecurity. He also graduated from Gonzaga University

School of Law and later received an LLM in National Security & U.S. Foreign Relations Law from The George Washington University Law School.

Sarah Freeman is an Industrial Control Systems (ICS) Cyber Security Analyst for the Cybercore Integration Center at Idaho National Laboratory (INL), where she provides U.S. government partners and private sector entities with actionable cyber threat intelligence, developing innovative security solutions for the critical infrastructure within the U.S. At INL, Sarah pursues innovative threat analysis and cyber defense approaches, most recently Consequence-driven Cyber-informed Engineering (CCE). As Principal Investigator on a laboratory discretionary research project, her current research is focused on new signatures and structured methods for cyber adversary characterization. Following the December 2015 electric grid attacks, Sarah participated in the DOE-sponsored training for Ukrainian asset owners in May 2016. She has also researched the Ukrainian 2015 and 2016 cyber-attacks and the Trisis/Hatman incident.

Ron Fisher, PhD is the Director of Infrastructure Assurance and Analysis (IAA) in the National & Homeland Security (N&HS) directorate at Idaho National Laboratory (INL). He provides over 20 years of critical infrastructure protection experience including serving on President Clinton's Presidential Commission on Critical Infrastructure Protection. Dr. Fisher has worked at INL for eight years, and prior to that, 26 years at Argonne National Laboratory serving as deputy director for the Laboratory's Infrastructure Assurance Center. Dr. Fisher attended Northern Illinois University and received a bachelor's degree in Finance and a Master of Business Administration in finance, economics, and management. He also attended Benedictine University and received a doctorate degree in organizational development.

References

Abela, Robert. (2021, February 10). Statistics Highlight the Biggest Source of WordPress Vulnerabilities. Available from WP WhiteSecurity: https://www.wp-whitesecurity.com/statistics-highlight-main-source-wordpress-vulnerabilities/.

Abrams, Lawrence. (2021, May 17). Ransomware Victim Shows Why Transparency in Attacks Matters. Available from Bleeping Computer: https://www.bleepingcomputer.com/news/security/ransomware-victim-shows-why-transparency-in-attacks-matters/.

Backman, Kent. (2021, May 18). When Intrusions Don't Align: A New Water Watering Hole and Oldsmar. Available from Dragos: https://www.dragos.com/blog/industry-news/a-new-water-watering-hole/.

Behr, Peter. (2019, February 25). Power Lines: The Next 'Green New Deal' Battlefront? Retrieved from E&E News: https://www.eenews.net/stories/1060122295.

Bertrand, Natasha, Evan Perez, Zachary Cohen, Geneva Sands, and Josh Campbell. (2021, May 13). Colonial Pipeline Did Pay Ransom to Hackers, Sources Now Say. Available from CNN: https://edition.cnn.com/2021/05/12/politics/colonial-pipeline-ransomware-payment/index.html.

Canfield, Kevin. (2021, August 14). Ransomware Group Conti Likely Responsible for City's Cyber-attack, Experts Say. Available from Tulsa World: https://tulsaworld.com/news/local/ransomware-group-conti-likely-responsible-for-citys-cyber-attack-experts-say/article_3cad1622-df57-11eb-b3c8-437f9866823f.html.

Cimpanu, Catalin. (2018, February 8). Hackers Pounce on Cisco ASA Flaw (CVE-2018-0101). Retrieved from Bleeping Computer: https://www.bleepingcomputer.com/news/security/hackers-pounce-on-cisco-asa-flaw-cve-2018-0101/.

CISA. (n.d.). Joint Cyber Defense Collaborative. Available from CISA: https://www.cisa.gov/jcdc.

CISA. (n.d.). Executive Order on Strengthening the Cybersecurity of Federal Networks and Critical Infrastructure. Available from CISA: https://www.cisa.gov/executive-order-strengthening-cybersecurity-federal-networks-and-critical-infrastructure.

CISA. (n.d.). Executive Order on Improving the Nation's Cybersecurity. Available from CISA: https://www.cisa.gov/executive-order-improving-nations-cybersecurity.

CISA. (n.d.). Recommended Practices. Available from CISA: https://www.cisa.gov/uscert/ics/Recommended-Practices.

CISA. (2009, October 6). Recommended Practice: Developing an Industrial Control Systems Cybersecurity Incident Response Capability. Available from CISA: https://www.cisa.gov/uscert/sites/default/files/recommended_practices/final-RP_ics_cybersecurity_incident_response_100609.pdf.

CISA. (2009, November 4). Understanding Denial-of-Service Attacks. Available from CISA: https://us-cert.cisa.gov/ncas/tips/ST04-015.

CISA. (2021, February 11). AA21-042A – Compromise of Water Treatment Facility. Available from CISA: https://us-cert.cisa.gov/ncas/alerts/aa21-042a.

CISA. (2021, October 14). AA12-287A – Ongoing Cyber Threats to U.S. Water and Wastewater Systems. Available from CISA: https://us-cert.cisa.gov/ncas/alerts/aa21-287a.

CISA. (2021, December 17). Emergency Directive 22-02 Mitigate Apache Log4J Vulnerability. Available from CISA: https://www.cisa.gov/emergency-directive-22-02.

CISOMAG. (2018, April 3). Energy Transfer Partners Reports Cyber Breach. Available from CISOMAG: https://cisomag.eccouncil.org/energy-transfer-partners-reports-cyber-breach/.

City Population (2021, August 28). State of Paraná. Available from City Population: https://www.citypopulation.de/en/brazil/cities/parana/.

Collier, Kevin. (2021, June 17). 50,000 Security Disasters Waiting to Happen: The Problem of America's Water Supplies. Available from NBC News: https://www.nbcnews.com/tech/security/hacker-tried-poison-calif-water-supply-was-easy-entering-password-rcna1206.

Colonial Pipeline. (2021, May 17). Media Statement Update: Colonial Pipeline System Disruption. Available from Colonial Pipeline: https://www.colpipe.com/news/press-releases/media-statement-colonial-pipeline-system-disruption.

Colonial Pipeline. (2021, August 1). Frequently Asked Questions. Available from Colonial Pipeline: https://www.colpipe.com/about-us/faqs.

Colonial Pipeline. (2021, August 13). Available from Document Cloud: https://www.documentcloud.org/documents/21043496-colonial-piepeline-bc-data-breach-notification.

Culafi, Alexander. (2021, June 9). Mandiant: Compromised Colonial Pipeline Password Was Reused. Available from Search Security: https://searchsecurity.techtarget.com/news/252502216/Mandiant-Compromised-Colonial-Pipeline-password-was-reused?.

Cyber Defense Magazine. (2021, April 22). China-linked APT used Pulse Secure VPN Zero-Day to Hack U.S. Defense Contractors. Available from Cyber Defense Magazine.com: https://www.cyberdefensemagazine.com/china-linked-apt/.

Defense.gov. (2020, July 22). NSA and CISA Recommend Immediate Actions to Reduce Exposure Across all Operational Technologies and Control Systems. Available from Defense.gov: https://media.defense.gov/2020/Jul/23/2002462846/-

1/-1/1/OT_ADVISORY-DUAL-OFFICIAL-20200722.PDF.

Defense.gov. (2021, July 1). Russian GRU Conducting Global Brute Force Campaign to Compromise Enterprise and Cloud Environments Cybersecurity Advisory. Available from Defense.gov: https://media.defense.gov/2021/Jul/01/2002753896/-1/-1/1/CSA_GRU_GLOBAL_BRUTE_FORCE_CAMPAIGN_UOO158036-21.PDF.

Dellinger, Michael. (2021, June 24). Tulsa Says Ransomware Attackers Accessed, Shared Personal Information. Available from Public Radio Tulsa: https://www.publicradiotulsa.org/post/tulsa-says-ransomware-attackers-accessed-shared-personal-information#stream/0.

Department of Energy. (n.d.). Cybersecurity Capability Maturity Model (C2M2). Available from United States Department of Energy: https://www.energy.gov/ceser/cybersecurity-capability-maturity-model-c2m2.

Energy Transfer.com. (2021, November 1). We are Energy. Available from Energy Transfer: https://www.energytransfer.com/about/.

Eaton, Collin. (2021, May 18). Colonial Pipeline Still Moving Fuel Despite Disruptions to Orders System. Available from The Wall Street Journal: https://www.wsj.com/articles/colonial-pipeline-ordering-system-disrupted-but-still-moving-fuel-11621358203.

Evans, Jack. (2021, February 8). Someone Tried to poison Oldsmar's Water Supply During Hack, Sheriff Says. Available from Tampa Bay Times: https://www.tampabay.com/news/pinellas/2021/02/08/someone-tried-to-poison-oldsmars-water-supply-during-hack-sheriff-says/.

FTC. (2022, January 4). FTC Warns Companies to Remediate Log4j Security Vulnerability. Available from US FTC: https://www.ftc.gov/news-events/blogs/techftc/2022/01/ftc-warns-companies-remediate-log4j-security-vulnerability.

Fung, Brian. (2021, August 16). Colonial Pipeline Says Ransomware Attack Also Led to Personal Information Being Stolen. Available from CNN: https://www.cnn.com/2021/08/16/tech/colonial-pipeline-ransomware/index.html.

Gjerstad, Kevin. (2021, September 16). Cybersecurity Roadmap: Volue After the Ransomware Attack. Available from Volue: https://www.volue.com/news/cybersecurity-roadmap-volue.

Greenberg, Andy. (2021, February 8). A Hacker Tried to Poison a Florida City's

Water Supply, Officials Say. Available from Wired: https://www.wired.com/story/oldsmar-florida-water-utility-hack/.

Greenberg, Andy. (2021, May 8). The Colonial Pipeline Hack Is a New Extreme for Ransomware. Available from Wired: https://www.wired.com/story/colonial-pipeline-ransomware-attack/.

Greenberg, Andry. (2020, October 19). U.S. Indicts Sandworm, Russia's Most Destructive Cyberwar Unit. Available from Wired: https://www.wired.com/story/us-indicts-sandworm-hackers-russia-cyberwar-unit/.

Greig, Jonathan. (2021, December 15). U.S. Senate Passes $768 Billion Defense Bill Without Cyber Incident Reporting Provisions. Available from ZDNet: https://www.zdnet.com/article/us-senate-passes-defense-bill-without-cyber-incident-reporting-provisions/.

Hemsley, Kevin, Fisher, Ron. (2018, December). History of Industrial Control System Cyber Incidents. Available from the Office of Scientific and Technical Information: https://www.osti.gov/servlets/purl/1505628/.

Hope, Alicia. (2021, July 8). NSA and GCHQ Warn That Russian Hackers Frequently Brute Force Passwords at Scale Using Kubernetes Clusters. Available from CPO Magazine.com: https://www.cpomagazine.com/cyber-security/nsa-and-gchq-warn-that-russian-hackers-frequently-brute-force-passwords-at-scale-using-kubernetes-clusters/.

Ilascu, Ionut. (2021, February 5). Eletrobras, Copel Energy Companies Hit by Ransomware Attacks. Available from Bleeping Computer. Available from: https://www.bleepingcomputer.com/news/security/eletrobras-copel-energy-companies-hit-by-ransomware-attacks/.

James, Timothy. (2021, May 17). Ransomware Victim Shows Why Attack Transparency Matters. Available from News Block: https://news-block.com/ransomware-victim-shows-why-attack-transparency-matters/.

Justice. (2017, November 21). Acting Manhattan U.S. Attorney Announces Charges Against Iranian National for Conducting Cyber Attack And $6 Million Extortion Scheme Against HBO. Available from United States Department of Justice: https://www.justice.gov/usao-sdny/pr/acting-manhattan-us-attorney-announces-charges-against-iranian-national-conducting.

Justice. (2021, October 28). Russian National Extradited to United States to Face Charges for Alleged Role in Cybercriminal Organization. Available from United

States Department of Justice: https://www.justice.gov/opa/pr/russian-national-extradited-united-states-face-charges-alleged-role-cybercriminal.

Kephart, Tim. (2021, May 19). Report: Oldsmar Water Hack Came After City Computer Visited Compromised Website. Available from ABC Action News: https://www.abcactionnews.com/news/region-pinellas/report-oldsmar-water-hack-came-after-city-computer-visited-compromised-website.

Kerner, Sean M. (2021, July 7). Colonial Pipeline Hack Explained: Everything You Need to Know. Available from What is Tech Target.com: https://whatis.techtarget.com/feature/Colonial-Pipeline-hack-explained-Everything-you-need-to-know.

Kovacs, Eduard. (2021, May 13). Green Energy Company Volue Hit by Ransomware. Available from Security Week: https://www.securityweek.com/green-energy-company-volue-hit-ransomware.

KSN.com. (2021, March 13). United States District Court Case No. 21-40029-HLT. Available from KSN.com: https://www.ksn.com/wp-content/uploads/sites/13/2021/03/travnichek-indictment.pdf.

Lyngaas, Sean. (2018, April 3). Major U.S. Pipeline Hit by Cyberattack on Transaction Software. Retrieved from CyberScoop.com: https://www.cyberscoop.com/major-u-s-pipeline-disrupted-cyberattack-transaction-software/.

Malware Remove. (2021, July 7). How to Remove Zucano Ransomware and Restore Files. Available from Remove Malware.com: https://malware-remove.com/blog/how-to-remove-zucano-ransomware-and-restore-files/.

Metropolitan Water District of Southern California. (2018, September 1). Metropolitan's Water Treatment Plants Safeguard Public Health. Available from Metropolitan Water District of Southern California: https://www.mwdh2o.com/media/4360/water-treatment-plants-fact-sheet-final_web.pdf.

Mitre.org (2021, October 18). APT28. Available at Mitre.org: https://attack.mitre.org/groups/G0007/.

Mitre.org (n.d.) WordPress Query. Available at Mitre.org: https://cve.mitre.org/cgi-bin/cvekey.cgi?keyword=wordpress.

Mills, Matt. (2021, May 19). Why Transparency is Important to Curb Ransomware. Available from ITGIC: https://itigic.com/why-transparency-is-important-to-curb-ransomware/.

Morgan, Lisa. (2021, April 9). Another Cyber Attack Affecting Water Supply. Retrieved from Cyber Security Hub.com: https://www.cshub.com/attacks/articles/another-cyber-attack-affecting-water-supply.

Novinson, Michael. (2021, June 5). Colonial Pipeline Hacked Via Inactive Account Without MFA. Available from CRN: https://www.crn.com/news/security/colonial-pipeline-hacked-via-inactive-account-without-mfa.

O'Donnell-Welch, Lindsey. (2021, April 2). Kansas Water Utility Attack Underscores Security Limitations in Municipalities. Retrieved from Decipher.com: https://duo.com/decipher/kansas-water-utility-attack-underscores-security-limitations-in-municipalities.

Osborne, Charlie. (2021, April 19). Everything You Need to Know About the Microsoft Exchange Server Hack. Available from ZDNet: https://www.zdnet.com/article/everything-you-need-to-know-about-microsoft-exchange-server-hack/.

Phillips, Sharon. (2021, July 22). Story Behind the Ransomware Attack on the City of Tulsa." Available from 2 News Oklahoma: https://www.kjrh.com/news/local-news/story-behind-the-ransomware-attack-on-the-city-of-tulsa.

Pulse Secure. (2021, April 1). SA44784 - 2021-04: Out-of-Cycle Advisory: Multiple Vulnerabilities Resolved in Pulse Connect Secure 9.1R11.4. Available from Pulse Secure.net: https://kb.pulsesecure.net/articles/Pulse_Security_Advisories/SA44784.

Rasmussen, Jeremy. (2021, April 5). Lessons Learned from Oldsmar Water Plant Hack. Available at Security Today: https://securitytoday.com/articles/2021/04/05/lessons-learned-from-oldsmar-water-plant-hack.aspx.

Reuters. (2021, February 4). Brazil's Eletrobras Says Nuclear Unit Hit with Cyberattack. Available from Reuters: https://www.reuters.com/article/us-eletrobras-cyber/brazils-eletrobras-says-nuclear-unit-hit-with-cyberattack-idUSKBN2A41JN.

Robertson, Jordan and Turton, William. (2021, May 10). Cyber Sleuths Blunted Pipeline Hack, Choked Data Flow to Russia. Available from Bloomberg: https://www.bloomberg.com/news/articles/2021-05-10/cyber-sleuths-blunted-pipeline-hack-choked-data-flow-to-russia?srnd=technology-vp.

Seals, Tara. (2021, February 5). Ransomware Attacks Hit Major Utilities Threat Post. Available from: https://threatpost.com/ransomware-attacks-major-utilities/163687/.

Solar Winds. (2021, April 6). SolarWinds Security Advisory. Available from Solar Winds.com: https://www.solarwinds.com/sa-overview/securityadvisory.

Stafford, Tony. (2020, August 13). Notice of Data Breach. Available from Camrosa Water District.com. https://oag.ca.gov/system/files/Camrosa%20-%20California%20Notification.pdf.

Suderman, Alan. (2021, June 15). MWD Among Targets in Large-Scale Cyber-Espionage Hack Blamed on China. Available from Los Angeles Times: https://www.latimes.com/world-nation/story/2021-06-15/critical-entities-targeted-suspected-chinese-cyber-espionage.

Teague, Courtney. (2021, June 18). FBI Investigating Hacker Attempt to Poison Bay Area Water: Report. (2021, June 18) Available from Patch.com: https://patch.com/california/san-francisco/fbi-investigating-hacker-attempt-poison-bay-area-water-report.

Thomas, Ian. (2021, June 9). The State of Ransomware Attacks across Latin America. Available from Iron Scales: https://ironscales.com/blog/ransomware-latin-america/.

Tomlinson, Kerry. (2019, May 9). What Happened to the U.S. Grid on March 5? Available from Archer: https://archerint.com/what-happened-to-the-us-grid-on-march-5/.

Tomlinson, Kerry. (2020, February 27). Power Plant Reportedly Hit by Mouse Ransomware Attack. Retrieved by Archer: https://archerint.com/power-plant-reportedly-hit-by-mouse-ransomware-attack/.

Varghese, Sam. (2021, May 11). Norwegian Firm Shows How Ransomware Attack Should Be Handled. Available from ITWire: https://itwire.com/security/norwegian-firm-shows-how-ransomware-attack-should-be-handled.html.

Volue.com (2021, July 12). Urgent Updates on the Cyberattack. Available from Volue.com: https://www.volue.com/urgent-updates.

Walsh, Joe. (2021, May 12). Colonial Pipeline Reportedly Won't Pay Hacker Ransom. Available from Forbes: https://www.forbes.com/sites/joewalsh/2021/05/12/colonial-pipeline-reportedly-wont-pay-hacker-ransom/?sh=2eee20e941c3.

Whaley, Sara. (2021, May 10). Ransomware Attack Targets City of Tulsa, Causing Technical Difficulties. Available from Fox News: https://www.fox23.com/news/local/tulsa-city-officials-ransomware-attack-causing-technical-difficulties/R4BXX

HIRVJCYDHUG6VAUFJB4BQ/.

Wilkie, Christina. (2021, June 9). Colonial Pipeline Paid $5 Million Ransom One Day After Cyberattack, CEO Tells Senate. Available from CNBC: https://www.cnbc.com/2021/06/08/colonial-pipeline-ceo-testifies-on-first-hours-of-ransomware-attack.html.

Policy Studies Organization Resources

The Policy Studies Organization (PSO) is a publisher of academic journals and books, sponsor of conferences, and producer of programs. There are numerous resources available for scholars, including:

Journals
Policy Studies Organization publishes dozens of journals on a range of topics:

Arts & International Affairs
Asian Politics & Policy
China Policy Journal
Digest of Middle East Studies
European Policy Analysis
Latin American Policy
Military History Chronicles
Popular Culture Review
Poverty & Public Policy
Proceedings of the PSO
Review of Policy Research
Risks, Hazards & Crisis in Public Policy
Ritual, Secrecy, & Civil Society
Saber & Scroll Historical Journal
Sculpture, Monuments, and Open Space (formerly Sculpture Review)
Sexuality, Gender & Policy
Security & Intelligence (formerly Global Security & Intelligence Studies)
Space Education and Strategic Applications
International Journal of Criminology
International Journal of Open Educational Resources
Journal on AI Policy and Complex Systems
Journal of Critical Infrastructure Policy
Journal of Indigenous Ways of Being, Knowing, and Doing
Journal of Online Learning Research and Practice
Indian Politics & Polity
Journal of Elder Studies
Policy & Internet
Policy Studies Journal
Policy Studies Yearbook
Politics & Policy
World Affairs
World Food Policy
World Medical & Health Policy
World Water Policy

Conferences

Policy Studies Organization hosts numerous conferences, including the Middle East Dialogue, Space Education and Strategic Applications, International Criminology Conference, Dupont Summit on Science, Technology and Environmental Policy, World Conference on Fraternalism, Freemasonry and History, AI – The Future of Education: Disruptive Teaching and Learning Models, Sport Management and Esport Conference, and the Internet Policy & Politics Conference. Recordings of these talks are available in the PSO Video Library.

Yearbook

The Policy Yearbook contains a detailed international listing of policy scholars with contact information, fields of specialization, research references, and an individual scholar's statements of research interests.

Curriculum Project

The Policy Studies Organization aims to provide resources for educators, policy makers, and community members, to promote the discussion and study of the various policies that affect our local and global society. Our curriculum project organizes PSO articles and other media by easily serachable themes.

For more information on these projects, access videos of past talks, and upcoming events, please visit us at:

ipsonet.org

Related Titles from Westphalia Press

The Limits of Moderation: Jimmy Carter and the Ironies of American Liberalism by Leo P. Ribuffo

The Limits of Moderation: Jimmy Carter and the Ironies of American Liberalism is not a finished product. And yet, even in this unfinished stage, this book is a close and careful history of a short yet transformative period in American political history, when big changes were afoot.

The Zelensky Method by Grant Farred

Locating Russian's war within a global context, The Zelensky Method is unsparing in its critique of those nations, who have refused to condemn Russia's invasion and are doing everything they can to prevent economic sanctions from being imposed on the Kremlin.

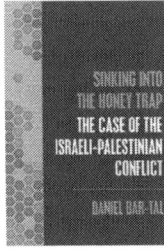

Sinking into the Honey Trap: The Case of the Israeli-Palestinian Conflict by Daniel Bar-Tal, Barbara Doron, Translator

Sinking into the Honey Trap by Daniel Bar-Tal discusses how politics led Israel to advancing the occupation, and of the deterioration of democracy and morality that accelerates the growth of an authoritarian regime with nationalism and religiosity.

Notes From Flyover Country: An Atypical Life & Career by Max J. Skidmore

In this remarkable book, Skidmore discusses his "atypical life and career," and includes work from his long life in academe. Essays deal with the principles and creation of constitutions, anti-government attitudes, the influence of language usage on politics, and church-state relations.

The Athenian Year Primer: Attic Time-Reckoning and the Julian Calendar
by Christopher Planeaux

The ability to translate ancient Athenian calendar references into precise Julian-Gregorian dates will not only assist Ancient Historians and Classicists to date numerous historical events with much greater accuracy but also aid epigraphists in the restorations of numerous Attic inscriptions.

Siddhartha: Life of the Buddha
by David L. Phillips,
contributions by Venerable Sitagu Sayadaw

Siddhartha: Life of the Buddha is an illustrated story for adults and children about the Buddha's birth, enlightenment and work for social justice. It includes illustrations from Pagan, Burma which are provided by Rev. Sitagu Sayadaw.

Growing Inequality: Bridging Complex Systems, Population Health, and Health Disparities
Editors: George A. Kaplan, Ana V. Diez Roux, Carl P. Simon, and Sandro Galea

Why is America's health is poorer than the health of other wealthy countries and why health inequities persist despite our efforts? In this book, researchers report on groundbreaking insights to simulate how these determinants come together to produce levels of population health and disparities and test new solutions.

Issues in Maritime Cyber Security
Edited by Dr. Joe DiRenzo III, Dr. Nicole K. Drumhiller, and Dr. Fred S. Roberts

The complexity of making MTS safe from cyber attack is daunting and the need for all stakeholders in both government (at all levels) and private industry to be involved in cyber security is more significant than ever as the use of the MTS continues to grow.

Female Emancipation and Masonic Membership: An Essential Collection
By Guillermo De Los Reyes Heredia

Female Emancipation and Masonic Membership: An Essential Combination is a collection of essays on Freemasonry and gender that promotes a transatlantic discussion of the study of the history of women and Freemasonry and their contribution in different countries.

Bunker Diplomacy: An Arab-American in the U.S. Foreign Service
by Nabeel Khoury

After twenty-five years in the Foreign Service, Dr. Nabeel A. Khoury retired from the U.S. Department of State in 2013 with the rank of Minister Counselor. In his last overseas posting, Khoury served as deputy chief of mission at the U.S. embassy in Yemen (2004-2007).

Managing Challenges for the Flint Water Crisis
Edited by Toyna E. Thornton, Andrew D. Williams, Katherine M. Simon, Jennifer F. Sklarew

This edited volume examines several public management and intergovernmental failures, with particular attention on social, political, and financial impacts. Understanding disaster meaning, even causality, is essential to the problem-solving process.

User-Centric Design
by Dr. Diane Stottlemyer

User-centric strategy can improve by using tools to manage performance using specific techniques. User-centric design is based on and centered around the users. They are an essential part of the design process and should have a say in what they want and need from the application based on behavior and performance.

Masonic Myths and Legends
by Pierre Mollier

Freemasonry is one of the few organizations whose teaching method is still based on symbols. It presents these symbols by inserting them into legends that are told to its members in initiation ceremonies. But its history itself has also given rise to a whole mythology.

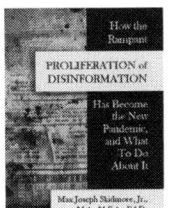
How the Rampant Proliferation of Disinformation has Become the New Pandemic by Max Joseph Skidmore Jr.

This work examines the causes of the overwhelming tidal wave of fake news, misinformation, disinformation, and propaganda, and the increase in information illiteracy and mistrust in higher education and traditional, vetted news outlets that make fact-checking a priority

Anti-Poverty Measures in America: Scientism and Other Obstacles
Editors, Max J. Skidmore and Biko Koenig

Anti-Poverty Measures in America brings together a remarkable collection of essays dealing with the inhibiting effects of scientism, an over-dependence on scientific methodology that is prevalent in the social sciences, and other obstacles to anti-poverty legislation.

Geopolitics of Outer Space: Global Security and Development
by Ilayda Aydin

A desire for increased security and rapid development is driving nation-states to engage in an intensifying competition for the unique assets of space. This book analyses the Chinese-American space discourse from the lenses of international relations theory, history and political psychology to explore these questions.

Contests of Initiative: Countering China's Gray Zone Strategy in the East and South China Seas
by Dr. Raymond Kuo

China is engaged in a widespread assertion of sovereignty in the South and East China Seas. It employs a "gray zone" strategy: using coercive but sub-conventional military power to drive off challengers and prevent escalation, while simultaneously seizing territory and asserting maritime control.

Discourse of the Inquisitive
Editors: Jaclyn Maria Fowler and Bjorn Mercer

Good communication skills are necessary for articulating learning, especially in online classrooms. It is often through writing that learners demonstrate their ability to analyze and synthesize the new concepts presented in the classroom.

westphaliapress.org

Made in the USA
Monee, IL
19 January 2024

51096782R10140